D0571993

The Theory and Practice of
Strategic Environmental Assessment

The Theory and Practice of Strategic Environmental Assessment

Towards a More Systematic Approach

Thomas B Fischer

London • Sterling, VA

First published by Earthscan in the UK and USA in 2007

Copyright © Thomas B. Fischer, 2007

All rights reserved

ISBN: 978-1-84407-452-5 (paperback)
        978-1-84407-453-2 (hardback)

Typeset by MapSet Ltd, Gateshead, UK
Printed and bound in the UK by TJ International, Padstow
Cover design by Andrew Corbett

For a full list of publications please contact:

Earthscan
8–12 Camden High Street
London, NW1 0JH, UK
Tel: +44 (0)20 7387 8558
Fax: +44 (0)20 7387 8998
Email: earthinfo@earthscan.co.uk
Web: **www.earthscan.co.uk**

22883 Quicksilver Drive, Sterling, VA 20166-2012, USA

Earthscan publishes in association with the International Institute for Environment and Development

A catalogue record for this book is available from the British Library

Library of Congress Cataloging-in-Publication Data

Fischer, Thomas B., 1965–
  Theory and practice of strategic environmental assessment : towards a more systematic
approach / Thomas B. Fischer.
     p. cm.
  Includes bibliographical references and index.
  ISBN-13: 978-1-84407-453-2 (hardback : alk. paper)
  ISBN-10: 1-84407-453-6 (hardback : alk. paper)
  ISBN-13: 978-1-84407-452-5 (pbk. : alk. paper)
  ISBN-10: 1-84407-452-8 (pbk. : alk. paper)
  1. Environmental impact analysis. 2. Strategic planning. I. Title.
  TD194.6.F575 2007
  333.71'4—dc22

                                                              2007005931

The paper used for this book is FSC-certified and
totally chlorine-free. FSC (the Forest Stewardship
Council) is an international network to promote
responsible management of the world's forests.

Mixed Sources
Product group from well-managed
forests and other controlled sources
www.fsc.org Cert no. SGS-COC-2482
© 1996 Forest Stewardship Council
FSC

For Stephanie and Moritz

Contents

Preface

It has been established practice for many years to take the environmental effects of projects into account in their design and authorization but this has generally resulted in mitigation rather than avoidance of adverse effects. Avoidance has been seen increasingly as the domain of 'strategic' environmental assessment (SEA). If there could still be any lingering doubt about the need to take systematic account of environmental effects in planning – and to do so in the widest, most inclusive manner possible – it must surely have been dispelled by the latest (February 2007) IPCC assessment of the science of climate change. This starkly demonstrates the consequences for the planet of our collective failures to have proper regard to the environmental effects of our plans and actions. In such a context, SEA is a tool that can help to make development more sustainable. SEA was given an enormous impetus in the European Union and beyond when the member states began to apply Directive 2001/42/EC in mid-2004. The legal basis now provided by the Directive has enormously widened and strengthened the application of SEA. But, as Thomas Fischer's book makes clear, it has been accompanied by doubts, often inspired by a lack of experience, about how to apply it to widely differing types of plan and programme, verging at one extreme on policies and at the other on projects; by a quest for examples of good practice; and sometimes by a failure to see how to embed SEA in different planning systems. Part of the importance of Fischer's book lies in addressing these issues and showing, by examples from recent practice, that SEA is not the arcane preserve of specialists alone but is in the mainstream of good planning. Fischer also warns against complacency: there is ample room for improvement in the application of SEA and especially in the assessment of alternatives and the provision of better follow-up of assessments if we are to achieve the high level of protection of the environment sought by the Directive.

David Aspinwall
Former policy advisor on SEA to the European Commission, DG Environment

Foreword

It takes specialized tools to manage the uncertainty inherent when developing strategic plans with extensive geographic scope and stakeholder interests. As this book admirably demonstrates, strategic environmental assessment has now finally moved from the 'untried' to the 'proven' column in the project management balance sheet. Through SEA we can identify the environmental and enviro-social risks at the earliest phases of strategic appraisal. Working through the range of potential alternatives, SEA can advise on potential outcomes and propose solutions involving future design, management and planning to avoid, reduce or remedy potential risks. For too long SEA has been viewed as a conceptual tool waiting its application, and as the following chapters record, there is now a growing and extensive body of recorded practice that justifies how the use of SEA can improve decision-making frameworks within government, non-governmental organizations (NGOs) and even industry.

One of the primary objectives of the International Association for Impact Assessment (IAIA) is to act as a networking organization for the exchange of ideas, concepts and best practice in impact assessment. Over the last few years, the IAIA has promoted increased contact between international SEA practitioners and interested parties. The results have been impressive: IAIA conferences, debates and papers have been charged with a dynamism, energy and vitality as the participants have explored the flexibility that SEA possesses across its various guises and international settings. We have been delighted to host many of the debates that help make up the contents of this book.

Dr Ross Marshall
President 2006–07
International Association for
Impact Assessment

About This Book

Strategic environmental assessment has been developing rapidly over the past two decades and continues to do so. However, to date, analysis of existing practice and associated reporting has remained far from systematic, lagging behind practical applications. Furthermore, SEA theory has remained poorly developed.

It is now commonly accepted that SEA should adapt to the specific situation of application, and therefore be applied in a flexible manner. Furthermore, there are basic generic principles that underlie any SEA. These principles are used in this book as the foundations for developing and promoting a more systematic approach to SEA. In this context, four objectives are pursued:

1   To portray current conceptual ideas and to develop them further,
2   To provide for an overview of the fundamental principles and rules of SEA,
3   To report on international SEA practice in a systematic manner,
4   To advance SEA theory.

The book is written for a wide international audience, including in particular students and practitioners who are new to SEA or who wish to refresh their knowledge of SEA. An evidence-based approach is used, aiming at filling a gap in the professional literature, which to date has relied too heavily on non-analytical case descriptions rather than on systematic review and empirical evidence. With the author being from Europe, the focus is on European examples. In this context, an update of the implementation and transposition status of the SEA Directive in the European Union member states is provided. However, on various occasions, reference is also made to non-European practice and a number of non-European SEA systems are reviewed. The book is based on various sources, including the international professional literature, as well as publications and research project results by the author. Furthermore, teaching materials, particularly from the University of Liverpool MA in Environmental Management and Planning have been considered.

The book is based on the following understanding of SEA:

- SEA is a systematic decision support process, aiming to ensure that environmental and possibly other sustainability aspects are considered effectively in policy, plan and programme making. In this context, SEA may be:
  - a structured, rigorous, participative, open and transparent environmental impact assessment (EIA) based process, applied particularly to plans and programmes, prepared by public planning authorities and at times private bodies,
  - a participative, open and transparent, possibly non-EIA-based process, applied in a more flexible

manner to policies, prepared by public planning authorities and at times private bodies, or

– a flexible non-EIA based process, applied to legislative proposals and other policies, plans and programmes in political/cabinet decision-making.

• Effective SEA works within a structured and tiered decision framework, aiming to support more effective and efficient decision-making for sustainable development and improved governance by providing for a substantive focus regarding questions, issues and alternatives to be considered in policy, plan and programme (PPP) making.

• SEA is an evidence-based instrument, aiming to add scientific rigour to PPP making, by using suitable assessment methods and techniques.

The book is organized into seven chapters. Chapter 1 explains what SEA is. In this context, the origins and development of SEA, current understanding and perceived benefits, differences with project EIA, rationale and theoretical thinking behind SEA, as well as context conditions and potential barriers to effective SEA are explained. Chapter 2 reports on the SEA process, making a distinction between EIA- and non-EIA-based approaches. Furthermore, descriptive, analytical and involvement methods and techniques are introduced. Chapter 3 deals with the question of how suitable alternatives can be identified in SEA. In this context, the importance of a tiered approach to SEA is stressed and explained, looking at transport and electricity transmission planning. Furthermore, tiering in spatial/land use planning is discussed. Chapter 4 provides for a comparative review of the performance of 11 established SEA systems in 10 countries globally, using context and methodological evaluation criteria introduced in Chapters 1, 2 and 3. Chapter 5 reviews implementation and transposition of the SEA Directive in the European Union member states. In this context, legislation and guidance documents are listed; in an annex to the chapter, references to emerging Directive-based case studies are also made. Chapter 6 introduces and reviews five spatial/land use SEAs, representing different levels of strategicness, focusing particularly on processes, methods and techniques used. Furthermore, whether perceived SEA benefits have been achieved is discussed. Finally, Chapter 7 draws conclusions and provides for recommendations for the future development of SEA. There are three annexes. Annex 1 presents a table for reviewing the quality of an environmental report, prepared according to SEA Directive requirements. Annex 2 lists emerging SEA case studies in EU member states. Annex 3, finally, is written for instructors, making suggestions for exercise questions.

Acknowledgements

The book is an outcome of the EC-funded Tempus Erasmus Mundus project PENTA – Promotion of European Education on Environmental Assessment, conducted from 2006 to 2007 (www.penta-eu.net). In this context, an especially big 'thank you' is due to my project partners Ingrid Belcakova, Paola Gazzola and Ralf Aschemann. Furthermore, I would also like to thank my colleagues from the Department of Civic Design, particularly those involved with environmental planning and assessment, including Urmila Jha-Thakur, Sue Kidd, Dave Shaw and Olivier Sykes, as well as my current SEA PhD students Paula Posas and John Phylip-Jones. Furthermore, I would like to thank all those from the SEA community who have inspired me, many of whom have become good friends over the years, including Jos Arts, Elvis Au, Adam Barker, Olivia Bina, Nick Bonvoisin, Lex Brown, Helen Byron, Aleh Cherp, Holger Dalkmann, Jiri Dusik, Lars Emmelin, John Glasson, Ainhoa Gonzalez, Natalia Gullon, Marie Hanusch, Sachihiko Harashina, Xu He, Mikael Hilden, Elsa João, Tuja Hilding-Rydevik, Hans Köppel, Lone Kørnøv, Mu Choon Lee, Einar Leknes, Simon Marsden, Ross Marshall, Angus Morrison-Saunders, Leonard Ortolano, Maria Partidário, Sandra Ruza, Barry Sadler, Frank Scholles, Wil Thissen, Paul Tomlinson, Riki Therivel, Rob Verheem, Wolfgang Wende and many others! Also, thanks to the people from the IAIA headquarters, particularly Rita, Jenny and Bridget.

Chapter 4 partly refers to information generated for a project for WBIEN, (the World Bank Environment and Natural Resources Program) in 2005. In this context, the author wishes to thank the following experts: Leonard Ortolano (USA), Richard Grassetti (USA), Bram Noble (Canada), Greg Wilburn (Canada), Angus Morrison-Saunders (Australia), Simon Marsden (Australia), Martin Ward (New Zealand), Kim Seaton (New Zealand), Francois Retief (South Africa), Wil Thissen (The Netherlands), Mikael Hilden (Finland), Jiri Dusik (Czech Republic), Paola Gazzola (Italy), Holger Dalkmann (Germany), Sue Kidd (UK) and John Phylip-Jones (UK).

Chapter 5 partly draws on information originally generated in the project 'Environmental Policy Advisory Service and Environmental Management', conducted for the Deutsche Gesellschaft für Technische Zusammenarbeit (GTZ) and the State Environmental Protection Agency (SEPA) of China in 2006. In this context, the author wishes to thank the following member states' experts for their contribution to compiling the information: Ulla Riitta Soveri (Finland), Veronika Vers (Estonia), Sandra Ruza (Latvia), Ruta Revoldiene (Lithuania), Joanna Mackowiak-Pandera (Poland), Lone Kørnøv (Denmark), Frank Scholles (Germany), Jos Arts (The Netherlands), Georges Guignobles (France), Ainhoa Gonzalez (Spain), Maria Partidário

(Portugal), Connor Skehan (Ireland), Paola Gazzola (Italy), Ralf Aschemann (Austria), Jiri Dusik (Czech Republic), Ingrid Belcakova (Slovakia), Efthymis Zagorianakos (Greece), Christina Pantazi (Cyprus) and Joe A Doublet (Malta).

Finally, I am particularly grateful to my wife, Stephanie, for her love, patience and support and my son, Moritz, who forced me into a more concentrated and focused working pattern – despite testing my ability to survive on very little sleep!

During the time of writing this book, Chris, a good friend of mine from Ottawa, was diagnosed with ALS, which is currently considered incurable. Whilst the reasons for the disease are still unknown, there are suspicions that environmental stresses, particularly related to heavy metals, may play an important role. I will donate 20% of the royalties of this book to the ALS Society of Canada (www.als.ca). My thoughts are with him, Leny, Maddie and Sarah at this very difficult time.

Thomas Fischer

Figures, Tables and Boxes

Figures

Tables

Boxes

Acronyms and Abbreviations

AAP	area action plan
AfS	Action for Sustainability
BPEO	best practical environmental option
CBA	cost–benefit analysis
CBR	cost–benefit relationship
CEAA	Canadian Environmental Assessment Agency
CESD	Commissioner of the Environment and Sustainable Development (Canada)
CO	carbon monoxide
COPR	California Governor's Office of Planning and Research
EA	environmental appraisal
EC TEN-T	European Commission Trans-European Transport Networks
EIA	environmental impact assessment
EPA	Environmental Protection Agency (Western Australia)
EREGoSum	Environmental thinking, effective Reasoning, Efficient decision-making, good Governance and Sustainable development
EU	European Union
FEARO	Federal Environmental Assessment Review Office (Canada)
FTIP	Federal Transport Infrastructure Plan (Germany)
GIS	geographical information system
GONW	Government Office of the North West of England
GTZ	Deutsche Gesellschaft für Technische Zusammenarbeit
IAIA	International Association for Impact Assessment
InChAR	Providing Information, Changing Attitudes and Routines
LCA	life-cycle assessment
LDD	local development document
LDF	local development framework
LTNZGA	Land Transport New Zealand Government Agency
LULU	locally unwanted land use
LUP	land use plan
MCA	multi-criteria analysis
MerITS	Merseyside Integrated Transport Study
MMS	mutil-modal studies
NEPA	National Environmental Policy Act (US)
NIMBY	not in my back yard
NIS	Newly Independent States
NMVOC	non-methane hydrocarbons
OECD	Organisation for Economic Co-operation and Development

OVOS	assessment of environmental impact requirements
PEIR	programmatic environmental impact report
PENTA	Promotion of European Education on Environmental Assessment
PPP	policy, plan and programme
PPG	planning policy guidance
PPS	planning policy statement
ProMtext	SEA Process, Methods and techniques and the overall context within which it is applied
REC	Regional Environment Center
RIA	regulatory impact assessment
RLTS	regional land transport strategy
ROA	Regional Body of Amsterdam
ROCOL	Review of Charging Options for London
RPG	regional planning guidance
RSS	regional spatial strategy
SA	sustainability appraisal
SEA	strategic environmental assessment
SEAN	strategic environmental analysis
SEPA	State Environmental Protection Agency (China)
SER	State Environmental Review (USSR)
SI	Statutory Instrument
SOER	state of the environment reporting
SPD	supplementary planning document
SWOT	strengths, weaknesses, opportunities and threats
SyProTEIn	Systematic, Pro-active, Tiered and Effective Involvement
UDP	unitary development plan
UNDP	United Nations Development Programme
UNECE	United Nations Economic Council for Europe
VROM	Ministry of Public Housing, Physical Planning and Environmental Affairs (The Netherlands)

What is Strategic Environmental Assessment?

In Chapter 1, the origins and development to date of strategic environmental assessment (SEA) are summarized. Furthermore, current SEA understanding and perceived benefits arising from SEA are outlined. The substantive focus of SEA is explained and its differences from project environmental impact assessment (EIA) are depicted. Furthermore, SEA's rationale is established. Why and when SEA is effective in improving the consideration of the environmental component in policy, plan and programme (PPP) making are explored. Context conditions for effective SEA are identified and, finally, a summary of the main points is provided.

Introduction

General environmental assessment requirements in public decision-making were first introduced in the US in 1970, based on the National Environmental Policy Act (NEPA), covering 'major Federal actions' (United States Government, 1969). While in 1978 the President's Council on Environmental Quality defined these 'actions' to include regulations, plans, policies, procedures, legislative proposals and programmes (Wood, 2002; Wright, 2006), in practice, NEPA-based assessment mainly revolved around project proposals.

Following NEPA, other countries started to establish environmental assessment requirements (see Dalal-Clayton and Sadler, 2005), such as: Canada (based on the Federal Environmental Assessment Review Process of 1973); Australia (based on the Commonwealth Government's Environment Protection [Impact of Proposals] Act of 1974); West Germany (based on the Principles for Assessing the Environmental Compatibility of Public Measures of the Federation of 1975); and France (based on the Law on the Protection of the Natural Environment of 1976). However, at the early stages of its development, in many systems, environmental assessment was used only occasionally rather than systematically. Furthermore, similarly to US practice, throughout the 1970s and 1980s, in most countries, environmental assessment was applied mainly to project planning (Fischer, 2002a). Finally, international aid organizations and development banks, such as the United Nations Development Programme (UNDP), the Organisation for Economic Co-operation and Development (OECD) and the World Bank started to promote environmental assessment application and training, particularly in developing countries in the 1980s (see, for example, Dusik et al, 2003; OECD, 2006; World Bank Group, 2006).

During the 1980s, within the environmental assessment literature, increasingly, a distinction was made between project and higher tiers of decision-making. In the member states of the European Union (EU), this distinction became formalized through the introduction of environmental impact assessment in 1985, based on Directive 85/337/EEC (European Commission, 1985), covering projects only. In a European context, therefore, the term EIA became used for project assessment. Due to a growing perception that environmental consequences also needed to be considered in decision-making above the project level, strategic environmental assessment was introduced in the second half of the 1980s (Wood and Djeddour, 1992). The decision-making tiers to which SEA is applied have become widely referred to as policies, plans and programmes (PPPs).

Initially, SEA was mainly thought of in terms of the application of project EIA principles to PPPs (Fischer and Seaton, 2002). However, subsequently different interpretations emerged that were connected in particular with:

- the different geographical and time scales of SEA and EIA (Lee and Walsh, 1992);
- the different levels of detail at strategic and project tiers (Partidário and Fischer, 2004);
- the different ways in which strategic decision processes are organized, when compared with project planning (Kørnøv and Thissen, 2000; Nitz and Brown, 2001).

SEA can be described as having the following three main meanings:

- SEA is a systematic decision support process, aiming to ensure that environmental and possibly other sustainability aspects are considered in PPP making. In this context, SEA may support, first, public planning

authorities and private bodies (including international aid organizations/development banks) to conduct:
  - structured, rigorous, participative, open and transparent EIA-based processes, particularly to plans and programmes;
  - participative, open and transparent, possibly non-EIA-based flexible processes to policies/visions and policy plans.

  Second, SEA may support cabinet-type decision-making, working as a flexible (non-EIA based) assessment instrument that is applied to legislative proposals and other PPPs.
- SEA is an evidence-based instrument, aiming to add scientific rigour to PPP making by applying a range of assessment methods and techniques.
- SEA provides for a structured decision framework, aiming to support more effective and efficient decision-making, sustainable development and improved governance by establishing a substantive focus, for example, in terms of the issues and alternatives to be considered at different systematic tiers and levels.

Within this book, SEA for public planning and private bodies is referred to as 'administration-led SEA', while SEA for cabinet-type decision-making is referred to as 'cabinet SEA'. The main focus of the book is on the former, namely, SEA conducted by public planning authorities and private bodies (including international aid organizations/development banks) because this is where SEA is mainly conducted and required globally, and because there is a much wider range of practical experiences with administration-led SEA than with cabinet SEA.

To date, SEA has been applied in a wide range of different situations, including trade agreements, funding programmes, economic development plans, spatial/land use and sectoral (for example, transport, energy, waste, water) PPPs. In this book, a wide range of practice examples are brought forward, mainly from spatial/land use, transport and electricity transmission planning. Numerous examples for other SEA applications can be found in the professional literature, for example for waste management (Arbter, 2005; Verheem, 1996), trade (Kirkpatrick and George, 2004), oil and gas extraction (DTI, 2001), economic development plans (Fischer, 2003c), wind farms (Kleinschmidt and Wagner, 1996; for offshore windfarms see Schomerus et al, 2006), water/flood management (DEFRA, 2004) and funding programmes (Ward et al, 2005). Finally, policy SEA has been the main focus of two recent publications, including Sadler (2005) and the World Bank (2005).

Currently, probably the best-known SEA 'framework law that establishes a minimum common procedure for certain official plans and programmes' (Dalal-Clayton and Sadler, 2005, p37) is the European Directive 2001/42/EC on the assessment of the effects of certain plans and programmes on the environment ('SEA Directive'; European Commission, 2001b). This Directive advocates the application of a systematic, pro-active EIA-based and participative process that is prepared with a view to avoiding unnecessary duplication in tiered assessment practice. In this context, however, policies and cabinet decision-making are not mentioned. At the heart of a Directive-based SEA process is the preparation of an environmental report, which is supposed to:

- portray the relationship with other PPPs;

- identify the significant impacts of different alternatives on certain environmental aspects;
- explain how the SEA was considered in decision-making;
- provide information on the reasons for the choice of a certain alternative.

Furthermore a non-technical summary needs to be prepared and monitoring arrangements for significant environmental impacts need to be put into place.

The implementation and transposition status of the SEA Directive in EU member states is described in Chapter 5. In its short lifetime to date, the SEA Directive has not only had an impact on EU member states, but also within a wider international context. It has been a reference point for practice, for example, in Asia, Africa and South America. Furthermore, the Kiev protocol to the Espoo Convention (UNECE, 2003) on trans-boundary SEA formulates almost identical requirements to the Directive, though it also explicitly mentions the possibility of applying SEA at the policy level. This protocol and the associated Resource Manual (UNECE, 2006) are likely to enhance SEA application in United Nations Economic Council for Europe (UNECE) states outside the EU.

The SEA process

Figure 1.1 shows an SEA Directive-based assessment process. This is EIA based and linked to plan and programme making stages in a continuous and integrated decision flow. This process is objectives-led (namely, trying to influence PPP making so that certain objectives can be reached) and baseline-led (namely, relying on baseline data to be able to make reliable projections in assessment), and reflects ideas of instrumental rationality (Faludi, 1973).

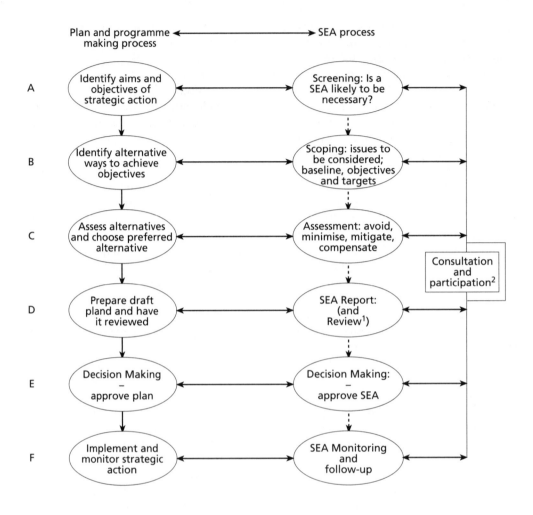

Notes: 1 not explicitly required by the Directive
       2 according to the Directive, at least at scoping and report stages of the SEA process

Source: Thomas Fischer; see also European Commission (2006)

Figure 1.1 *EC SEA Directive-based process for improving plan and programme making*

If applied in the way shown in Figure 1.1, the SEA process is thought to be able to influence the underlying plan and programme making process, with a view to improving it from an environmental perspective. Furthermore, an SEA that is applied in this manner may reshape the plan and programme decision flow, supporting not only the consideration of environmental issues at each stage of the process, but also leading to improved transparency and governance (Kidd and Fischer, 2007). The generic SEA process is explained in further detail in Chapter 2.

Describing non-EIA-based SEA, applied in policy and cabinet decision-making situations (at times also referred to as 'policy assessment'-based SEA), is not as straightforward, as this is normally portrayed as being flexible, adaptable and at times communicative (reflecting ideas of communicative rationality; see Healey, 1997). However, even non-EIA-based SEA is normally perceived as being a systematic process, which may take different forms (see Kørnøv and Thissen, 2000). To date, attempts to define non-EIA-based SEA in a generic way have either led to a somewhat blurred picture of SEA or, ironically, have made it look similar to EIA-based SEA. This was described by Fischer (2003a), based on observations made by Tonn et al (2000) and Nielsson and Dalkmann (2001). Generally speaking, non-EIA-based assessment approaches are considered to be less methodologically rigorous than EIA-based processes, and descriptions of non-EIA-based SEA frequently mention the following core elements:

- Specifying the issue (problem identification);
- Goal setting (what are aims, objectives and targets);
- Information collection;
- Information processing and consideration of alternatives;
- Decision-making;
- Implementation.

Whilst there are a range of non-EIA-based systems (see Chapter 4), there is currently hardly any empirical evidence available for what makes non-EIA process-based SEA effective. In this context, research is urgently needed.

Current understanding and perceived benefits from SEA

SEA's main aim is to ensure due consideration is given to environmental and possibly other sustainability aspects in PPP making above the project level.

Furthermore, it is supposed to support the development of more transparent strategic decisions. It attempts to provide relevant and reliable information for those involved in PPP making in an effective and timely manner. As mentioned above, the exact form of SEA will depend on the specific situation and context it is applied in. Procedurally, differences are particularly evident between administration-led SEA and cabinet SEA. Regarding the substantive focus (that is, the issues and alternatives to be considered), differences may exist between different administrative levels (for example, national, regional, local), strategic tiers (for example, policy, plan and programme) and sectors (for example, land-use, transport, energy, waste, water). While certain key elements are likely to be reflected in every SEA system, others will differ depending on established planning and assessment practices, as well as on the specific traditions of the organizations preparing PPPs and SEAs. Based on what has been laid out in the previous section, Box 1.1 presents an up-to-date definition of SEA.

Generally speaking, a range of benefits are supposed to result from the application of SEA. In this context, SEA aims at supporting PPP processes, leading to environmentally sound and sustainable development. Furthermore, it attempts to strengthen strategic processes, improving good governance and building public trust and confidence into strategic decision-making. Ultimately, it is hoped that SEA can lead to savings in time and money by avoiding costly mistakes, leading to a better quality of life. Box 1.2 shows those SEA characteristics, based on which benefits are thought to result. Conceptually, this may be expressed by the term 'SyProTEIn' (Systematic, Proactive, Tiered and Effective Involvement).

BOX 1.1 DEFINITION OF SEA

SEA aims to ensure that due consideration is given to environmental and possibly other sustainability aspects in policy, plan and programme making above the project level. It is:

- A systematic, objectives-led, evidence-based, proactive and participative decision-making support process for the formulation of sustainable policies, plans and programmes, leading to improved governance; it can function as:
  - a structured, rigorous and open project EIA-based administrative procedure in public and, at times, private plan and programme making situations;
  - a possibly more flexible assessment process:
    - in public and at times private policy-making situations;
    - in legislative proposals and other policies, plans and programmes, submitted to cabinet decision-making.
- A policy, plan and programme making support instrument that is supposed to add scientific rigour to decision-making, applying a range of suitable methods and techniques.
- A systematic decision-making framework, establishing a substantive focus, particularly in terms of alternatives and aspects to be considered, depending on the systematic tier (policy, plan or programme), administrative level (national, regional, local) and sector of application.

Focus of SEA and differences from project EIA

SEA is applied in strategic decision-making contexts that precede project decisions. Being associated with decisions on aims and objectives for future development, SEA may deal with issues such as need and demand management, evaluating, for example, different fiscal, regulatory or organizational and spatial development options. Project EIA, by contrast, deals with detailed decisions that are normally concerned with the location and design of a project. In practice, project EIA has been frequently shown to revolve around measures for mitigating negative environmental impacts. Alternatively, SEA would normally aim at preventing negative impacts and at proactively enhancing positive developments. Furthermore, whereas in project EIA alternatives to be assessed are often limited to minor variants, SEA may address a broad range of alternatives covering different sectors.

SEA can be applied in a range of situations that may differ in terms of their 'strategicness', and the range of different SEA applications is much wider than the range of project EIA applications. Table 1.1 summarizes the changing focus of SEA, depending on how far away from the project level it is applied, that is, how 'strategic' it is. This shows a transition in the shape that SEA is likely to take from lower tiers of decision-making to higher tiers. Whereas at lower tiers, SEA is likely to be based on a more rigorous EIA-based approach, at higher tiers it is likely to be more flexible (and possibly non-EIA based). Methods and techniques applied vary, depending on the specific situation of application. At lower tiers, methods and techniques typically used in EIA (for example, field surveys, overlay mapping and multi-criteria analysis (MCA) for comparing different spatial alternatives)

**BOX 1.2 CHARACTERISTICS OF SEA, BASED ON
WHICH BENEFITS ARE THOUGHT TO RESULT**

1   SEA allows for a more systematic and effective consideration of wider environmental impacts and alternatives at higher tiers of decision-making, leading to more effective and less time-consuming decision-making and implementation.
2   SEA acts as a proactive tool that supports the formulation of strategic action for sustainable development.
3   SEA increases the efficiency of tiered decision-making, strengthens project EIA and identifies appropriate and timely alternatives and options; in this context, it helps to focus on the right issues at the right time and aims to uncover potentially costly inconsistencies.
4   SEA enables more effective involvement in strategic decision-making, creating knowledge at low costs.

Source: adapted from Fischer (1999a) and Dusik et al (2003).

---

may be useful and appropriately applied. At higher tiers, methods and techniques typically applied within policy making may be more appropriate, such as forecasting, backcasting and visioning (see also Chapters 2 and 6). Furthermore, there are methods and techniques that may be applied at both, higher and lower tiers, including, for example, checklists, matrices and impact trees. Generally

Table 1.1 *The changing focus of SEA from lower tiers to higher tiers*

SEA **EIA**

	'Higher tiers' / 'Lower tiers'	
Decision making level	Policy ⟶ Plan ⟶ Programme ⟶ Project	
Nature of action	Strategic, visionary, conceptual	Immediate, operational
Output	General	Detailed
Scale of impacts	Macroscopic, cumulative, unclear	Microscopic, localised
Timescale	Long to medium term	Medium to short term
Key data sources	Sustainable development strategies, state of the environment reports, vision	Field work sample analysis
Type of data	More qualitative	More quantitative
Alternatives	Area wide, political, regulative, technological, fiscal, economic	Specific locations, design, construction, operation
Rigour of analysis	More uncertainty	More rigour
Assessment benchmarks	Sustainability benchmarks (criteria and objectives)	Legal restrictions and best practice
Role of practitioner	Mediator for negotiations	Advocator of values and norms Technician, using stakeholder values
Public perception	More vague, distant	More reactive (NIMBY)

Source: adapted from Partidário and Fischer (2004)

speaking, quantification within assessment is more difficult to achieve at higher tiers that come with a greater degree of uncertainty. However, this does not mean that it is impossible to apply more quantitative techniques, as the frequent use of scenario analysis and mathematical modelling have shown (see Fischer, 2002a).

Rationale for applying SEA

The rationale for applying SEA is connected with current shortcomings of PPP making. In this context, the need for SEA results from:

- the need for a stronger representation of strategic environmental thinking in PPP making;
- the need for more effective reasoning in decision-making;
- the need for more efficient decision-making;
- the need for better support of good governance and sustainable development in decision-making.

Conceptually, the rationale for applying SEA may be expressed by the term EREGoSum (Environmental thinking, effective Reasoning, Efficient decision-making, good Governance and Sustainable development).

The need for a stronger representation of strategic environmental thinking in PPP making

The main reason for introducing SEA has been the perceived weak representation of environmental aspects in PPP making (Dusik et al, 2003; Morrison-Saunders and Fischer, 2006). In this context, and despite of the widespread claim by policy makers and planners in many countries that a balanced evaluation is achieved, non-material, cultural, social and ethical values have tended to be underrepresented due to utilitarian and economistic views prevailing in planning (Ortolano, 1984). Having identified this as a problem, many countries now have introduced formal environmental assessment requirements, aiming to improve the consideration of the environmental dimension in decision-making. However, despite the efforts made, environmental issues – and particularly those that are of a strategic nature – are still frequently treated as simple 'add-ons' that are taken into account not during, but after PPP processes have been conducted. This means that environmental issues are dealt with in a reactive way. A reactive approach, however, means that the main focus of assessment is on mitigation of negative environmental impacts, rather than on proactively finding ways for avoiding negative impacts and enhancing positive impacts. Furthermore, applying SEA in a reactive manner means that environmental standards – if available – are unlikely to be effectively used to guide PPP making.

In current PPP making practice, concrete quantitative environmental thresholds are only rarely available. Also, if they do exist, they are frequently not respected (Fischer, 2002a). In addition, there are indications that long-term visions of sustainable development and associated aims and objectives, with time horizons of between 20 to 30 years are not consistently followed through (Fischer, 2004a; see also Chapter 3 and

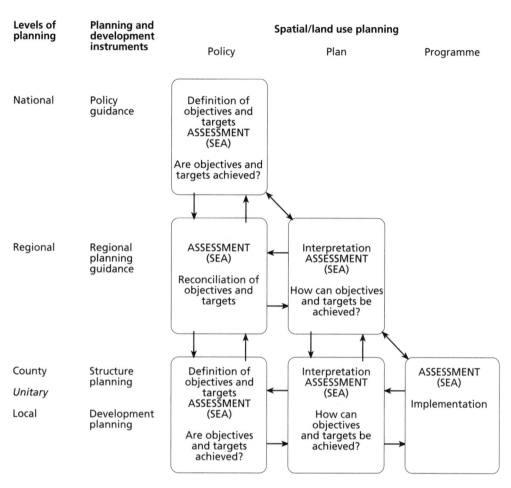

Source: adapted from Barker and Fischer (2003)

Figure 1.2 *SEA for reconciling aims and objectives:*
The example of the pre-2004 English planning system

Chapter 6). Rather, short-term political interests frequently appear to prevail. This problem is closely connected with the duration of election cycles. Finally, a consistent consideration of thresholds within the whole planning system, that is, throughout all sectors and administrations, is normally difficult because in most countries and systems, different planning tiers, levels and sectors are isolated rather than effectively integrated and may have different aims and objectives (Stead et al, 2004). In this context, SEA may be used as a reconciliatory tool of different administrative levels, systematic tiers and sectors. How this might happen was discussed by Barker and Fischer (2003) for the pre-2004 English spatial/land use planning system (see Figure 1.2).

The need for more effective reasoning in decision-making

SEA is more than the application of prediction techniques and methods within an assessment process. Rather, it can provide for a systematic decision-making framework, identifying tasks to be addressed at different tiers and administrative levels (Fischer, 2006a). In this context, SEA can help decision-makers ask questions relevant to a specific tier, leading to more effective reasoning in decision-making. A generic SEA framework can thus guide decision-makers in systematically addressing, for example:

- initial 'why' and 'what' questions; typically at the policy (or vision) tier of decision-making:
  - identifying and/or defining underlying – *sustainability* – objectives and targets;
  - supporting identification of possible development scenarios and policy options;
  - enabling the assessment of impacts of policy options on objectives and targets;
- subsequent 'what', 'where' and 'how' questions; at the plan tier of decision-making:
  - proactively developing possible – *spatial* – development options;
  - enabling the assessment of impacts of these options on objectives and targets;
- 'where' and 'when' questions at the programme tier of decision-making:
  - supporting ranking of possible projects and/or alternatives in terms of, for example, benefits and costs.

Figure 1.3 shows a strategic planning framework that can be provided by SEA, specifying tasks and issues to be addressed

at different tiers (following Marshall and Fischer, 2006). The stages introduced by a tiered SEA framework are similar to the basic stages of corporate planning frameworks (see, for example, McNamara, 2006). How a tiered approach to SEA can potentially play an important role for detecting gaps in existing planning systems and the identification of suitable alternatives is discussed in further detail in Chapter 3.

The value of a tiered approach to SEA lies in its potential to enable greater transparency and integration, supporting more effective streamlining of strategic planning. Furthermore, connections with other PPPs may be made explicit, thus helping to avoid duplication. Tiering within PPP making and SEA is not just a conceptual idea; this is evident when looking at current practice, for example, in transport planning in northern and western European countries (Fischer, 2006a). Here, practice has been observed to fall into one of four main categories, which may be dubbed policy SEA, network-plan SEA, corridor-plan SEA and programme SEA. This is further explained in Chapter 3. In this context, whereas transport policy SEAs have been found to address initial 'why' and 'what' questions, network-plan SEAs were found to revolve around subsequent 'what' and 'where' questions. Corridor-plan SEAs were found to address 'where' and 'how roughly' questions, and programme SEAs, finally, were found to focus on 'when' questions. At times, categories are combined, for example, policy and network plans (as was the case with the regional Dutch transport strategies in the 1990s; see Fischer, 2002a) or corridor plans and programmes (as done within the German Federal Transport Infrastructure Plan; see Chapter 3); in other words, in practice boundaries are often flexible.

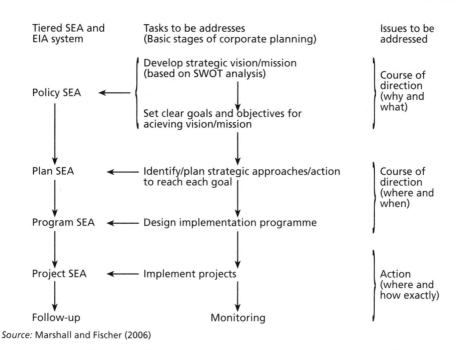

Source: Marshall and Fischer (2006)

Figure 1.3 *Strategic planning framework provided by SEA*

Tasks may not only be allocated to different systematic tiers (policies, plans or programmes), but also to different administrative levels. In the spatial/land use planning system in England, for example, the national level (central government) sets the context for 'why' and 'what' questions through general policy and planning guidance, the regional level for 'what' and 'where' questions through regional spatial strategies, and the local level for 'where' and 'how' questions through local development frameworks (Fischer, 2006a; see also Chapter 3).

The need for more efficient decision-making

SEA can support more efficient decision-making, particularly by, first, helping to achieve more structured decision-making frameworks, thus creating the context for more focused PPP making and subsequent project planning and EIA (see previous section and Chapter 3), and second, by supporting more systematic PPP processes (see Figure 1.1 and Chapter 2). A systematic decision-making framework may support addressing 'the right issues at the right time' at different tiers, as explained above. Ultimately, a framework, within which different tiers and levels address different issues, tasks and alternatives, may help avoid delays in subsequent project preparation. In this context, SEA should help to address problems early enough in order to be able to proactively solve them, thus maximizing positive impacts and preventing damage rather than only aiming at mitigating negative impacts. A proactive decision support process, as shown in Figure 1.1 can be used to achieve more proactive decision-making.

Acting as a proactive decision framework and supporting more systematic PPP processes, SEA may help to detect not

11

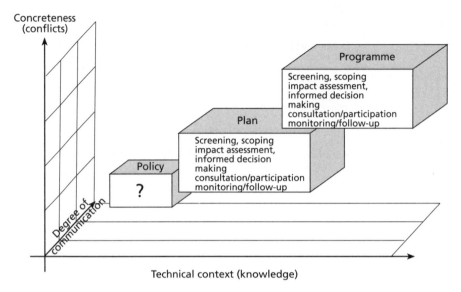

Source: adapted from Fischer (2003)

Figure 1.4 *Identifying a communication-based 'acting strategy'*

only direct, but also indirect, cumulative and synergistic effects. Providing for a participative process, SEA may enable the effective gathering of information and inputs from a wide range of stakeholders. Furthermore, providing for a tiered decision framework, SEA may support decision-makers to ask the right questions at the right time. In this context, SEA can also advise decision-makers and assessors on how to act, based on the technical knowledge and the expected potential conflicts in a certain situation, therefore helping them to act more efficiently. 'Acting strategies' may revolve around: first, mediation, for example, in more vague policy situations, where 'why' and 'what' questions are addressed; second, advocacy in planning situations in which 'where' and 'how' questions are addressed and in which policies are supposed to be implemented; and third, technical approaches, where 'when' questions are addressed (based on, for example, MCA and cost–benefit analysis (CBA); see

Chapter 2). Figure 1.4 shows, in a simplistic manner, how a systematic SEA framework may provide the basis for decision-makers to identify a strategy for acting, depending on the expected degree of communication, using the strategic planning framework provided by SEA introduced in Figure 1.3. Whilst advocative and technical approaches may work well in structured EIA-based processes, they may be less helpful in processes, in which the assessor needs to act as a mediator, requiring a higher degree of flexibility. Required skills in the context of mediation are less technical and include communication and negotiation capabilities (Heikinheimo, 2003).

The need for supporting good governance and sustainable development in decision-making

More recently, the use of SEA has been discussed in the context of its potential for improving governance (Kidd and Fischer,

2007). This is mainly based on its capability to increase transparency, participation and inclusiveness by advocating a participatory and structured assessment process. In SEA, communication, participation and reporting have an important role to play by introducing perspectives and inputs of different stakeholders to the PPP making process. Expected achievements can be subdivided into two main streams:

1   Long-term public empowerment:
    –   leading to, for example, conflict resolution, gain of public support for future actions, increased public confidence in decision-making and in politicians, development of social ownership and belonging.
2   An improved and more effective PPP process:
    –   leading to, for example, the identification of public concerns and the introduction of new ideas for possible solutions;
    –   ensuring that alternatives are considered and that decision-makers and proponents are accountable;
    –   providing opportunity to share expertise and to benefit from local knowledge and fresh perspectives on the SEA process.

The practice of public participation in SEA should anticipate and, if possible, help to avoid NIMBY (not in my back yard) and LULU (locally unwanted land use) situations, that often occur at project levels of decision-making. Ultimately, this should lead to reduced costs and avoidance of decision delays. The results to be achieved through communication, participation and reporting in SEA are likely to differ from those achievable in EIA. In this context, it is important to acknowledge that the general public is unlikely to be equally interested in all strategic issues, which at times may appear too unclear and unspecific.

By providing for a systematic decision-making framework, SEA may lead to increased effectiveness and efficiency of decision-making. Ultimately, if applied in a systematic, participative and structured manner, SEA should lead to increased accountability, better integration, increased responsiveness and resilience of decision-making, thus supporting good governance. As explained above, SEA works as an effective decision-making support instrument for sustainable development. In this context, various authors have shown that it is potentially able to support PPP formulation for sustainable development by providing for an objectives-led, alternatives-focused and participatory instrument (Sheate, 1992; Fischer, 1999b). This is why SEA is thought to be able to change planning processes that are insufficiently open.

What PPP making towards sustainable development is thought to look like is shown in Figure 1.5, also indicating corresponding SEA stages. In addition to those, there are also substantive requirements. However, these differ depending on the country, region and locality, as well as underlying value systems and attitudes. The range of definitions of sustainable development has been said to stretch from technocentric – *cornucopian* – approaches, where natural capital can be fully substituted by man-made capital. to ecocentric – *deep green* – approaches, where use of natural resources is only permitted if they can be fully replaced (Tait, 1995). Having a good understanding of the values and attitudes of those involved in SEA is vital for achieving an effective process (Valve, 1999). How SEA can act as an instrument for integrating environmental, social and economic

PPP making framework in support of sustainable development   SEA stages

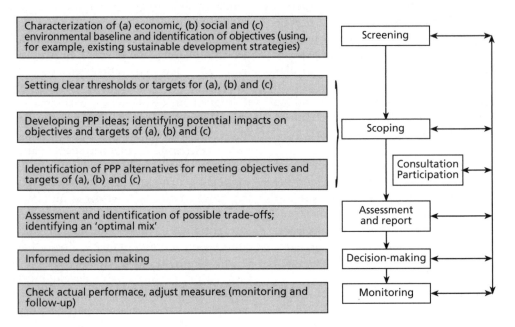

Source: adapted from Fischer (1999b)

Figure 1.5 *PPP making framework in support of sustainable development and corresponding SEA stages*

aspects is explained in the next section.

Generally speaking, what makes defining sustainable development difficult is not just different attitudes and value systems, but also different dimensions and speeds of the various sustainability aspects to be considered. While, for example, fens or moorlands can take up to 1000 to 10,000 years to develop fully, in business planning, a time horizon of 10 to 20 years would in many cases already be considered strategic. Modern shopping centres, for example, are built for a life span of about 15 years. Planning for

sustainable development can therefore only be considered effective if clear objectives are in place for what a society wants to achieve in the short-, medium- and long-terms (see also below and Chapter 3). Furthermore, it is important to appreciate that planning for sustainable development is frequently controversial, coming with great uncertainties. How SEA can act as an instrument for integrating environmental, social and economic aspects in order to achieve sustainable development is further discussed in the next section.

SEA as an instrument for integrating environmental, social and economic aspects in order to achieve sustainable development

In order for sustainable development to be achieved, economic, social and environmental aspects need to be effectively considered in decision-making (Lee, 2006). As a consequence, substantive integration is raising a lot of interest among decision-makers, practitioners and academics worldwide (Fischer, 1999c; Kidd and Fischer, 2007), and there have been suggestions by some authors that SEA should be converted into integrated or sustainability appraisal (Smith and Sheate, 2001; Carter et al, 2003). The argument is that if SEA acts as an instrument for sustainable development, by addressing interdependencies, an improved balance of the different assessment aspects in decision-making should result. There have also been claims that an integrated approach to impact assessment will assist in a better implementation of all thematic PPPs (Scholten and Post, 1999). Furthermore, integration is supposed to help effectively address overlapping areas of concern, reduce duplication of efforts and make assessments more user-friendly (Milner et al, 2003). Ultimately, through integration of different aspects in SEA, it is hoped that integrated and joined-up thinking can result, leading to deliberative processes and thus to more inclusive, informed and transparent decision-making (Buselich, 2002; Cowell and Martin, 2003).

Integration in assessment started to be promoted in the early 1980s, with the World Conservation Strategy (IUCN, 1980) calling for an 'inter-disciplinary approach to the evaluation of policies, programmes and projects', arguing that different assessment aspects needed to be considered simultaneously. This was confirmed by the OECD (1990), asking for a greater integration between sectoral policies and management regimes to be achieved, hoping that this would lead to a 'systematic consideration of many diverse elements... in conceiving, designing, implementing, maintaining and terminating a policy' (OECD, 1990, p.39). Furthermore, the Rio Earth Summit's Local Agenda 21 (UNCED, 1992) asked for an integration of economic, social and environmental considerations in decision-making at all levels.

Over the past decade, a range of assessment instruments has been developed in various countries, institutions and sectors, aiming to integrate economic, social and environmental aspects in decision-making for sustainable development (Dalal-Clayton and Sadler, 2005). While a number of authors have made suggestions for what SEA that integrates different aspects should look like in terms of process, substantive focus and methodology (George 2001a, 2001b; Dovers, 2002; Pope et al, 2004; Lee, 2006), empirical evidence for what makes integration effective in order to really lead to more balanced decision-making has remained thin. For this reason, the usefulness of the integration of different substantive aspects through SEA is currently more an assumption than a proven fact. Currently, no clear generic recommendation can therefore be given on how to integrate environmental, economic and social aspects in a specific situation.

Substantive integration has often been approached through qualitative assessment, for example through the collection of expert opinions, which are subsequently portrayed within impacts/goals achievement matrices (see Figure 2.3). Quantitative aggregation of data has been approached mainly through CBA and MCA (see, for example, Fischer, 2002a; Dalkmann and Bongardt, 2004 and Chapter 2). However, whilst there are these methods of aggregation, how exactly the different dimensions should best be combined and trade-offs be achieved has largely remained unclear. Furthermore, whether outcomes of integrated assessments are indeed meaningful is currently subject to a controversial debate (More et al, 1996).

Joint databases that put environmental, social and economic aspects next to each other exist in various countries, regions and municipalities.[1] Whilst these normally define overall economic, social and environmental objectives, they mostly do not provide much support for assessors when attempting to deal with the necessary trade-offs. A particular problem here is that databases normally do not specify what non-negotiable minimum thresholds should be. For example, in current local spatial/land use policy/plan SEA practice in England, economic, social and environmental aspects are normally considered next to each other in qualitative, expert-based assessment. In this context, while sustainable development strategies often provide the objectives and targets for assessment, these are not necessarily compatible and trade-offs are often insufficiently addressed and dealt with.

Broadly speaking, three main conceptual approaches for SEA to act as an instrument for achieving sustainable development can be distinguished, as follows:

1 Reactive, ex-post approaches for minimizing negative effects;[2]
2 Objectives-led approaches that are supposed to indicate movements towards or away from sustainable development, attempting to maximize positive impacts;
3 Minimum thresholds approaches that are based on the assumption that actions cannot be permitted, if they lead to minimum sustainable development thresholds not being reached.

Approach 1 is the least ambitious in terms of actually aiming to achieve sustainable development aims and objectives, as the focus is not on proactive forward thinking but only on reacting to negative impacts. Whilst approach 2 may indicate a direction of change, whether and how sustainability objectives can be reached remains unclear, similarly to approach 1. Both, approaches 1 and 2, do not give any clear indications of how trade-offs should be dealt with. Approach 3, finally, is the most ambitious, attempting to calculate the distance of a proposed PPP from defined sustainable development aims and objectives. In this context, approach 3 has also been referred to as an actual 'assessment for sustainability' (Pope et al, 2004). Its aim is to seek positive gains over all sustainable development principles and over the long term. In order to be able to do so, sustainability criteria or thresholds need to be defined that should not be crossed (Gibson, 2004).

Why is SEA thought to be effective in improving the consideration of the environmental component in PPP making?

This section focuses on the question of how SEA is thought to be effective in leading to a better consideration of the environmental component in PPP making. Overall, this effectiveness is thought to be connected with three main functions:

1 SEA provides decision-makers with better information;
2 SEA enables attitudes and perceptions to change through participation and involvement;
3 SEA changes established routines.

All these functions (which, conceptually, may be expressed by the term *InChAR – Providing Information, Changing Attitudes and Routines*) are closely related to individual as well as institutional learning. They are subsequently described in further detail, introducing relevant decision-making models (following Fischer, 2005a).

SEA provides decision-makers with better information (information function)

SEA is supposed to support and influence PPP making by providing better information on the impacts of alternatives in a proactive and systematic manner. According to the 'information processing model' (Bartlett and Kurian, 1999), good information may lead to better decisions. While over recent years, the validity of the information processing model has been questioned, based on its 'rational' nature (see, for example, Tonn et al, 2000), all EIA-based SEA requirements worldwide continue to be directly connected with it,

as provisions are usually formulated for a systematic decision process with a report as a key element. Accepting the information processing model means SEA can be evaluated, among other things, through the quality of the environmental report (Lee et al, 1999). Annex 1 presents an environmental report review package, which is based on EC SEA Directive requirements.

There is some empirical evidence that good quality information can indeed influence decisions and actors. While clear cause–effect relationships between SEA and project implementation are normally difficult to establish (Perdicoúlis et al, forthcoming), it is hoped that the instrument does not only have a positive impact in procedural but also substantive terms. In this context, in order for better information to influence PPP making, it is important that processes are open and not marked by major controversies (Schijf, 2002; Fischer, 2003a). However, in situations of major conflict, 'rational' information has also been observed to be corrupted by powerful actors (Bras-Klapwijk, 1999), who have been found to use scientific evidence for political purposes. 'Facts' have therefore been observed to be bent towards particular interests (Sabatier and Jenkins-Smith, 1993). This may become a problem if no effective external review mechanisms are in place. In this context, Nooteboom and Teisman (2003) observe that 'rational knowledge is often available through impact assessment, but not used in decision making'. At times, this may not even be done on purpose, but may simply 'reflect a "mental distance" between those responsible for the two processes [ie PPP and SEA]' (Hilden et al, 2004, p.529).

In order to reduce 'mental distances', the roles different actors play, their interests and attitudes need to be understood when conducting SEA. The information function of SEA is closely connected with aspect 2 of the definition of SEA, provided in Box 1.1: 'SEA is a PPP-making support instrument that is supposed to add scientific rigour to decision-making'.

SEA enables attitudes and perceptions to change through participation and involvement (changing attitudes function)

SEA supports and influences PPP making by enabling attitudes and perceptions to change through facilitation of increased participation and involvement in structured processes. This means SEA can bring together diverse goals and values of actors and stakeholders. Two models explain the importance of participation and involvement: the 'external reform model' (see, for example, Culhane et al, 1987) and the 'pluralist politics model' (Bartlett and Kurian, 1999). Disagreement over underlying aims and objectives has been described as a reason for SEA not going beyond initial screening and scoping stages. In this context, the role of SEA can also be understood as a 'social learning process' among different actors. This is important because 'many of the decisions are not matters of expertise but matters of opinion, of values rather than facts' (Banister, 1994, p.129).

For project EIA, Schijf (2002) showed that attitudes and perceptions of those involved in assessment processes had indeed changed (see also Sadler, 1996; Wood and Jones, 1997). Furthermore, the introduction of SEA in transport planning was observed to have 'opened up minds...

about the need and potential for a stronger traffic policy with environmental objectives' (European Commission, 1997, p.327).

A transparent and systematic process is the basis for effective participation and involvement. As a consequence, SEA can be evaluated based on the quality of the participative process. The changing attitudes function of SEA is closely connected with aspect 1 of the definition of SEA, provided in Box 1.1: 'SEA is a systematic, objectives-led, evidence-based, proactive and participative decision-making support process for the formulation of sustainable policies, plans and programmes, leading to improved governance'.

SEA changes established routines (changing routines function)

SEA supports and influences PPP making by changing established routines that favour environmentally unsustainable PPPs, potentially leading to a greater environmental awareness in an authority or agency. SEA may thus create a 'preventive effect' for future action (Van den Berg and Nooteboom, 1994). Two theoretical models explain why SEA may lead to changing established routines: the 'organizational politics model' and the 'institutionalist model'.

The organizational politics model (Bartlett and Kurian, 1999) says that organizational culture will change if interaction within organizations is being structured, directed and biased. The institutionalist model suggests that formal SEA may ultimately be able to lead to an institutionalization of its values (following Taylor, 1984; see also Czada, 1998), particularly through institutional learning. Institutions – on which SEA can have an effect – consist of 'routines, procedures, conventions, roles, strategies, organizational forms and technologies around which political activity is constructed' (March and Olsen, 1989, p.22).

In this context, SEA may be found to play an important role for the rationalization of decision-making, particularly in fragmented societies of pluralist democracies. In order to do so, 'why', 'what', 'where', 'how' and 'when' questions need to be explicitly addressed, possibly within a tiered decision framework (see Figure 1.3 and Chapter 3). The changing routines function of SEA is closely connected with aspect 3 of the definition of SEA, provided in Box 1.1: 'SEA is a systematic decision-making framework, establishing a substantive focus'.

As changes to routines and to established decision-making cultures are likely to need some time (Schön and Rein, 1994), SEA might turn out to be effective only in the long term. In this context, behaviour and values of actors may change due to systematization of planning and social learning. The likelihood of indirect, long-term effects in PPP making led Faludi (2000) to suggest that strategic plans are probably best evaluated not on the basis of direct, concrete material outcomes, but rather on the basis of how they improve understanding of decision-makers of current and future problems. As a consequence, SEA might only become fully effective in subsequent PPPs (see Chapter 3). Evidence for long-term effectiveness has been found in The Netherlands, where environmental awareness in administrations was observed to be enhanced through EIA and SEA (Van Eck and Scholten, 1997). In order to establish whether SEA is effective, long-term monitoring of decision-making systems is therefore essential. Accepting the changing routines function means SEA can be evaluated, based on the 'why', 'what', 'how', 'where' and 'when' questions framework it is working within.

SEA effectiveness criteria

In this section, SEA effectiveness criteria, as advocated in the professional literature, are introduced and discussed. This is followed by a list of context evaluation criteria for effective SEA application that is used to evaluate 11 SEA systems in Chapter 4.

SEA effectiveness criteria advocated in the professional literature

SEA effectiveness criteria first appeared in the international professional literature in the mid-1990s. In this context, terminology used has varied and includes 'basic elements for effective SEA' (Sadler and Verheem, 1996), 'SEA good practice elements' (Partidário, 1997), 'basic principles of SEA' (DETR, 1998), 'conditions of effectiveness for SEA' (Nooteboom, 1999), 'principles for SEA guidelines' (CSIR, 2000), 'factors for SEA effectiveness in decision-making' (Furman and Hilden, 2001), 'SEA performance criteria' (IAIA, 2002) and 'SEA principles' (Fischer, 2002a). Box 1.3 draws together effectiveness criteria advertised by the authors mentioned above, revolving around issues of objectives-led, efficient, relevant, accountable, transparent, iterative, adaptive, flexible, integrated and sustainable decision-making.

Criteria that support effective SEA application consist of SEA procedural aspects, as well as appropriate methods and techniques. They also include context-related enabling criteria. A good

---

> **BOX 1.3 SEA EFFECTIVENESS CRITERIA ADVERTISED IN THE PROFESSIONAL LITERATURE**
>
> - SEA should be effective in ensuring environmental aspects are given due consideration in PPP making;
> - SEA should be integrated and sustainability-led, supporting a proactive planning process that is driven by clear goals and objectives; apart from environmental aspects, SEA should also consider economic and social aspects;
> - SEA should be carried out with professionalism and those conducting it should be made accountable; SEA should document and justify how environmental and sustainability objectives are considered in PPP practices in a transparent and simple manner; in this context, quality control is said to be of great importance;
> - SEA should be stakeholder-driven, explicitly addressing the public's inputs and concerns, ensuring access to relevant information of the PPP making process;
> - SEA should provide sufficient, reliable and usable information in a cost- and time-efficient manner;
> - SEA should be iterative, being part of an ongoing decision cycle (that is, within a tiered PPP framework); it should inspire future planning through the potential amendment of strategic decisions; in this context, SEA needs to be applied in a tiered manner with effective project EIA within an established PPP framework;
> - SEA should be flexible and adaptive to the PPP process.
>
> *Source:* following Fischer and Gazzola (2006a).

quality process and a high technical standard of methods and techniques come with a high degree of accountability and quality control in SEA. In this context, a focused, participative, iterative and adaptable SEA process that is open to external input is desirable. Furthermore, cost- and time-efficient generation of sufficient, reliable and usable information on environmental baseline, impact and alternative assessments in SEA making are vital. While the SEA process, methods and techniques are further elaborated on in Chapter 2, context criteria are listed in the next section. Context criteria revolve around an established institutional framework for the effective consideration of the environment in PPP making, an awareness of environmental problems, and the existence of a sustainable development framework that provides for SEA objectives. Furthermore, a tradition of effective cooperation and public participation in PPP making, and an effective project EIA system with which SEA can be tiered, are important.

Context criteria for effective SEA application

Context criteria for effective SEA are established in this section. These are used for evaluating 11 SEA systems from throughout the world in Chapter 4. Criteria are summarized under six headings, as is shown in Box 1.4 (following Fischer, 2005a). The absence or non-consideration of any of these criteria may pose a barrier to effective SEA application.

> # BOX 1.4 CONTACT EVALUATION CRITERIA FOR EFFECTIVE SEA APPLICATION
>
> 1 Formal requirements and clear provisions to conduct and effectively consider SEA;
> 2 Clear goals for assessment;
> 3 Appropriate funding, time and support;
> 4 Achievement of a willingness to cooperate; consideration of traditional decision making approaches;
> 5 Setting clear boundaries – addressing the right issues at the right time and defining roles of assessors;
> 6 Acknowledging and dealing with uncertainties.

Formal requirements and clear provisions to conduct and effectively consider SEA

Formal requirements are of importance for ensuring SEA is applied in a consistent manner, giving certainty to the actors involved in both SEA and PPP processes. Formal requirements are normally laid out in legislation and guidance. Regulations and directives are also at times the basis for SEA. In this context, it is vital that there are explicit and clear provisions for SEA results to be considered in decision-making and to justify the decision taken in the light of the assessment results. An allocation of clear responsibilities and enforcement, for example, by a specific agency, legal threats or independent review, are important, ensuring that practice is complying with requirements and SEA results are actually considered in PPP making.

If PPP makers are not accountable for possible environmental effects, SEA is bound to have a weaker status than otherwise. However, to establish clear accountabilities at strategic levels of decision-making is not as straightforward as at the project level, where causes and effects can be connected more easily. Based on current knowledge, for example, it would be close to impossible to calculate the possible environmental damage due to global climate change caused by CO_2 emissions connected with a specific transport policy.

Clear goals for assessment

Clear goals coming out of a common value system provide guidance for action in SEA. In this context, sustainable development strategies and linkages to existing environmental objectives that are accepted by all actors involved in PPP making and SEA have been shown to be particularly important. SEA should not simply be used in a reactive way to mitigate environmental impacts of actions that have already been decided upon. Instead, it should proactively inform decision-making by providing for suggestions on what alternatives to consider. Furthermore, it should help to identify the most favourable alternatives for minimizing negative environmental impacts within the decision process, thus enhancing positive effects and changing the thinking on possible solutions of those involved in the decision process. Consistent sets of substantive aims and objectives across all sectors and administrations are normally difficult to find. In this context, at times, economic and environmental objectives may turn out to be incompatible, for example, 'achieving constant and high levels of GDP growth' versus 'an effective protection of the environment' (for an in-depth discussion, see Jansson et al, 1994). An important role of SEA is to clearly pinpoint incompatibilities and to identify possible trade-offs.

Appropriate funding, time and support

Appropriate funding, time and support are of essential importance to conduct SEA in a meaningful manner. In this context, appropriate also means 'sufficient' to achieve desired outcomes. In order to add scientific rigour to PPP making and to be able to apply the SEA process effectively, appropriate time will need to be made available. In this context, looking at spatial/land use and transport SEA practice in the UK, The Netherlands and Germany, Fischer (2002a) found a statistically significant correlation between the time spent on an SEA and its perceived effectiveness. This indicates that if an effort is made to produce a good quality SEA, the willingness to have SEA influence PPP making may increase.

Appropriate support mechanisms help PPP makers and assessors to deliver an effective and efficient SEA process. Support can be provided, for example, by suitable agencies, centres of expertise or coordination units (German Presidency of the EC Council, 1999, point 12). Other possibilities include advisory bodies that are jointly established by several ministries or departments, bringing together different networks of experts and different sectors. Finally, education and training are important, particularly in the interest of social learning, and a commitment of the different actors to be involved in SEA.

Achievement of a willingness to cooperate: Consideration of traditional decision-making approaches

An insufficient political and administrative will to cooperate in SEA is a barrier to its effective application. This may take some time to overcome. In this context, if there is initial resistance to using SEA, it may turn out to be effective only in the long term by slowly changing attitudes, once its application is perceived by PPP makers to indeed support better decision-making. If there is insufficient political and administrative will, but there is a well-developed environmental consciousness in society, there may be public pressure to apply SEA. However, if public support is lacking, SEA may turn out to be weak and ultimately ineffective.

Compartmentalized organizational structures and bureaucratic prerogatives may be in the way of effective SEA application. If, for example, spatial and transport planning departments of a country, a region or a municipality do not cooperate in PPP preparation, it is unlikely that SEA results can be effectively implemented (see also Chapter 3). In this context, careful consideration of decision-making traditions, and a willingness to change identified weaknesses for achieving better cooperation and coordination of PPP and project planning is vital for being able to achieve effective SEA.

In order to achieve a willingness to cooperate in strategic decision-making, all those involved (that is, administrations, agencies, politicians and others) need to perceive themselves as *real* actors in the PPP and SEA process. In this context, two types of learning need to be addressed by SEA: cognitive learning, where knowledge is the dominant variable, and social learning, where communication between different actors and their values may lead to the reformulation of policy issues. This is going to be easier to achieve in the presence of a tradition of transparency and cooperation. In this context, a sound public, legal, administrative and political support base is going to be crucial. In societies/communities with a well-developed environmental consciousness, it is likely to be easier to influence decision-making and to enhance cooperation on environmental issues. The absence of a clear understanding of needs, objectives, values, processes and methods poses a barrier for effective SEA application. In this context, training and support of those involved in PPP and SEA making is also important.

Setting clear boundaries: Addressing the right issues at the right time and defining roles of assessors

If there are no clear and/or consistent aims and objectives available in a PPP making system, SEA might indicate differences in opinions, rather than leading to clear solutions (Hilden et al, 2004). Setting clear boundaries at the outset of SEA application helps to create situations in which PPP actors struggle less with defining the issues to be considered, but rather with dealing with solutions. In this context, the definition of clear tasks is important. If applied within a transparent, structured decision-making framework, SEA can help to shorten and simplify not only PPPs, but ultimately EIA and project planning, thus saving time and money. In this context, the existence of an effective project EIA system is important. Whereas proactive assessment means that the process should be open to

all feasible alternatives, in developed decision systems, alternatives are unlikely to be considered all together in one 'mega' PPP/SEA process (as is suggested by the strategic environmental analysis, or SEAN, approach, developed for developing countries that do not have established planning systems in place; see Kessler, 2000). Rather, they are probably best addressed at different tiers, as described above. Taking the example of strategic transport planning, when dealing with transport infrastructure network extensions, it is important that 'obviating development' options are firstly considered, namely, reasonable policy options that would make, for example, extensive road construction unnecessary (ODPM, 2005a; see also Chapter 3).

Acknowledging and dealing with uncertainties

It is important that all actors involved in the SEA process are aware of and acknowledge that uncertainties and unforeseeable impacts are likely to occur in all planning situations, particularly at higher tiers. If uncertainties are not explicitly acknowledged, actors might be disappointed with the outcomes of SEA and, as a consequence, the influence of subsequent SEAs may be greatly reduced. Uncertainty follow-up is an important post-SEA process activity (see Chapter 2). Whereas accepting uncertainty is important, there is also a need to develop a better understanding of cause–effect relationships, thus ultimately aiming at reducing uncertainties. In this context, monitoring, evaluation and publication/distribution of experiences is of particular importance.

Summary and outlook

SEA's origins lie within a project EIA-based assessment approach first brought about by the US National Environmental Policy Act in 1969. The main procedural stages in this context include screening, scoping, assessment of alternatives, report preparation and review, decision-making, follow-up and monitoring, consultation and participation. In the 1990s, suggestions started to be made that this process may be too rigorous and inflexible for decisions made at higher strategic tiers (namely, the policy level) and for cabinet decision-making. As a consequence, subsequently, a distinction started to be made between plan and programme making by public authorities, and at times, private bodies, on the one hand, and policy preparation, as well as cabinet decision-making, on the other.

Whereas for plans and programmes, EIA-based approaches are normally said to work well, less rigorous and more adaptable, flexible processes are now frequently advocated within policy and cabinet decision-making. However, in this context, empirical evidence for what makes this type of SEA effective remains thin to date.

This introductory chapter has provided explanations for:

- SEA's rationale, ie leading to a stronger presentation of environmental issues; more effective reasoning; more efficient decision-making; supporting good governance and sustainable development.
- The way in which SEA works; as a decision support process, as an information generating instrument and as a systematic decision framework.
- How SEA functions, providing for better information; enabling attitudes and perceptions to change through participation and involvement; changing established routines.
- Context evaluation criteria for effective SEA; namely, formal requirements and clear provisions, clear goals of assessment, appropriate funding, time and support, achieving a willingness to cooperate, setting clear boundaries, and an awareness of uncertainties.

Context criteria introduced above will be used in order to review 11 SEA systems in Chapter 4. Furthermore, the ability of SEA to meet perceived benefits (see Box 1.2) will be used in the evaluation of five spatial/land use SEA case studies in Chapter 6. These include:

- More systematic and effective consideration of wider environmental impacts and alternatives;
- Proactive support of strategic action for sustainable development, helping to focus on the right issues at the right time;
- More efficient and tiered decision-making and strengthening of project EIA;
- More effective involvement in strategic decision-making.

Other evaluation criteria for Chapters 4 and 6 will include SEA procedural aspects and appropriate methods/techniques. These are introduced and discussed in further detail in Chapter 2.

Notes

1   See, for example, the national UK sustainable development indicators (www.sustainable-development.gov.uk) and the North West of England Region's 'Implementing Action for Sustainability – an Integrated appraisal Toolkit for the North West' (www.actionforsustainability.org).

2   While at times this is referred to as the 'EIA-based' approach, it is suggested here that this notion should be avoided, as even project EIA should not be applied in a reactive and ex-post manner. In this context, it is also important to acknowledge that in a number of systems EIA has shown to be of good quality (see, for example, Barker and Wood, 2001). Within these systems, to refer to EIA as a reactive tool that is applied in an ex-post and ineffective manner would likely result in some considerable confusion and would be counterproductive.

2

Strategic Environmental Assessment Process, Methods and Techniques

In Chapter 2, the role and purpose of the SEA process are first explained. In this context, structured and rigorous EIA-based and flexible non-EIA-based SEA processes are discussed. Methods and techniques to be used in SEA are then introduced, including descriptive, analytical, involvement and other methods and techniques.

The SEA process: Its role and purpose

As has been explained in Chapter 1, in a generic sense, SEA is a procedural support instrument that aims to achieve a better integration of environmental and possibly other sustainability considerations into PPP making processes. In this context, SEA is supposed to help moving towards achieving objectives and targets, rather than moving away from problems.

While a 'good' PPP making process is normally portrayed as one that provides for a balanced view of all relevant aspects, in reality, and opposite to what many PPP makers claim, certain issues tend to be subordinated to others, including particularly those that are of an environmental and social nature. In this sense, SEA works as an advocate tool, which is supposed to 'reorient' strategic planning processes towards achieving more environmentally sound and sustainable decisions.

In order to be able to act as an effective decision-making support instrument for the development of environmentally sustainable PPPs, SEA needs to be able to proactively influence all preparation stages of the PPP to which it is applied. In this context, in order to establish the most

appropriate SEA process, assessors need to be aware that besides enabling a more effective incorporation of the environmental component into a PPP, the SEA process should also allow for:

- the timely gathering and analysis of the information necessary for sound decision-making, including input from relevant stakeholders (information function and changing attitudes function; see Chapter 1);
- the timely evaluation of the likely significant environmental effects of strategic alternatives and proposed actions (changing routines function; see Chapter 1);
- the setting of conditions for environmentally sound implementation of strategic decisions (information function and changing routines function; see Chapter 1).

The SEA literature has identified two main types of SEA processes (Sadler and Verheem, 1996; Fischer, 2002a). Following Chapter 1, these include: first, a structured and rigorous EIA-based process of predefined steps for plans and programmes, prepared by public planning authorities and at times private bodies; and second, a more flexible assessment process for policies, prepared by public planning authorities, and at times private bodies, and for cabinet decision-making (for example, legislative proposals and other PPPs).

Subsequently, these two types of processes are discussed in further detail. In practice, hybrids of the two types may also exist and the boundaries between the two may not always be clear cut (Scrase, 2006). This is further explained below.

EIA-based SEA

Figure 2.1 shows a typical EIA-based SEA process, as applied at lower tiers of strategic decision-making in public authorities', and at times private bodies' (including international aid organizations/development banks) plan and programme making. An EIA-based process is applied to certain plans and programmes in EU member states, following the requirements of the SEA Directive (see also Figure 1.1).[1] The main stages of what may be termed the 'classical' SEA process, shown in Figure 2.1, are subsequently explained.

Screening

The screening stage is used to decide if SEA is needed. In this context, the first question to be asked is whether there are any specific legislative requirements for SEA and whether those PPPs for which SEA is needed are specified. Second, if a PPP as such was not formerly specified to require SEA by leading to certain environmental thresholds being crossed, SEA may still be needed. Thresholds may include, for example, the area covered (size), the sensitivity of the nature affected (protected species) or the PPP action. Finally, in the absence of any specified PPPs and thresholds, SEA screening may be done on a case-by-case basis. In this context, the potential impact significance may be assessed individually with a subsequent decision to conduct or not to conduct SEA. Questions to be asked may include:

- What are the characteristics of the receiving environment?
- What are the overall – development and protection – objectives? Are significant environmental effects likely, considering the anticipated PPP? What are the characteristics of the potential effects?
- If SEA is needed, what type of SEA should be conducted (for example, policy, plan or programme related; see Chapter 3)?

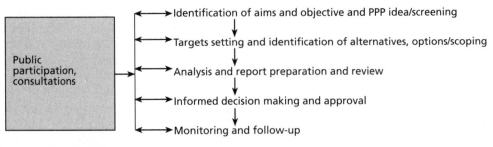

Source: Dusik et al (2003)

Figure 2.1 *The EIA-based SEA process*

Scoping

The scoping stage determines the likely extent (geographic, temporal and thematic) and level of detail of the assessment, the information to be included in the SEA and the environmental report. In this context, baseline information and data needs have to be established. Existing sources and gaps need to be identified and environmental problems and protection objectives described. In order to be able to draw a realistic picture of the situation, it is important not only to consider the biophysical environment, but also to take economic and social development objectives into account. Objectives and indicators can be based on, for example, legislative requirements, sustainable development or other strategies. Other PPPs and projects that may be of importance in order for the SEA need to be identified and described. In this context, the consistency of different sustainability objectives and targets needs to be checked. At the scoping stage, different development alternatives should be identified that may be available for meeting environmental, economic and social objectives. Furthermore, suitable methods and techniques for the assessment, as well as potential stakeholders/actors need to be identified. Finally, at the scoping stage, consultation and participation should be conducted. Scoping experiences with project EIA in the UK have lately been reported on by Wood et al (2006).

Analysis, environmental report and review

This stage is at the heart of the SEA process. The analysis needs to be sufficiently (*scientifically*) robust and transparent to convince stakeholders and the public that the results are state-of-the-art and as reliable as possible. The analysis should involve prediction and evaluation of possible impacts. Furthermore, it should show how remaining impacts can be minimized, mitigated and compensated. A wider analysis, also considering economic and social aspects, provides scope for identifying trade-offs in SEA. In this context, a 'best practical environmental option' (BPEO) (see Bond and Brooks, 1997) may be identified. Methods and techniques that may be used in analysis are further discussed below.

The environmental report documents the findings of the assessment of the various proposed alternatives and the predicted impacts upon the environment. It usually serves as a basis for consultation and public participation and should be one of the considerations to be taken into account in decision-making. The environmental report should not only establish the significant environmental impacts of the different development options and alternatives, but should also fulfil a range of other tasks. This includes the justification of the assessment methods and techniques used in SEA. Furthermore, it should establish how other documentation was taken into account, describe how consultation and participation was conducted up until that point and how the results of these exercises were considered in the SEA. Finally, the environmental report should provide for some recommendations to decision-makers in terms of preferred alternatives and regarding possible measures for avoiding, minimizing, mitigating and compensating any potentially remaining impacts.

At the review stage (which is not explicitly required by the SEA Directive), the adequacy of the environmental information collected during the SEA process and presented in the environmental report is supposed to be checked. In this context, uncertainties and contradictions should be identified and any bias, if possible, should be counteracted. While review can take different forms, it should always be done by an independent person or body, for example, an environmental authority or assessment commission. The quality of the environmental report may be reviewed with the help of a review package. A review package for environmental reports prepared under the requirements of the European SEA Directive is provided in Annex 1 (following Fischer, 2005b).

Decision-making and approval

At the main decision-making stage, economic and social matters are weighed against the environmental considerations brought forward by SEA. Within decision-making, due consideration to the environment should be given and the decision-maker should explain how a decision was reached and what information was used. The European SEA Directive asks decision-makers to justify their decisions in the light of the findings of the environmental report and the consultations conducted. Effective integration of SEA into decision-making is vital if SEA is to be meaningful and beneficial.

Follow-up and monitoring

SEA should neither be conducted in a reactive manner, nor should it be an exercise that informs the PPP process only at one stage. Rather, SEA should be used as a proactive environmental management instrument. In this context, it needs to reach beyond the decision-making stage. While an important task of environmental assessment follow-up is to try to establish cause–effect relationships, in SEA this may frequently be difficult to achieve, particularly due to the abstract nature and the time gap with project implementation (Fischer, 2004a; Perdicoúlis et al, forth-

coming). Post-SEA activities can take the following forms (following Partidário and Fischer, 2004):

- Conformance follow-up – complying with agreed PPP/SEA objectives, regulatory requirements, standards and conditions;
- Performance follow-up – checking the satisfactory environmental and possibly sustainability performance at subsequent stages of decision-making and following implementation; attempting to connect causes and effects;
- Uncertainty follow-up – managing actual impacts; reviewing the effectiveness of any possible mitigation or compensation measures and possibly modifying activities in case of unpredicted harmful effects;
- Dissemination follow-up – providing feedback for the design of new PPPs.

In the member states of the EU, SEA Directive-based practice currently requires follow-up/monitoring in terms of what has been introduced above as conformance and performance follow-up (European Commission, 2001a). Whereas there is currently very little practice of uncertainty monitoring, Holling (1978) outlined how uncertainty could potentially be managed, applying an 'adaptive environmental management' approach. There is currently a particular need for improving dissemination follow-up in order to improve understanding of the effectiveness of the measures and action proposed in PPPs. This book is, in effect, a dissemination follow-up effort, based on various practical SEA experiences. Box 2.1 outlines what the four types of SEA follow-up and monitoring may comprise.

Box 2.1 Four types of SEA follow-up

1 *Conformance* follow-up

This includes regular observations of developments in order to demonstrate verification of compliance with objectives, regulatory requirements and applicable standards or criteria established in PPP SEA. Conformance follow-up can potentially take place within monitoring programmes. It is likely to be rather difficult in policy situations with large time gaps between policy making and implementation, particularly as political changes may have led to new policy objectives that differ from those originally formulated.

2 *Performance* follow-up

This includes regular observations and measurements of environmental and possibly sustainability parameters/indicators with the purpose of attempting to establish cause–effect relationships with those activities laid out in the PPP SEA. Whilst performance follow-up should be comparatively straightforward, in policy situations it may prove to be difficult, due to technical and institutional problems, particularly when large time gaps between policy making and implementation are present.

3 *Uncertainty* follow-up

Uncertainty follow-up calls for an environmental impact management programme to be in place in order to ensure uncertain and unexpected effects can be identified. This includes reporting on inspections and checks on the environmental impacts of the PPP implementation at subsequent tiers of decision-making, providing an opportunity to any changes being reviewed or reassessed in a comprehensive and cumulative manner. Uncertainty follow-up may prove particularly fruitful in policy situations, in which changing political or institutional circumstances may ask for flexible reactive mechanisms to be in place.

4 *Dissemination* follow-up

Experience with previous SEA needs to be widely disseminated in order to improve future practice. Feedback is needed in order to adjust the design of new PPPs, or the methods and approaches of implementation. Furthermore, feedback is necessary to improve impact prediction and mitigation practices at all tiers of decision-making.

Source: following Partidário and Fischer (2004)

Consultation, participation, communication and reporting

A well-performed SEA effectively informs and involves interested and affected stakeholders throughout the assessment process. Furthermore, it addresses the general public's input, making it explicit in reporting, and supporting its effective consideration in the decision-making process. It also provides for effective communication. Finally, effective SEA ensures the general public is given sufficient access to information. Participation processes in public decision-making have been strengthened by the Aarhus Convention on Access to Information, Public Participation in Decision-making

---

Box 2.2 Definitions for participation, consultation, communication and reporting

Participation

Engagement process, in which external persons (for example, the public) are called to contribute to the decision-making process by exchanging information, predictions, opinions, interests and values.

Consultation

Engagement process, in which external persons (for example, the public) are called to comment on documentation.

Communication

One-way process, in which the objective is to inform and assist third parties and the public towards understanding of problems, alternatives, opportunities and solutions.

Reporting

Documentation process in which results are made available in a written document, on the basis of which third parties/the public can make their comments, providing for feedback on the analyses made, alternatives and decisions.

---

and Access to Justice in Environmental Matters (UNECE, 2004).

Whilst frequently, the terms 'participation', 'consultation', 'communication' and 'reporting' are used in an interchangeable way, they do mean different things, representing different degrees of involvement, ranging from simple information to the full involvement of actors, as shown in Box 2.2.

Stakeholders and relevant interest groups (for example, industry, households, businesses, services and religious groups/churches) should be fully engaged in decision-making processes. The extent to which the general public will want to be involved is likely to depend on the specific PPP making situation. Whereas, for example, in more policy-related situations, the general public may not necessarily show a great degree of interest, once more project-related decisions are considered, this is likely to be different.

One example known to the author in this context is the National Spatial Plan of Denmark. Here, in a public consultation exercise in the mid-1990s, only roughly 160 comments were received for the plan, covering the whole country with a population of about 5 million (European Commission, 1997). In this context, the most likely reason was that the plan was perceived as being too abstract.

The international professional literature suggests that public input should occur throughout the whole SEA process, that is, public participation and communication should be an integral part of SEA. In this context, interest groups as well as the general public can contribute to the following tasks:

- defining SEA objectives (screening, scoping),
- supporting comprehensive baseline information (scoping),

- identifying alternatives (scoping),
- choosing between alternatives (assessment and report),
- identifying mitigation measures (assessment and report),
- ensuring the effective implementation of the proposed PPP (follow-up).

From the very early stages of strategic decision processes, namely, when setting the context for PPP making and SEA, decisions on who should be involved in the process need to be made (including the public, NGOs and public administration/authorities). Information should be communicated with a view to the groups involved in SEA and PPP making. Reporting should include a description of this process, thus providing authorities, NGOs, consultants and the general public with a documented basis for following up the environmental and sustainability considerations that have been taken into account. However, the exact information to be included in the environmental reports will vary according to legal requirements. Reporting may either occur at the end of the decision-making process with the preparation of a final document, or throughout the various stages of the SEA process with the writing-up of smaller reports, which are ultimately brought together in a final report. Reporting may also occur through information bulletins and websites.

The SEA process in cabinet decision-making and policy making

As explained in Chapter 1, SEA applied in cabinet decision-making (for example, when drafting legislation or other PPP initiatives) and in public authorities' and at times private bodies' policy making is currently unlikely to follow the same rigorous process as EIA-based SEA

applied in plan and programme making. However, understanding of what makes a flexible SEA process effective is not yet fully developed and, to date, little empirical evidence has been brought forward. While in both cabinet decision-making and policy making, SEA needs to be adapted to the specific situation of application, most likely requiring a more flexible format of application, experiences indicate that this increased flexibility does not necessarily mean that certain core stages and core principles are abandoned altogether (Elling and Nielsen, 1997; Dalal-Clayton and Sadler, 2005; Verheem, 2005).

SEA in cabinet decision-making

There are a range of cabinet SEA systems globally, including Canada (based on a Cabinet Directive from 1990, amended 1999), Denmark (based on Prime Minister's Circulars from 1993, 1995, amended 1999, 2004), Finland (based on guidelines on EIA of legislative proposals from 1998), Hong Kong (based on a Governor's Policy Address from 1992), The Netherlands (based on a Cabinet Order environmental e-test of draft regulations from 1995, amended 2003), Norway (based on an Administrative Order on Assessment of White Papers and Government Proposals from 1995), the Czech Republic (based on the national EIA Act of 1992, amended 2004) and the US (based on the National Environmental Policy Act from 1969). There is often an assumption in the professional literature that at the policy level and in cabinet decision-making, SEA looks different from the plan/programme level. However, while certain systems are indeed set up in a non-EIA-based manner (for example, Canada, Denmark, The Netherlands and Norway), others are based on EIA requirements (Finland, Hong Kong and the US), and even in non-EIA-based systems there are certain common, systematic aspects. SEA systems from Denmark, The Netherlands and Canada, for example, use a number of core questions as a basic assessment framework (Elling and Nielsen, 1997; see also Chapter 4). These include:

- Is SEA necessary? (based on overall aims and objectives, that is, screening)
- What should SEA consider? (substantive aspects, alternatives, that is, scoping)
- What are the effects of different policy options? (analysis)
- Has the assessment been effectively considered in decision-making? (documentation)

While many authors have underlined the necessity of a high degree of flexibility, the evidence that is available indicates that flexibility should not mean 'vague', as this appears to result in a toothless rather than an effective instrument (Verheem, 2005). Furthermore, while cabinet SEA does not include public participation, the possibility and feasibility of including the public has been stressed, for example, by Elling and Nielsen (1997) reflecting on Danish experiences with cabinet SEA. While two cabinet SEA systems are reviewed in Chapter 4 (the Canadian SEA and the Dutch e-test), what follows is a brief summary of Danish environmental assessment of bills and other government proposals.

Danish environmental assessment of bills and other government proposals
Requirements for an environmental assessment of bills and other government proposals were introduced in Denmark, based on the Administrative Order No. 31 of 26 February 1993 (later replaced by Administrative Order No. 12 of 11

January 1995). A guidance document was also released by the Danish Ministry of Environment and Energy (1993). Box 2.3 summarizes requirements, as laid out in the guidance.

In the Danish cabinet SEA system, the focus is on the prediction and evaluation of possible significant environmental impacts. There is no rigorous and formalized process in place. Furthermore, there are no requirements for the delivery of recommendations on how to offset impacts or on how to mitigate or compensate them. To date, enforcement has been weak and there is no public participation. As a consequence, there is a low degree of transparency (documentation is not publicly available). Finally, the quality of the SEA appears to depend very much on the goodwill of the ministry conducting SEA.

Interestingly, and despite the limited scope of this cabinet SEA system, a study from 1996 on Danish practice (Elling and Nielsen, 1997, p.vi) concluded that:

Nevertheless, one crucial conclusion of the project's testing is that the five internationally recognised principles of environmental... assessment – documentation, procedure, significance, alternatives and the involvement of the public – can be applied to parliamentary bills without any major or fundamental obstacles.

Furthermore, regarding the controversial issues of public participation and more concrete methodological requirements, the same study suggested that:

- *... it is possible to involve the general public in the environmental assessment procedure. This would strengthen the overall*

BOX 2.3 REQUIREMENTS FOR AN ENVIRONMENTAL ASSESSMENT OF BILLS AND OTHER GOVERNMENT PROPOSALS IN DENMARK

- The ministry putting forward a proposal is responsible for evaluating and explaining whether the bill/government proposal has significant environmental effects and for undertaking the assessment of environmental effects, if necessary.
- The Ministry of Environment and Energy provides advice on the assessment, however, the ministry putting forward the proposal decides on whether advice is wanted.
- The SEA should include an evaluation of the beneficial and adverse changes in pollution and health and the possible effects on resources, natural and cultural conditions regarding the local, regional and global environment.
- The SEA includes the following stages:
  - Determining the need for an SEA (screening), using a checklist, which includes questions regarding effects on:
    i   surface and groundwater,
    ii   air,
    iii climate,
    iv surface of the earth, soil and percolations,
    v   flora and fauna, including habitats and biodiversity,
    vi landscapes,
    vii other resources,
    viii waste,
    ix historical buildings,
    x   population's health and well-being, production,
    xi handling or transport of hazardous or toxic substances;
  - Scoping of environmental assessment;
  - Detailed analysis for those issues from the checklist, for which effects are considered to be significant.

Source: Danish Ministry of Environment and Energy, 1993.

---

process by adding weight behind joint propositions to the competent authorities.

- *Letting the general public take part in scoping and assessment may also prevent the authorities in charge of preparing legislation from attributing importance a priori to certain interested parties, which potentially enables the authorities to take control of incoming suggestions.*

- *If it were also made obligatory for the authorities to consider all incoming suggestions, they would – unlike today – be barred from neglecting the presentation of the conclusions reached by an environmental... assessment in the observations on the bill.*

- *More explicit demands on the assessment's contents and scope may help to get the information on a bill's environmental effects* presented *to decision-makers.* (Elling and Nielsen, 1997, p.vii.)

These conclusions indicate that even in cabinet SEA, a structured assessment approach may enhance rigour and SEA effectiveness.

Policy SEA

Policy SEA application in public authorities' and at times private bodies' decision-making is frequently conducted in what has been referred to as visioning exercises or development outlook plans. Visions aim to address fundamental 'why' and 'what' questions, and to set the context for subsequent plans and programmes. Frequently, there is full integration of the visioning and SEA processes. This was observed for spatial/land use and transport examples from The Netherlands, Germany and the UK (Fischer, 2002a).

While policy (vision/development outlook) making processes are normally conducted in a flexible (that is, individually designed) manner, there are also some common features. Thus, processes tend to be highly participative, with external bodies and the general public being given extensive opportunities for involvement. Furthermore, policy and SEA processes are normally fully integrated. Full integration is the reason why SEA as such is frequently not recognized. Also, normally, there are no formal requirements in place for assessment in policy making. Evaluation of various policy development options is done informally, allowing the consideration of issues and alternatives across sectoral and administrative boundaries. A policy SEA example, the Development Vision for Noord-Holland, is introduced in Chapter 6.

Procedural integration of PPP and SEA

While there is some consensus among those working on SEA that integration of SEA and PPP making processes is desirable, there is currently disagreement over the extent to which this should happen. In this context, while many protagonists appear to favour full integration (see, for example, Thérivel and Partidário, 1996), critics have argued that merging both processes fully may be problematic due to the different functions that PPP making and SEA have (Fischer 2003a; 2006b).

There is a range of possibilities to integrate PPP making and SEA, as is indicated by the following four types of integration:

1   SEA and PPP are fully integrated, that is, there is no separate SEA process.
2   SEA and PPP are parallel processes that connect at various core stages (also called the 'concurrent model' by Glasson and Gosling, 2001).
3   SEA and PPP are independent processes; SEA feeds into the PPP making process at one stage only, for example, before PPP consent is given (this has also been called the 'stapled model' by Glasson and Gosling, 2001).
4   SEA and PPP are independent processes, SEA is applied quasi ex-post, that is, SEA does not have an immediate impact on the PPP.

While option 4 has at times been applied, it is clear that this should not be the preferred choice because SEA is going to be largely ineffective if applied after PPP preparation. If used in the way described by option 3, SEA is also going to be of limited value because it is unlikely that SEA can influence the choice of alternatives, objectives and aspects to be considered. The specific situation of application is likely to rest on whether options 1 or 2 should be applied. Whereas in policy situations, for example, both processes may be fully integrated (see Chapter 3), in plan situations, a concurrent approach may be preferable, particularly in the interest of a balanced view on the various assessment aspects and transparency.

Methods and techniques used in SEA

SEA is not just a systematic process, as has been explained above. It also provides for a structured decision framework and acts as an evidence-based instrument, generating information through the use of appropriate methods and techniques, thus adding scientific rigour to the PPP making process. This means that predictions need to be rigorous and as exact as possible. However, in SEA, this may be difficult to achieve because of the nature of action and impacts, which frequently may be of a cumulative and synergistic nature.[2]

This section first explains what methods and techniques should aim to achieve in SEA. Second, the most commonly used methods and techniques in SEA are introduced and briefly explained. In this context, possible differences between EIA-based and non-EIA-based SEA are highlighted. Descriptive, analytical and involvement methods and techniques are introduced. For EIA-based SEA, suitable methods and techniques for the main procedural stages (see Figure 2.1) are summarized. Finally, some other methods and techniques, which are currently used infrequently but which may be useful in SEA, are introduced.

What methods and techniques should aim to achieve in SEA

Methods and techniques used in SEA should help to achieve various goals:

- Methods and techniques should aim at simplifying the frequently complex issues under consideration at strategic decision-making levels.
  - An overlay map applied in spatially defined SEA provides for a good example of how this may be achieved, summarizing spatial sensitivities of various environmental aspects, based on data, for example, for fauna and flora, soils, water, protected areas and other aspects.
- Methods and techniques should add rigour to the SEA process.
  - If, for example, different policy options are available for reducing CO_2 emissions, the technique enabling identification of the best option should allow for some reliability in reaching a judgement based on past evidence. In this context, evidence-based forecasting and backcasting techniques may be helpful.
- Methods and techniques should support the identification and evaluation of the direct and indirect environmental and possibly sustainability effects of a reasonable range of alternatives.
  - In strategic situations above the project level, even direct impacts may be difficult to establish quantitatively. In this context, one technique allowing to compare different alternatives is MCA

BOX 2.4 CONDITIONS THAT SEA METHODS AND TECHNIQUES SHOULD MEET

SEA methods and techniques should:

- Be fit for purpose, that is, be able to address relevant/key issues and fit into the decision-making process and timetable;
- Allow for the integration of various aspects, that is, substantive aspects, different administrations, sectors and procedures;
- Allow uncertainties to be addressed;
- Be transparent, robust, relevant and practical;
- Be understandable to all those involved in SEA;
- Be cost-effective.

(multi-criteria analysis). The evaluation of indirect effects will normally pose even greater problems. In this context, an experienced assessor may be able to identify at least some of the indirect effects based on past observations (see, for example, Jonsson and Johansson, 2006).

- Methods and techniques should prove to be useful and effective in facilitating consultation and participation. In this context, transparency is crucial.
  - A prediction model that can only be understood by the programmer, but no one else, is not likely to support effective involvement; in this context, some authors have argued that qualitative techniques may be preferable to quantitative techniques, however, relying entirely on qualitative techniques may also lead to people questioning the validity of the SEA due to a lack of evidence and scientific rigour.
- Methods and techniques should support cost- and time-effective SEA, that is, unnecessary costs should be

avoided and the SEA should provide value for money.
  - If SEA is perceived as wasting both time and money, it is not likely to be perceived positively; value for money therefore needs to be an important goal for SEA.

Based on these goals, application of SEA methods and techniques should meet a range of conditions. These are listed in Box 2.4.

There are also certain limits to what methods and techniques can achieve. These are connected in particular with:

- The frequently indirect nature of PPP effects (see above);
- The difficulty of jointly assessing aspects that have different dimensions; this is especially a problem if substantive integration is to be achieved (that is, environmental, economic and social aspects; see Chapter 1);
- The absence of sets of compatible objectives from different areas (that is, environmental, economic and social; see Chapter 1).

Most commonly used methods and techniques

A large number of methods and techniques are available for use in SEA. Lee (2006) mentions 350 methods and techniques that were identified in an investigation of Dutch ministries in the early 1980s (VROM, 1984). However, despite this extensive choice, in practice only a very limited range of methods and techniques is used. This has been shown by various authors, for example Therivel and Wood (2004), Fischer (2002a) and Therivel and Partidário (1996). The most commonly used methods and techniques in SEA include:

- Descriptive methods and techniques – indicators, checklists, impact matrices and impact triangles;
- Analytical methods and techniques – impact trees/cause–effect diagrams or networks, multi-criteria/cost–benefit analysis, overlay maps, SWOT analysis, forecasting and backcasting (modelling);
- Involvement (consultative and participative) methods and techniques – visioning exercises, workshops and expert surveys.

These methods and techniques are described in further detail below, however, in addition to these three types of methods and techniques, the importance of data and field surveys should be stressed because these provide for the necessary baseline, allow for evaluation and generating follow-up data for assessment. Data/field surveys may rely on existing documentation or may involve the generation of SEA-specific information. Data/field surveys may be useful in different situations and for different purposes. At the policy level, for example, data may need to be generated in the context of forecasting and backcasting (explained further below). At the plan level, site-specific data may need to be generated, for example, in order to achieve a better understanding of how severance caused by a motorway network may impact a population of protected species. In order to determine the adequacy of factors used in MCA and CBA at the programme level (see also Chapter 3), follow-up data/field surveys are vital.

Descriptive methods and techniques

Indicators

Indicators are widely used in all assessment situations and at all SEA stages. They are applied, for example, in order to decide on whether SEA is needed (screening), and to define a baseline for establishing whether significant environmental effects are likely (for example, whether a PPP would be unlikely to lead to a fulfilment of CO_2 reduction targets). Furthermore, they can be used at the scoping stage, for example, in order to support decisions on the alternatives to be considered in the light of existing sustainable development indicators. Indicators may also provide an important evidence base when making a decision. Finally, monitoring activities are normally connected with selected indicators.

There are different types of indicators, including state, pressure and response indicators (see Bell and Morse, 2003). State indicators show, for example, how a certain impact develops over time (for example, CO_2 concentrations or particulate matter). Pressure indicators require a comparison of actual developments and environmental targets (for example, reduction of CO_2 emissions by 30 per cent between 1990 and 2020). Response indicators, finally, involve predefined regulative action in case a target is not reached. This may, for example, take the form of penalties or the introduction of certain management measures. In this context, in many privatized rail systems worldwide, if certain predefined minimum safety or delay thresholds are not met, operators have to pay penalties to the regulators. Figure 2.2 shows an example of a pressure indicator, as established by the second Transport Structure Plan (SVVII) in The Netherlands in 1989 (MVW, 1989). The 'policy effect measuring report' from 1995 (MVW, 1995) shows that whereas the declared target was to reduce CO_2 emissions from transport by 25 per cent by the year 2010, annual data indicated that the implementation of policies to reach that target was insufficient and that an increase in CO_2 emissions was observed.

A compatible set of indicators may be difficult to achieve and, frequently, the assessment process may reveal inconsistencies. In this context, necessary trade-offs for different alternatives should

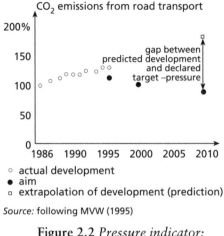

Figure 2.2 *Pressure indicator: The Dutch SVVII target*

Source: following MVW (1995)

be established by SEA.

Checklists

Checklists are used in most SEAs. Regulations, for example, may include threshold checklists to enable screening. Furthermore, scoping checklists may take the form of questionnaires for those involved in the process, and monitoring checklists may simply list those aspects that are to be monitored. Box 2.5 shows a threshold checklist for screening based on the EC SEA Directive.

Impact matrices

Impact matrices may be used in different assessment situations, for example, for indicating what impacts may occur through defined action. Some SEA systems are largely based on a 'matrix approach' to impact assessment. This includes the land use (development) plan making system in England. Figure 2.3 shows an example of a goals achievement matrix routinely used in England. Within this matrix, possible effects of statements of development intent (in England

---

Box 2.5 EC SEA Directive threshold list (for screening)

SEA shall be conducted for:

- Plans and programmes that set a framework for future development consent of projects listed in Annexes I and II to Council Directive 85/337/EEC (The EIA Directive);
- Plans and programmes that have been determined to require assessment pursuant to Council Directive 92/43/EEC (Flora-Fauna-Habitat Directive);
- Those plans and programmes that determine the use of small areas.

Criteria	Global sustainability					Natural resources				Local environmental quality					
	1	2	3	4	5	6	7	8	9	10	11	12	13	14	15
Proposed policies/action	Transport energy efficiency	Transport trips	Housing energy efficiency	Renewable energy potential	CO_2 fixing	Wildlife habitats	Air quality	Water conservation	Soil quality	Minerals conservation	Landscape	Rural environment	Cultural heritage	Public access to parks	Building quality
Urban regeneration	✔	✔	✔	✔	✔	✔	✔	✔	X?	•	✔	•	✔	✔?	✔
Improved trams	✔	✔	?	✔?	✔	•	✔	•	•	•	•	•	✔	?	✔
Use of brownfield sites	•	•	•	✔?	✔	X?	•	•	X?	✔	✔	?	✔	✔	✔

Legend:
- • No relationship or insignificant impact
- ✔ significant beneficial impact
- ✔? likely but unpredictable beneficial impact
- ? uncertainty of prediction or knowledge
- X? likely but unpredictable adverse impact
- X significant adverse impact

Source: Fischer (2004b)

Figure 2.3 *Goals achievement matrix as used in plan making SEA in the UK*

referred to as 'policies' – for example, urban regeneration) on indicators (for example, transport energy efficiency) are presented.

Another example for an impact matrix is provided by Table 2.1 (following Annandale et al, 2003). Here, a cost–benefit impact matrix has been used for comparing different waste management solutions: conventional landfill, incineration and composting/residual landfill, in terms of capital cost, employment, the land required and the possibility of groundwater pollution.

Impact triangles

Impact triangles allow for an easy-to-understand presentation of impact magnitudes of different alternatives relative to each other. An example is provided by Figure 2.4, which shows the extent to which environmental, social and economic sustainable development objectives may be met (following Fürst et al, 1999), comparing two spatial development concepts as examples: first, the compact city concept (namely, concentrated development in towns and cities); and second, the edge city concept (namely, concentrating development on the edges of towns and cities). Here, the compact city was presented as being more environ-

Table 2.1 *Cost–benefit impact matrix*

	Conventional landfill	Incineration	Composting and residual landfill
Capital cost (in M €)	20	30	10
Employment (in thousands)	20	10	50
Area of land required (in km²)	100	10	30
Possibility of groundwater pollution	High	Very low	Low

Source: following Annandale et al (2003)

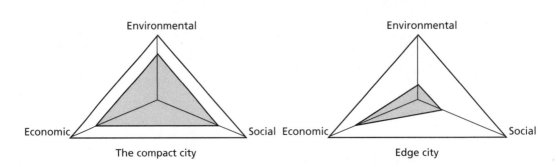

Source: following Fürst et al (1999)

Figure 2.4 *The sustainability triangle: An application to the compact and edge city concepts*

mentally and socially sustainable than the edge city, with similar scores being reached for economic sustainability. The impact triangle may also take the form of a hexagon or a star, depending on the number of aims and objectives to be represented.

Analytical methods and techniques

Impact trees, networks and flow charts

Flow charts, networks and impact trees indicate cause–effect chains and relationships for identifying different environmental and other aspects. They are suitable techniques for identifying those aspects and issues that may be potentially affected by development. Figure 2.5 shows an example, focusing on socio-cultural impacts of a PPP. Particularly due to the complexity of the issues under consideration at strategic decision-making levels, in practice, impact trees, flow charts and networks are used only infrequently. However, they may be usefully applied, particularly for screening and scoping purposes: for screening, in order to determine whether SEA is needed, and for scoping, in order to identify the issues to be covered in assessment.

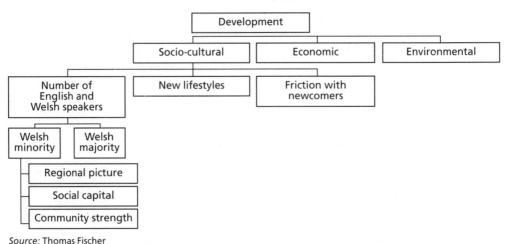

Source: Thomas Fischer

Figure 2.5 *Impact tree, showing a cause (development)–effect (on Welsh minority) chain*

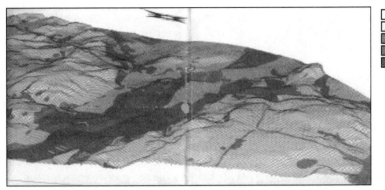

Increasing sensitivity
of bio-physical
environment

Source: Fischer et al (1994)

Figure 2.6 *A GIS overlay map showing sensitivities*

Cost–benefit analysis and multi-criteria analysis

Both, CBA and MCA are frequently used in assessment, comparing different alternatives, based on either monetarized (CBA) or non-monetarized (MCA) factors. CBA is normally understood in terms of the sum of all benefits minus the sum of all costs. CBA is applied in a range of sectors and in a range of situations. In transport programme making, for example, costs to be considered may include construction, maintenance and running costs, and benefits may include higher traffic security, improved accessibility and regional economic effects. Cost–benefit relationships (CBRs) are calculated as:

$$CBR = Bc - Cc$$

where Bc is the sum of all benefits (expressed in monetary terms) and Cc is the sum of all costs (expressed in monetary terms). MCA works in a very similar way to CBA, only that non-monetary factors are used. A problem with both CBA and MCA is that they frequently imply a preciseness in prediction (particularly regarding monetary impacts) that is not really there, particularly as the components used in evaluation are frequently arbitrarily chosen. They should therefore only be used for comparative purposes, for example, in order to identify projects that should receive priority in public funding within programmes (see Chapter 3).

Overlay mapping and geographical information systems

Overlay maps are used frequently in SEA, particularly when various area-wide themes are to be brought together, for example, for indicating environmental sensitivities in a plan area ('vulnerability analysis'). Overlay maps are widely used in spatial/land use and sectoral plan assessment. Figure 2.6 shows a geographical information system (GIS)-based overlay map indicating environmentally sensitive areas. The map shown here was prepared based on a range of underlying themes, including water, soils, biodiversity and others. In this case, the use of GIS would have also allowed the evaluation of impacts by comparing site sensitivities with impact magnitudes of different proposed alternatives. GIS-based overlay mapping also allows the evaluation of effects caused by severance and land partitioning on species (land partitioning analysis), for example, when considering impacts of infrastructure network extensions (network SEA; see Chapter 3).

SWOT (strengths, weaknesses, opportunities and threats) analysis

Hilden (2005) reported on qualitative SWOT (strengths, weaknesses, opportunities and threats) analyses being frequently used in Finnish SEAs, particularly at scoping and analysis stages, for example, as the basis for scenario analysis. SWOT analysis originally comes from strategic management of companies. A SWOT analysis aims at establishing strengths and weaknesses of the current situation, for example, in a sector, in order to portray opportunities and threats for future development. In this context, strengths and weaknesses are internal factors that are normally identified considering other areas or localities. Furthermore, opportunities and threats are external factors that are normally identified, taking trends and obstacles into account.

Forecasting and backcasting

Forecasting of impacts in SEA may be done qualitatively, for example, based on surveys with experts, or quantitatively, for example, with the help of statistical modelling in scenario analysis. Figure 2.7 shows a simple example for how results of a forecasting exercise may be presented using a 'forecasting cross'. Here, expected impacts on a local community are portrayed in terms of more or less housing and greater or smaller increases in employment. Each corner of the forecasting cross presented may include bullet point lists of, for example, expected impacts on land use or traffic.

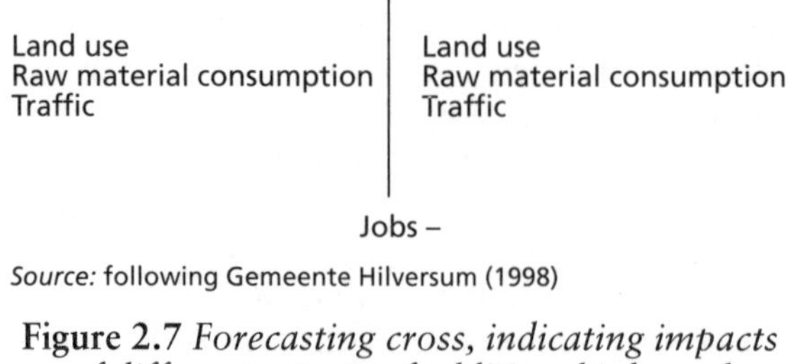

Backcasting is related to forecasting. The main difference is that backcasting aims at identifying those alternatives that will help achieve stated environmental objectives and targets. Ecological footprinting may be used as the basis for backcasting. This technique aims at identifying how much productive land and water area is required to support a region's population indefinitely at present consumption levels. Furthermore, it aims at showing how the required land (for generating resources and offsetting emissions) compares to the land that is actually available. The ecological footprint of a place (for example, a region, a county or a town) is the area size required to sustain its current lifestyle in terms of both, inputs (for example, food production, resources) and outputs (for example, waste, emissions). Figure 2.8 provides an example, comparing the geographical size of The Netherlands and its ecological footprint. This was calculated based on consumption, emission and waste levels, and indicates that The Netherlands uses more resources and produces more emissions and waste than they

Jobs +

Land use	Land use
Raw material consumption	Raw material consumption
Traffic	Traffic

Housing – ———————————|——————————— Housing +

Land use	Land use
Raw material consumption	Raw material consumption
Traffic	Traffic

Jobs –

Source: following Gemeente Hilversum (1998)

Figure 2.7 *Forecasting cross, indicating impacts of different extents of additional jobs and housing*

are able to sustain (for further information see Wackernagel and Rees, 1996; Barrett, 2002).

Involvement methods and techniques

A large number of involvement (consultation and participation) and communication/ reporting methods and techniques are available for use in SEA (see Box 2.6). The choice of appropriate methods and techniques in a specific situation depends on a range of factors, most importantly the desired degree of empowerment and the resources available. Whereas fully fledged participation can actively empower those involved in the assessment process, simple communication only informs those interested in the assessment, without actively involving them, thus being a one-way exercise. Consultation, finally, goes further than simple communication in aiming to obtain opinions of consultees. It comes with less empowerment than participation (see also Box

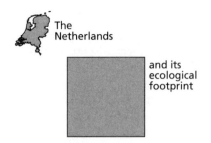

The Netherlands

and its ecological footprint

Source: following Rees and Wackernagel (1994)

Figure 2.8 *The Netherlands and its ecological footprint*

2.2).

Whereas full public participation may be difficult to achieve in many PPP making and SEA processes, effective consultation is likely to be easier to facilitate and may also have many positive effects, as explained above. Three frequently used involvement methods/techniques in SEA are discussed in further detail below, namely visioning exercises, workshops and surveys with experts, stakeholders and the general public.

Visioning exercises

Visioning exercises have been conducted in many countries and planning systems (see above, Chapter 6 and Figure 3.3). Visions started to emerge at the end of the 1980s and are examples of complex participation exercises, within which a range of other methods and techniques may be used. While in the first half of the 1990s, their application was particularly widespread in The Netherlands ('visies'; see Chapter 6), they were also used in

---

BOX 2.6 PARTICIPATION, CONSULTATION AND REPORTING METHODS AND TECHNIQUES

Participation

Advisory groups, workshops, visioning exercises, citizen juries

Consultation

Workshops, public meetings, questionnaire/interview surveys

Communication/reporting

Leaflets, newsletters, newspapers, television and radio, site visits, exhibitions, telephone helplines, fact sheets, websites, open houses

---

other countries. Visioning exercises are highly participative in nature, attempting to identify aspirations, aims and objectives of a society/community. Frequently, they aim at comparing different development scenarios, for example, in terms of a 'best' and 'worst' environmental result. A visioning exercise normally aims at developing ideas for preferred development options.

Workshops

Workshops are used in many planning and assessment situations. Within workshops, joint ideas for suitable solutions may be developed. Generally speaking, workshops are suitably used within an assessment process in order to develop a better understanding for possible problems, different opinions, attitudes and values. They are particularly useful in situations where there is no common understanding of issues and problems. Workshops should be organized in a way that allows everyone wishing to contribute to do so by raising questions, providing information, establishing answers and possible solutions. Some authors have described SEAs that were largely based on workshops. In Vienna, for example, a round-table approach was followed in order to establish environmentally sustainable waste management. This exercise had the aim of generating consensus among all round-table participants (Arbter, 2005).

Expert, stakeholder and public surveys

Surveys allow for the collection of information on opinions, attitudes and knowledge and are used widely in SEA. Surveys with experts, stakeholders and the general public can take the form of interviews, postal questionnaires and emails. Expert opinions on possible effects are frequently generated in SEA through surveys, particularly in situations that are

complex and where the assessment is supposed to be done quickly and at low cost. In this context, the careful choice of suitable experts is of particular importance in order to ensure credibility. Furthermore, expert surveys may be helpful for achieving a better understanding of possible future development, particularly in situations that are marked by a high degree of uncertainty. Surveys with stakeholders allow the identification of different interests in PPP making processes. Finally, surveys with the general public may indicate resistance or support for certain PPPs. Furthermore, local knowledge may be generated at low cost.

Additional methods and techniques

There are a number of other methods and techniques that may be beneficial in SEA, but that are currently used infrequently. In this context, three analytical methods and techniques are introduced here that may be usefully applied, particularly at the policy level. These include technology assessment, life-cycle analysis and risk assessment.

Technology assessment

Technology assessment is used for assessing the effects of new technologies, including environmental, social and economic effects. This type of assessment can be particularly helpful at the policy level when establishing what basic options may be available for meeting overall sustainable development aims and objectives. In transport planning, for example, technology assessment allows an examination of the role of new technologies, such as hydrogen engines. This may include an estimation of when it can be expected to be economically feasible to introduce new technologies and whether there is likely to be a societal support

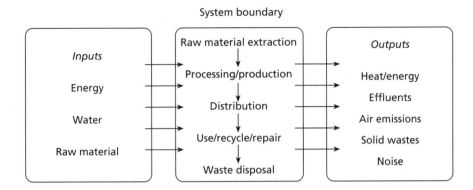

Source: Petts (1999)

Figure 2.9 *The industrial life-cycle system*

base. A suitable way to portray the extent to which different aims and objectives are met, once established, is the use of a 'sustainability triangle' (see above).

Life-cycle analysis

Life-cycle analysis helps to identify impacts over the whole life cycle of a product, project, or in the case of SEA, a PPP. In transport policy making, for example, life-cycle assessment (LCA) can help to identify impacts of different means of transport. Assessing the impact of cars, for example, goes far beyond simply measuring fuel consumption per kilometre and includes:

- consideration of extraction of raw materials for producing the car,
- transport of those materials,
- the production process,
- actual use of the car (fuel consumption and emissions),
- disposal.

When planning for a new road, applying life-cycle assessment means not only considering effects such as severance, noise disturbance and land use, but also, for example, the extraction and transport of the raw materials for construction. At

times, life-cycle assessment receives other names, such as 'eco-balancing', 'cradle to grave analysis' or 'eco-profiling'. Within life-cycle assessment, various other techniques may be used, particularly input–output techniques. Figure 2.9 depicts a basic industrial life-cycle system, identifying what the system involves, as well as possible inputs and outputs (following Petts, 1999). However, as a word of caution, Hilden (2005) suggests that because of the costs involved with conducting life-cycle analysis, it is unlikely to be used frequently in SEA.

Risk assessment

Risk assessment is a technique that is supposed to provide information to decision-makers about the anticipated frequency and severity of possible adverse environmental impacts of new technologies and developments. Whilst risk assessment is a discipline in its own right, it may be usefully combined with SEA. Similarly to SEA, the risk assessment process is normally portrayed as being proactive, aiming at reducing and subsequently managing risk. A typical risk assessment process includes risk estimation, evaluation and auditing of related activities at core stages. Risk assessment

---

BOX 2.7 METHODS AND TECHNIQUES AT DIFFERENT SEA STAGES

Screening

Indicators, checklists, expert opinions, communication/reporting

Scoping

Indicators, checklists, matrices, surveys, participation, communication, consultation, expert opinions, SWOT analysis

Impact assessment/report

Indicators, matrices, surveys, communication/reporting, participation, consultation, networks, statistical analyses, overlay maps, forecasting, expert opinions, SWOT analysis

Review

Indicators, consultation, participation, expert opinions

Monitoring

Indicators, surveys, communication/reporting, expert opinions

---

as a discipline has evolved since the 1980s and there is an extensive associated literature (see, for example, United States Environmental Protection Agency, 1998; Petts, 1999; Bina, 2003).

Use of suitable methods and techniques in different SEA situations

The use of suitable methods and techniques in SEA is determined by a range of aspects. Most importantly, these include:

- the stage in the assessment process,
- the sector SEA is applied in,
- the systematic tier, namely, policy, plan or programme (see Chapter 3).

Box 2.7 shows methods and techniques that may be used at the various stages of an EIA-based SEA process. In this context, most widely used are indicators, checklists and matrices, surveys, and communication/reporting. In non-EIA-based SEA, methods and techniques that are most frequently used include:

- in cabinet PPP making: matrices, checklists, expert opinions;
- in public authority/private body policy making: visioning, forecasting, backcasting, expert opinions, matrices.

Methods and techniques applied at different systematic tiers are introduced in Chapter 3. Furthermore, in Chapter 6, methods and techniques used in five spatial/land use SEAs are described.

Summary and conclusions

This chapter introduced and discussed the SEA process, as well as a range of methods and techniques that are used in SEA. Why the process is important was explained. In this context, the main purpose was described to be the proactive influencing of all preparation stages of a PPP in order to effectively incorporate the environmental component. A detailed description of the role and content of the SEA process was provided next. In this context, the importance of considering core procedural stages was underlined. For EIA-based SEA, these include screening, scoping, environmental report preparation and review, decision-making, follow-up and monitoring, consultation and public participation. For public authority/private body policy making and cabinet decision-making (legislative proposals and other PPPs), the process is often portrayed as being less rigorously defined and more flexible. However, even here, certain core procedural elements should also be in place, including at least screening, scoping and analysis.

Also in this chapter most commonly used methods and techniques were identi-fied and explained. These include descriptive, analytical and involvement methods and techniques. The first group includes indicators, checklists, impact matrices and sustainability triangles. The second group includes impact trees/networks, flow charts, multi-criteria and cost–benefit analyses, overlay mapping, forecasting and backcasting and SWOT analysis. The third group includes visioning exercises, workshops and surveys of experts, stakeholders and the general public. Finally, expert consultation is important in most SEAs. The importance of data/field surveys for generating information in order to be able to assess, evaluate and monitor PPPs was also stressed. Other methods and techniques that are not yet frequently used, but that may prove to be particularly useful in SEA include technology, life-cycle and risk assessment. While in this chapter, the different procedural stages of SEA were connected with suitable methods and techniques, allocation to the different systematic tiers (policies, plans, programmes) is discussed in Chapter 3.

Notes

1 In Directive-based SEA, no formal review stage is required and consultation and participation might only take place at scoping and report stages.

2 For guidance on how cumulative and synergistic effects may be considered, see CEAA (1999).

Identifying Appropriate Issues and Alternatives to be addressed in SEA: The Importance of a Tiered Approach

Chapter 3 shows how appropriate issues and alternatives may be identified in SEA. In this context, it fills the gap identified in Chapter 2, focusing on different systematic tiers of decision-making. In this chapter, the third part of the definition of SEA provided in Box 1.1 is addressed: 'SEA is a systematic decision-making framework, establishing a substantive focus, particularly in terms of alternatives and aspects to be considered, depending on the systematic tier, administrative level and sector of application'.

The chapter is subdivided into six sections. First, the importance of identifying appropriate issues and alternatives for SEA is explained. This is followed by a discussion on how a more systematic approach may be possible in transport planning. A practical example on the consideration of issues and alternatives in private sector electricity transmission planning and tiered SEA is provided. Furthermore, tiering in spatial/land use planning is explained, looking at practice in England and Germany. Potential problems with tiering are discussed, and finally, conclusions are drawn.

The importance of addressing appropriate issues and alternatives

The benefits that are supposed to result from SEA application are closely related to the consideration of appropriate issues and alternatives at the right time, as discussed in Chapter 1. Ultimately, by supporting the identification of appropriate issues and alternatives in systematic, objectives-led, evidence-based, proactive, transparent and participative processes, it is hoped that SEA can lead to savings in time and money, particularly by avoiding costly mistakes (see Chapter 1). Developing a better understanding of what issues and alternatives may be suitably addressed in a specific situation

of application is vital for SEA to be able to support better PPP making. In this context, suitable methods and techniques may also be defined.

The European SEA Directive requires the identification, description and evaluation of reasonable alternatives. While it does not explain what reasonable alternatives may be, it asks those conducting SEA to outline the reasons for selecting alternatives. Those reasons are likely to be connected with the sector, administrative level and systematic decision tier SEA is applied to. Whether SEA is applied by a public planning authority or in cabinet

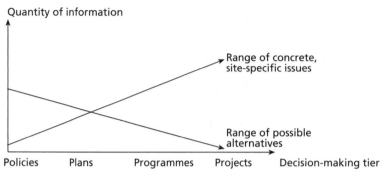

Source: Fischer (2006a)

Figure 3.1 *Quantity of information provided by different SEA types*

decision-making should be irrelevant. Figure 3.1 provides for a basic conceptual understanding of how alternatives may be developed, based on the systematic decision tier at which SEA is applied. In this context, the range of possible alternatives differs, depending on whether SEA is applied to a policy, plan or programme. Fewer alternatives are available when the range of concrete, site-specific issues is large in more project-related situations. More alternatives, by contrast, are available in policy-related situations. Whereas in project-related situations, alternatives are likely to revolve around specific locations, design, construction and operation, in policy-related situations, alternatives may be area-wide, political, regulative, technological, fiscal and economic (see also Table 1.1). Issues to be considered (substantive aspects, indicators, other PPPs) are closely connected with the consideration of appropriate alternatives. This is further discussed in the remainder of this chapter.

In order to explain how appropriate alternatives for use in SEA may be deter-mined. To this end, first, a conceptual SEA framework is introduced. Besides spatial/land use planning, transport is the sector in which SEA application has been most extensive to date. This is why trans-port is used as the example for identifying appropriate issues and alternatives to be addressed at different decision tiers. In this context a generic transport SEA framework is designed, based on the evidence provided by transport planning practice in northern and western European countries. The framework is used to evaluate transport PPP making and SEA in Germany. Second, a tiered SEA system developed by the privatized former public utility ScottishPower is introduced for electricity transmission planning, showing the applicability of tiered SEA frameworks in sectors other than transport. Evidence for the consider-ation of different alternatives at different spatial/land use planning tiers is then provided, looking at the examples of England and Germany. Finally, problems that may arise with SEA tiering and possi-ble barriers are highlighted.

Transport SEA[1]

In this section, a generic tiered transport SEA framework is introduced, allowing for the identification of appropriate alternatives in specific assessment situations. In this context, assessment issues, types of impacts to be considered and roles of the different administrative levels are identified. Apart from helping practitioners to conduct SEA in a more systematic manner, the framework may be used for evaluating existing practice. Furthermore, it may serve as the basis for developing context-specific guidance. The framework may help to make dividing lines 'between policies on one hand and plans and programmes on the other', that may currently be 'difficult to specify' clearer (Hilden, 2005, p.63). To show how the framework may be used, transport PPP making and SEA in Germany is evaluated.

Generic transport SEA framework

The generic transport SEA framework consists of four main strategic decision tiers, including policies, network plans, corridor plans and programmes. The framework is based on empirical observations in a range of northern and western European countries, mainly the Scandinavian countries (Jansson, 2000), Germany, The Netherlands and the UK (Fischer, 2000) and Belgium (Van Straaten et al, 2001). The existence of different systematic SEA types is also supported by the evidence provided by Bina (2001), referring to European Commission Trans-European Transport Networks (EC TEN-T) pilot studies in Sweden, the UK, Austria, Italy and France.

Using the framework for identifying suitable alternatives requires the initial analysis of a transport planning system. Based on this analysis, gaps in the existing system may be identified, including, for example, the absence of certain tiers or the non-consideration of certain types of alternatives. This knowledge may subsequently be used to amend an 'incomplete' system, either by introducing new tiers or by extending existing tiers. The four strategic decision tiers of the framework are explained in further detail below.

As a word of caution, it is important to add here that the framework is not meant to advocate a strictly hierarchical, rigid and inflexible approach to PPP making; SEA needs to adapt to the specific system it is applied in. Rather than working strictly top-down, a system may, for example, also consist of decision flows that work in both top-down and bottom-up directions. By introducing the framework, there is no suggestion that there may not be deviations regarding concrete project implementation from what was originally intended in earlier PPPs. Rather, the underlying assumption is that changes should be made in a conscious manner. It is important that any decision to construct a concrete transport infrastructure project would normally be associated with other policy, plan, programme and project decisions. Feedback to subsequent PPP making and assessment practice is therefore of particular importance. Finally, the framework is aimed at helping those working together on SEA to agree on those issues to be addressed in a specific situation. If there is no agreement on what to address, 'some stakeholder [may] attempt to raise broad strategic issues while others wish to make the whole exercise a technical listing of observations, which can be used to justify specific (predetermined) choices' (Hilden, 2005, p.61).

Policy (vision)

At the policy (vision) level, overall – consistent and compatible – transport aims and objectives are to be identified, setting the context for subsequent action. At this stage, the role of SEA is to assess different available policy options. Alternatives to be considered may, for example, be of an organizational, regulatory, fiscal or infrastructure nature. At the policy level, any considerations are going to be highly cross-sectoral and cross-thematic in nature, with effective cooperation of different administrations and stakeholders being of crucial importance. Ideally, transport policy making should involve the preparation of integrative, participative, administration-led visioning exercises. However, in practice, transport policy is frequently fragmented and decided upon in a non-transparent manner. Generally speaking, transport policy would normally be expected to be decided upon by elected decision-makers (see also Chapter 2).

Examples of public planning authorities' policy SEAs are provided by a range of regional transport and traffic plans in The Netherlands. In the province of Noord-Holland, for example, fully integrated visions/assessments were conducted throughout the 1990s, for example Noord-Holland Noord, Haarlem-IJmond, the Regional Body of Amsterdam (ROA), and Gooi en Vechtstreek (Fischer, 2002a). Furthermore, they include local examples from the UK (Merseyside Integrated Transport Study – MerITS; Merseyside Passenger Transport Authority, 1993), Germany (the Hamburg Transport Development Plan – *Verkehrsentwicklungsplan*, Freie und Hansestadt Hamburg, 1995) and Finland (Helsinki Metropolitan Area Transport System Plan, 1998; see Kaljonen, 2000). There

are other more recent policy-type documents focusing on assessing the effectiveness of certain policy aspects, for example, road charging (see the report of the Review of Charging Options for London – ROCOL working group; ROCOL, 2000).

Regarding the substantive issues to be considered, at the policy level, empirical evidence shows that SEA normally tends to focus on a selected number of key aspects, including energy consumption and CO_2. Furthermore, NO_x/SO_2 emissions are frequently considered (Fischer, 2002a). According to the European Commission (1999), other possible aspects that may be included are CH_4, N_2O and land take. Considering the difficulties in assessing comprehensive and complex policies, for example, at national levels of decision-making, for practical reasons, it may be preferable to focus on one or two indicators only, for example, energy consumption and CO_2 emissions.

Network plans

Transport policies set the basis for considerations within transport infrastructure networks (namely, network plans). Depending on the specific administrative level (national, regional or local), alternatives to be considered may revolve, for example, around road, railway, water and air transport infrastructures. Considering that different parts of a transport infrastructure network may fall into different responsibilities, a systematic and comprehensive evaluation of the entire network is likely to be difficult. Therefore, for network planning to be effective, all those authorities responsible for the different parts of the network will need to be involved and cooperate closely. The role of a central body (for example a transport ministry) to act as a facilitator, mediator and/or advocate is of particular importance (Fischer, 2003a; see also Figure 1.4). Network plan SEAs are likely to address issues such as energy consumption, CO_2, severance and biodiversity. NO_x/SO_2 may also be considered and other possible aspects to be addressed at this stage include non-methane hydrocarbons (NMVOC), carbon monoxide (CO) and land take (European Commission, 1999). It is important to add that if there is no systematic assessment taking place at the policy stage, network plans may need to compensate for associated omissions.

Corridor plans

Network plans are likely to lead to the establishment of concrete transport infrastructure needs and further evaluation may take place in transport corridor plans.[2] If, in a transport planning system, intermodal alternatives are addressed at policy and network plan levels, a deliberate decision may be made to only consider one transport mode within a specific corridor plan. Assuming agreement among different stakeholders, the tasks to be performed may vary, depending on whether or not policy and/or network plans and associated assessments have been conducted. If this is not the case, the corridor plan may need to compensate for gaps elsewhere. Normally, corridor plan SEAs can be expected to address issues such as severance and biodiversity, harmful emissions and land take. In case intermodal alternatives are assessed, close cooperation of those administrations responsible for the different modes under consideration is vital. Overall policy aims and objectives should set the context for plan making and assessment.

Programmes

Concrete infrastructure projects resulting from corridor plan making and assessment may subsequently be collected and ranked by a transport administration, using MCA or CBA. This may take place within a comprehensive transport programme making process and/or within programmes of a limited number of linked projects. Those projects achieving the highest multi-criteria or benefit–cost ratios would subsequently become priority projects (or priority alternatives) in terms of administrative and financial support. Key issues to be considered in this context are likely to include concrete local/regional impacts.

The framework

In summary, the system-based SEA framework consists of four main tiers:

- Transport policy-related SEA – visioning, objectives and policies setting.
- Transport network plan-related SEA – establishing and evaluating intermodal network solutions (based on transport policies).
- Transport corridor plan-related SEA – assessing concrete network needs in transport corridors.
- Transport (investment) programme-related SEA – identifying priority projects based on MCA or CBA.

Following on from these four SEA tiers, transport project-related EIA would be conducted, dealing with project specific issues. Figure 3.2 summarizes, in a conceptual way, the four tiers of the SEA framework.

As explained later, in current transport planning practice in many countries, certain decisions, for example, regarding major infrastructure projects, may be reached in a different manner than based on policies, network plans, corridor plans and programmes. However, even here, the existence of a generic framework would still be useful, for example, providing an

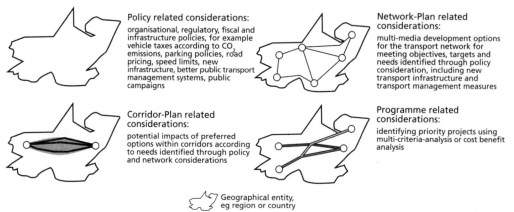

Policy related considerations:
organisational, regulatory, fiscal and infrastructure policies, for example vehicle taxes according to CO_2 emissions, parking policies, road pricing, speed limits, new infrastructure, better public transport management systems, public campaigns

Network-Plan related considerations:
multi-media development options for the transport network for meeting objectives, targets and needs identified through policy consideration, including new transport infrastructure and transport management measures

Corridor-Plan related considerations:
potential impacts of preferred options within corridors according to needs identified through policy and network considerations

Programme related considerations:
identifying priority projects using multi-criteria-analysis or cost benefit analysis

Geographical entity, eg region or country

Source: Fischer (2006a)

Figure 3.2 *The four SEA tiers of the system-based transport planning framework*

important basis for evaluation. It is also acknowledged that certain systems may combine different tiers, for example corridor plan and programme (as in the case of the German Federal Transport Infrastructure Plan – FTIP) or network plans and corridor plans (as in the case of the UK multi-modal studies – MMSs). Furthermore, in smaller countries or regions, it may be difficult to distinguish between network and corridor levels.

Figure 3.3 summarizes the substantive focus, the tasks to be performed, the alternatives to be considered, the role different administrations are likely to play and possible core issues (indicators) to be addressed at each tier, based on the discussion provided above. Furthermore, possible SEA methods and techniques are listed. Even if actual transport planning practice does not strictly follow this framework, it can encourage consideration of a wide range of issues and alternatives that might otherwise be ignored.

Practical application of the framework

This section is subdivided into two parts.

First, based on the assumption that the SEA framework should always adapt to existing practice, different approaches to transport planning in EU member states are outlined. A good understanding of these approaches is vital in order to be able to tier SEA and to use the framework effectively, not just regarding the questions of what impact SEA can be expected to have and who to involve in the PPP/SEA making process, but also in order to establish where and when SEA should be introduced. Second, the existing transport planning system in Germany is evaluated, based on the framework.

Approaches to transport planning in EU member states

In EU member states, national ministries of transport are mostly responsible for national transport planning, and associated agencies are responsible for construction and maintenance of nationally administered infrastructure. Normally, a number of transport documents are prepared reflecting the different systematic tiers introduced above. National transport planning may take the following forms (Fischer, 2006a):

Systematic decision-making tier	Focus	Tasks and alternatives to be considered	Types of impacts to be considered (indicators)	Role of different administrations	Possible methods and techniques
Policy and vision	All policy options that might lead to overall policy objectives and targets	• analysis of current situation • listing existing economic, social and environmental objectives and targets and adaptations to transport • identifying different development scenarios (eg economic and spatial) • identifying different policy options[1] that may lead to objectives and targets • evaluating options in the light of scenarios, indicating trade-offs for achieving objectives and targets, policy assessment • monitoring actual developments • adjusting policies regularly	• Energy consumption and CO_2 • Other possible indicators include NO_x and/or SO_2, CH_4, N_2O and land take	• Can only be effective if the various administrations cooperate closely (different sectors and levels; need to analyse responsibilities first • Combination of cabinet decision making and administration-led policy making likely	• Indicators • Checklists • Data surveys • Impact matrices • Forecasting and backcasting (modelling) • Impact trees and networks • Visioning • Workshops • Expert surveys • Technology assessment • Risk assessment • Life-cycle assessment • SWOT analysis
Network plans	National or regional infrastructure development options leading to specific projects	• analysis of current situation • identifying – inter-modal – development options according to needs identified in policies within the network • assessing impacts on different options to achieve objectives and targets, network-assessment; indication of possible trade-offs • feedback to policies • monitoring actual developments • adjusting network plans regularly	• Energy consumption and CO_2 • Severance and biodiversity • Other possible indicators include NO_x and/or SO_2, NMVOC, CO, severance, land take	• Can only be effective if the administrations responsible for different transport infrastructures co-operate closely	• Indicators • Checklists • Data surveys • Impact matrices • Overlay maps • Workshops • Expert surveys • SWOT analysis
Corridor plans	Spatial alternatives within corridors	• analysis of current situation • potential impacts of preferred options, possibly uni-modal (only if multi-modal alternatives are addressed at both policy and network level), corridor-assessment • monitoring actual developments • feedback to policies and networks	• severance and biodiversity • land take and harmful emissions • other possible indicators include noise and visual impacts	• depends on higher levels; if vision/policy and network aspects are fully covered, one administration may be the main actor	• Indicators • Checklists • Data surveys • Impact matrices • Overlay maps • Workshops • Expert surveys
Programmes	Identify priority projects	• analysis of current situation • identifying priority projects using multi-criteria-analysis or cost-benefit analysis, programme-assessment • monitoring actual developments • regular adjustment of programmes • feedback to previous tiers	• concrete environmental damage translated into factors (MCA) or costs (CBA)	• One administration may be the main actor	• Indicators • Checklists • Data and field surveys • Expert surveys • Multi-criteria/cost-benefit analysis
Projects	Project design	• analysis of current situation • optimise project design in terms of policy objectives and targets (project-assessment) • monitoring actual developments • feedback to previous tiers	• Localised impacts	• One administration may be the main actor	• Project planning related methods and techniques (see Glasson et al, 1999)

Note: 1 Options may include taxes, subsidies for motor vehicles, parking policies, road pricing, speed limits, access restrictions, new infrastructure, better public transport, transport management systems, public campaigns and others

Source: adapted from Fischer (2006a)

Figure 3.3 *Focus, tasks, alternatives, impacts, role of different administrations and methods/techniques within the system-based SEA framework*

1   A national government with its transport ministry and responsible agencies are the main drivers for national transport planning; the planning system works in a quasi top-down manner of decision-making:

a   Proposals for potential projects are the result of careful policy, network-plan, corridor-plan and programme evaluations;

b   While proposals may also be the result of suggestions from, for example, regional and local authorities, industry or other interest groups, the national transport ministry and responsible agencies aim to ensure a close fit between proposals and national transport aims and objectives.

2   The national government with its transport ministry and responsible agencies mainly act as 'collectors' of project ideas from local and regional administrations or other bodies; these are subsequently retrofitted through, for example, a transport programme into the planning system, in other words, the system works more bottom-up than top-down:

a   The national government has an overall policy/vision for the development of transport infrastructure in place, setting the framework for the selection of the most suitable projects;

b   Projects are chosen largely on the basis of financial considerations; in this context, CBA is likely to be the key assessment technique.

3   The regional level acts as the main driver for national transport PPP making with the national level taking on a coordinating role between different regions.

At least theoretically, other forms of transport planning and hybrids of the above are also possible, with, for example, the local level becoming the main driver.

In the EU, countries with a tradition of centralized planning tend to fall into the first category. Based on what has been reported in the literature, the Czech Republic would fall into category 1a, pursuing a centralized top-down planning approach, with central government making project proposals based on various strategic considerations and subsequently driving proposals forward (Zdrazil and Martis, 2001). Up until a few years ago, England would have also fallen into this category. However, more recent changes to transport planning mean that many Highway Agency (the agency responsible for national roads planning) schemes must now compete with other transport projects for regional priority, that is, the regional level has gained in importance and the English system currently appears to be moving more towards category 3. Whereas The Netherlands have a centralized top-down approach to national transport planning (Niekerk and Voogd, 1996), there is some substantial input from third parties, particularly the provinces. It can therefore be said to fall into category 1b. In the interest of effective national PPP making, it would therefore be crucial to involve them throughout the SEA process. In Germany, the federal decision-making tradition means that suggestions for potential projects come from either local or state administrations or from regional road construction agencies (Fischer, 2002a; Dalkmann and Bongardt, 2004). Federal transport planning therefore falls into category 2, with certain aspects of the two sub-categories a and b also being present. Administrations and agencies will need to be fully involved in national PPP making and SEA. While central government formulates overall transport development aims and objectives, their connection with actual projects frequently remains unclear. Finally, Italy and Belgium are examples of countries falling into category 3. Here, the regional level plays a key role in national transport infrastructure planning. In Italy, national transport infrastructure is developed mainly on the back of regional transport plans and national government only takes on a coordinating role between the various regions (Diamantini and Geneletti, 2004). This coordination role may be supported by SEA, as has been indicated for spatial/land use planning in Figure 1.2. Exceptions to this rule are certain national projects that are pushed forward by central government. An example is the Messina bridge motorway between the Italian mainland and Sicily (*Repubblica*, 9 April 2004).[3] In Belgium, finally, the three regions of Flanders, Wallonia and Brussels are responsible for the planning of national transport infrastructure, with the national government only having a moderating role (Van Straaten et al, 2001). Again, SEA may be helpful in this context, at least for checking that regional transport objectives are compatible with national aims.

Transport planning and SEA in Germany

Figure 3.4 portrays transport planning in Germany, using the systematic SEA framework described above. While there is national transport policy, currently no comprehensive federal transport policy document or transport vision is prepared. Federal transport policy making can therefore be said to be fragmented. The main federal transport document is the Federal Transport Infrastructure Plan (FTIP – BMV, 1992). While this mentions some strategic objectives, such as a reduction of CO_2 emissions, it does not include an evaluation of different policy options

of how this might be achieved (in other words, there is no policy SEA). Rather, the FTIP is a project-focused programme, which, when it was last prepared in 1992 (updated in 2003), revolved around the presentation of 1600 concrete projects. These were based on suggestions from state, regional and local planning bodies. In the FTIP, projects were ranked using CBA. Draft SEA guidance for the implementation of the SEA Directive in the transport sector was released in 2004 (FGSV, 2004).

Policy tier

Examples of how transport policy may be developed and subsequently presented in a comprehensive policy document are provided by a number of state and local transport visions/policies that were prepared during the 1990s. However, to date, their impact has remained somewhat unclear. In this context, the city of Hamburg (Freie und Hansestadt Hamburg, 1995) is a good practice example (see Figure 3.4). Here, a transport vision was prepared in the first half of the 1990s that identified overall transport objectives, and that provided for an assessment of 40 policy measures. These consist of 16 pricing/administrative measures, 14 infrastructure development measures and 10 organizational measures.[4]

Furthermore, responsibilities for the different measures were identified in terms of federal (national) and municipal (local) responsibilities, stressing the need for cooperation of different administrations. Overall effectiveness of the three types of measure on reducing anticipated transport growth is shown in Figure 3.5. It needs to be added that the underlying model for predictions was not explained properly and predictions are therefore not transparent. Here, more of an effort should be made to explain what the model is based on and how it works.

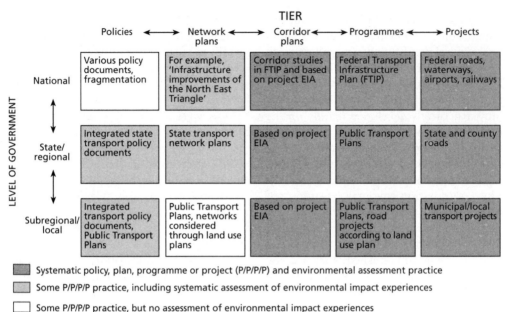

Figure 3.4 *Transport planning system in Germany*

Network plan tier

Regarding the network plan tier, there are experiences at different administrative levels of decision-making. An example with importance for the federal transport network is the 'North-East Triangle' road infrastructure improvement study (Ministerium für Wohnungswesen, 1995) for the area between Hamburg, Hanover and Berlin. This provided for a comprehensive assessment of various spatial options in terms of social, economic and environmental criteria. Overlay mapping was the main technique, using GIS. Only uni-modal considerations were considered, however, focusing on federal motorways and highways. The underlying assumption was that poor accessibility within the triangle area would need to be remedied. Figure 3.6 shows the different spatial road options.

Taking a follow-up perspective, it needs to be added here that the results of this network plan were not well reflected in the most recent FTIP update (BMVBW, 2003), which includes a motorway project (the A39) that was not favoured by the network plan. This may be the result of powerful state administrations and regional road construction agencies pushing certain infrastructure proposals forward (see also Fischer, 2004a), despite the results from studies like the North-East Triangle. This example also underlines the importance of having all important stakeholders cooperating closely in network plan preparation, as is indicated in Figure 3.3.

Other network type plans have been prepared that consider intermodal infrastructure solutions at the state level, including, for example, the North-Rhine Westphalia (Minister für Stadtentwicklung, 1990) or Baden-Württemberg (Verkehrsministerium, 1995) transport plans. They aimed mainly at identifying lists of potential transport projects taking a multi-modal perspective.

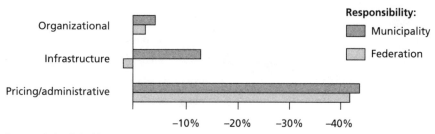

Source: Fischer (2002b)

Figure 3.5 *Effectiveness of three types of measures on reducing anticipated transport growth*

In this context, however, different transport modes have tended to be regarded in separation, making intermodal assessment impossible. At the local level, transport networks are considered (at least in a purely physical way) in the preparation processes of statutory land use plans. Furthermore, since the end of the 1990s, public transport plans have been prepared at local/regional levels. However, currently, these do not include any assessment of environmental impacts.

Corridor plan tier

Regarding corridor plan assessment practice at the federal level, there are two approaches. Preliminary corridor studies are conducted within the Federal Transport Infrastructure Plan (FTIP) preparation process. The approach applied in this context is called 'ecological risk analysis'. This practice has been described on previous occasions (European Commission, 1999). In the 1992 FTIP, corridor-based ecological vulnerability studies were conducted for those 100 projects from the 1600 proposals that were over 10km long. Information on land cover and on potential risks of conflicts within protection areas were the basis for evaluation. In case of expected significant impacts, projects within the

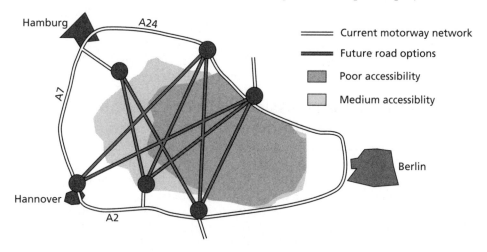

Source: following Ministerium für Wohnungswesen (1995)

Figure 3.6 *Network improvement study 'North-East Triangle'*

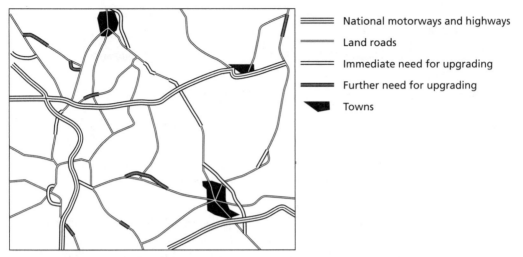

National motorways and highways

Land roads

Immediate need for upgrading

Further need for upgrading

Towns

Source: Thomas Fischer, following Land Brandenburg (1995)

Figure 3.7 *Section of the state roads development plan, Land Brandenburg*

FTIP were said to have been downgraded or entirely abandoned (European Commission, 1999). Similar approaches have also been applied at the state level, for example in North-Rhine Westphalia (Stein et al, 1993). In addition to these corridor SEA type studies, at the project level, corridor evaluation is a routine part of EIA procedures (Knieps and Welp, 1991). In the planning process of a bypass, for example, various spatial (unimodal) alternatives have to be considered and evaluated.

Programme tier

Regarding programme assessment practice, the FTIP ranks potential motorways and other federal roads according to their benefits and costs. In this context, various development scenarios are considered regarding economic and population growth. Similar practice also exists at the state level for state roads planning. Figure 3.7 shows an example of a resulting action map (based on Land Brandenburg, 1995). Finally, transport programmes are also prepared at the county (*Kreis*) levels. This is discussed by Fischer (2001) for the County Oder-Spree.

Electricity transmission network planning and tiered SEA[5]

Whereas the application of SEA has been suggested to be desirable not just for the public, but also for the private sector (Linderhof et al, 2003), how the rigours of a formalized SEA process can ultimately benefit private companies has not yet been clearly established. Suggestions that SEA

may not only help to effectively address environmental aspects in strategic decision-making, but also support effective governance (Jones and Mason, 2002; Kidd and Fischer, 2007) are an indication that some yet largely unanticipated benefits may also result from SEA application to private sector plans and programmes. To date, the professional literature has reported on only a few private sector SEA cases, including oil and gas extraction (Glasson et al, 1999) and offshore windfarms (DTI, 2005). Furthermore, there have been some suggestions, dating back to the beginning of the 1980s, that environmental assessment procedural frameworks similar to SEA can improve corporate decision-making (House of Lords Select Committee, 1981). More recently, Cherp (2004) provided a theoretical discussion on the linkages between SEA and corporate environmental management.

This section reports on practice in the privatized, formerly public, electricity company ScottishPower. Here, SEA was applied voluntarily to electricity transmission planning, based on the perceived benefits that are supposed to result. SEA was applied within a tiered planning system, with different tiers focusing on different alternatives. SEA applied to the electricity sector has been discussed on various occasions, however, mostly in only a generic way (for example by Sheate et al, 2004). In terms of case-specific reporting, Sadler and Verheem (1996) introduced the SEA for the Dutch Second Structure Plan Electricity Supply, which was prepared on the basis of the national EIA Act. A concrete SEA methodology for electricity transmission planning had been developed and described earlier by Noble and Storey (2001). This was also used by ScottishPower, as is shown below.

Background

ScottishPower is one of three UK companies who hold a statutory licence under the Electricity Act 1989 to 'develop and maintain an efficient, co-ordinated and economical transmission system of electricity supply' (HMSO, 1989). The

company's licensed transmission and distribution service area includes southern Scotland, the north west of England and north Wales.

Two factors triggered the initial debate on whether SEA should be applied. First, ScottishPower was interested in finding effective and efficient ways to include the consideration of environmental factors into its existing overhead line routeing programmes (Marshall and Baxter, 2002), promoting good corporate governance and better internal decision-making management, particularly to avoid potentially costly environmental damage. In this context, the company had already sought to develop internal management systems to promote a corporate culture that included the consideration of the environment into its planning and decision-making frameworks, notably through ISO 14001 management systems and corporate environmental governance programmes (ISO, 1996; PowerSystems, 2003). SEA was considered a suitable instrument for complementing the existing frameworks in terms of network planning. Second, there was experience with project EIA, which overall was perceived to be positive. Therefore, a lot of ScottishPower's personnel did not feel uncomfortable with SEA and were open to it.

While there was an early acknowledgement that plans and programmes resulting in statutory transmission projects under the European EIA Directive (European Commission, 1985) would probably fall under the scope of the SEA Directive, ScottishPower was particularly interested in establishing how SEA could make good business sense (which is the precondition for the private sector to embrace SEA). In this context, decision-makers were interested in establishing whether SEA could contribute to the long-

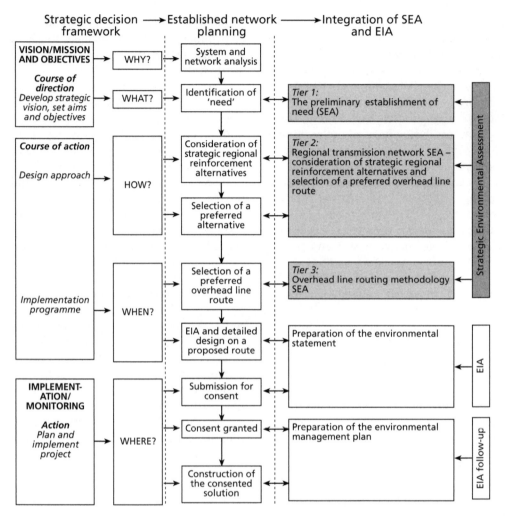

Source: Marshall and Fischer (2006)

Figure 3.8 *Regional electricity network planning and SEA*

term prosperity of the company and increase its ability to manage complex projects, for example, by enhancing cooperation, input and interaction between internal business groups and professional disciplines across management structures.

In the ScottishPower debate on whether any strategic advantage would lie in the voluntary up-take and examination of SEA prior to formalized requirements, particular focus was put on the question of how SEA and the underlying plan or programme process should be integrated. Early on, it was felt that the existing regional transmission network planning frameworks could actually facilitate the incorporation of SEA. Furthermore, it was thought that SEA would be able to consolidate and improve the existing procedures and influence deliverability of plans and programmes, as is explained in further detail below.

SEA framework developed by ScottishPower

An SEA system was designed, taking into account the established planning system within ScottishPower, as well as new ideas surrounding strategic economic planning and tiered SEA. This system consisted of:

- A 'preliminary establishment of need SEA' stage;
- A 'regional transmission network SEA' stage;
- An 'overhead line routeing methodology SEA' stage.

Figure 3.8 shows the anticipated integration of SEA into the various existing electricity network planning stages. Project planning with EIA and follow-up/monitoring are also included. The three anticipated SEA tiers, marked in grey in Figure 3.8, are explained in further detail below.

SEA tier 1: The preliminary establishment of need

The 'preliminary establishment of need' has been identified as the initial assessment stage in transmission network planning. At this stage, SEA application is likely to be most complex. Ultimately, 'need' will be used as the justification to grant statutory consent to construct a preferred option. Generally speaking, 'need' is thought to arise from:

- existing conditions and forecasted energy demand on existing network systems;
- quality and security of supply to customers;
- age and condition of its infrastructure;
- demands of new generators seeking connection to the electricity transmission grid.

At the early stages of planning, it was crucial to acknowledge that certain issues of energy demand, particularly regarding energy saving, technical or tax-based measures (that is, different policy alternatives) cannot be properly addressed by privatized companies. Rather, they need to be dealt with in political decision-making processes, possibly at the national level. Acknowledging this limitation, ScottishPower devised an internal guidance procedure to help engineering staff conduct this first planning tier. This stated that the purpose of the 'preliminary assessment of need' procedure is to 'guide the initial collation of data, to enable the earliest comparison of alternatives and to address the parameters that dictate the 'need' for a specific regional network programme' (PowerSystems, 2003, p.1).

The planning process of this tier consists of a simple series of questions and comparison tables and sets the baseline context for the subsequent tier – the identification of strategic regional reinforcement alternatives (namely, network 'location' alternatives). In this context, methods and techniques used included forecasting, workshops and impact matrices.

SEA tier 2: Regional transmission network

The objective of the second tier was to allow the company to identify the range of feasible strategic regional reinforcement alternative solutions that should be considered in securing the electrical supply to or demand within a region or user group. The anticipated SEA methodology is shown in Table 3.1. The methodology is founded on the key principles and attributes laid out in Noble and Storey's (2001) generic seven-phase methodological framework for SEA in Canadian energy sector planning, which

Table 3.1 *Methodological framework for transmission network SEA*

Phase	Attribute	Summary description
1	**Scoping** the assessment **issues**	Problem identification, setting the context within which the assessment will take place
2	**Describing** the **alternatives**	Identification of PPP alternatives, notably alternatives to identify as strategy for action
3	**Scoping** the assessment **components**	Specifying the criteria that will be used to evaluate the environmental implications of the various alternatives
4	**Evaluating** the potential **impacts**	The evaluation and assessment of whether the effect of an alternative will be adverse or beneficial
5	Determining the **impact significance**	Determining the extent of the change within the context of identified impact, the cumulative intensity or severity of impacts across the scope of the alternative and their perceived importance to stakeholders
6	**Comparing** the **alternatives**	Determination of the preferred strategic option or PPP direction
7	Identify **best practical environmental option**	The development of an overall strategy for action based on the possible alternatives and evaluative criteria assessed

Source: Marshall and Fischer, 2006; based on Noble and Storey, 2001.

was specifically developed for network SEA. The seven 'gateways' introduced by this framework made rational sense to in-house personnel and senior management unfamiliar with the concept and practice of SEA.

The regional transmission network process starts with scoping the assessment issues, where problems are identified and the context is set within which the assessment will take place. Location alternatives (that is, different basic network options) are established and criteria are specified for evaluation of their environmental implications. Evaluation of impacts and determination of impact significance are followed by the determination of the preferred strategic option. Finally, a BPEO is identified. In addition to the seven procedural phases, SEA made use of a combination of methods and techniques for identifying strategic alternatives, evaluating those alternatives against specific assessment criteria, and determining a preferred course of strategic action.

SEA tier 3: Overhead line routeing methodology

The third planning tier utilized an already existing in-house approach to the routeing of overhead transmission lines (ScottishPower, 2001; Marshall and Baxter, 2002). Developed during the early 1990s, its objective is to strategically evaluate geographic route options in order to select a final preferred route for the transmission corridor, and following consultation with stakeholders, to identify a proposed route for EIA. The procedure, summarized in Figure 3.9, is based on the simple premise that in the defence of its transmission network proposals, the company is best advised to have a robust and clearly defendable approach to route-ing in place, based on which line placement may be justified. The objective of the exercise is to bridge the gap between the selection of a preferred strate-gic alternative and the final design project submitted for EIA/developmental consent

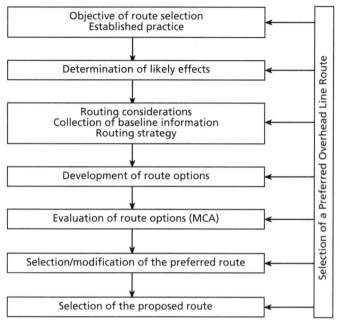

Source: Marshall and Fischer (2006)

Figure 3.9 *Scope of ScottishPower's strategic routeing methodology*

(that is, geographical 'location' options are refined).

The process is iterative and the steps may be revisited several times before a balance is achieved between technical, economic and environmental considera-

tions, using MCA. Critically, consultation is carried out throughout the process, with professional judgement being used to establish explicitly the balance between the various factors.

Spatial/land use SEA tiering

This section looks at a third area of SEA tiering, namely spatial/land use planning. Constrasting with the previous two sector examples (transport and electricity transmission planning), in spatial/land use planning, systematic decision tiers are frequently synonymous with administrative levels. This is shown below through describing practice in two countries with different planning traditions, including England (unitary system with a discretionary planning approach) and Germany (federal system with a non-discretionary

land allocation approach) (see Fischer, 2002a). Five spatial/land use SEA case studies are introduced and evaluated in Chapter 6. These show that there may be different levels of 'strategicness' in spatial/land use SEA.

Spatial/land use PPP tiering in a unitary system: The case of England

In spatial/land use planning in England, environmental assessment started to be conducted at the beginning of the 1990s at the local level (Fischer, 2004b). At this time, the term environmental appraisal (EA) was used, which took the form of a qualitative 'matrix evaluation' for *local* spatial/land use (development) plans. EA usually focused on biophysical aspects only and was done by one person, frequently ex-post, in a 'tick-box' manner (using impact matrices; see Chapter 2) for the four main stages of plan preparation: evaluation of the old plan, consideration of development options, plan deposit draft and plan final version. No alternatives were considered in assessment. Instead, development statements of intent (here called policies) were attempted to be optimized. The England-specific spatial/land use plan approach can therefore also be expressed as 'policy-plan making'. In the context of local spatial/land use plan appraisal, the earliest government guidance, *Environmental Appraisal of Development Plans: A Good Practice Guide*, was released in 1993 (DoE, 1993).

Towards the mid-1990s, EA increasingly also considered socio-economic aspects and several persons were often involved in a quasi ex-post assessment of the four main stages of development plan preparation. Also, at the *regional* level, assessments started to be conducted for regional planning guidance (RPG), following central government guidance from 1998 (DETR, 1998), which used the term sustainability appraisal (SA). The same approach used for local spatial/land use plans was followed, that is, no alternatives were assessed but development policies were optimized. Towards the end of the 1990s, environmental appraisal at the local level also frequently became called SA, which at this stage was conducted in an ex-ante manner by several persons, often including external consultation. Towards the beginning of

the 2000s, environmental and sustainability appraisals at both local and regional levels were conducted in an objectives-led assessment team process, making reference to sustainable development strategies (see, for example, NWRA, 2003).

Since 21 July 2004, SEA needs to be formally conducted in spatial/land use planning at regional and local levels, based on the SEA Directive and within the context of SA (ODPM, 2005a). Since the reforms of the planning system in 2004 (see OPSI, 2004), spatial/land use planning in England is formally organized in a tiered way, with responsibility being distributed among three administrative levels:

1 National level – government policy (as formulated through planning policy statements – PPSs) and development targets (as formulated through different policy documents, for example, on housing); no SEA conducted at this level;
2 Regional level – regional spatial strategies (RSS – statutory development plans); SEA integrated with SA, following government guidance on *Sustainability Appraisal of Regional Spatial Strategies and Local Development Documents* (ODPM, 2005a);
3 Local level – local development frameworks (LDFs – statutory development plans); SEA integrated with SA, following guidance on *Sustainability Appraisal of Regional Spatial Strategies and Local Development Documents* (ODPM, 2005a), consisting of:
   – local development documents (LDDs) including core strategy and site specific allocations of land;
   – supplementary planning documents (SPDs) on issues such

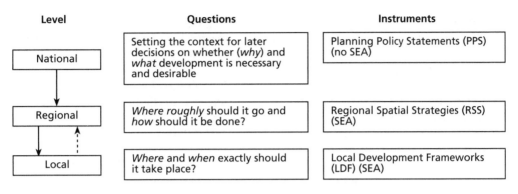

Level	Questions	Instruments
National	Setting the context for later decisions on whether (*why*) and *what* development is necessary and desirable	Planning Policy Statements (PPS) (no SEA)
Regional	*Where roughly* should it go and *how* should it be done?	Regional Spatial Strategies (RSS) (SEA)
Local	*Where* and *when* exactly should it take place?	Local Development Frameworks (LDF) (SEA)

⟶ Main decision flow   ------▶ Some scope for influencing decisions

Source: Thomas Fischer

Figure 3.10 *Spatial/land use planning hierarchy in England*

as design, waste and transport policy;

– area action plans (AAPs) for areas where specific action is thought to be required.

Government guidance on SA/SEA mentioned above (ODPM, 2005a) states that a hierarchy of questions on alternatives should be the backbone of every assessment process, consisting of questions regarding need (is it necessary?), mode or process (how should it be done?), and location (where should it go?). However, in practice, this hierarchy can only be addressed partly because, for example, at the local level, questions regarding need ('why' and 'what'; see Chapter 1) frequently do not fall within the remit of local authorities. In the south-east region of England, for example, local authorities can only decide on where they may build the several hundreds of thousands of new homes introduced through RSSs by central government (see HM Treasury, 2004). Whilst *in theory*, at the local level at least, core strategies of the LDDs should also deal with 'why' questions, in reality, their scope is rather limited. A clear allocation of assessment tasks and alternatives to different

decision-making levels would have helped tackle this problem. However, even then there would have been major gaps due to national government policy, where mainly 'why' and 'what' questions are addressed, not being subject to SEA. Spatial/land use planning in England can therefore be said to have a rather strict hierarchy in place, with the local level having limited scope to influence national policy. This means that certain fundamental issues remain insufficiently addressed and assessed. Figure 3.10 summarizes the main aspects of the spatial/land use planning hierarchy in England. Current SEA requirements are also indicated.

Spatial/land use PPP tiering in a federal system: The case of Germany

In Germany, in spatial/land use planning up to 21 July 2004 (the date by which the SEA Directive had to be transposed), most procedural aspects of SEA were reflected in plan making itself. Furthermore, many substantive SEA aspects were covered in the landscape planning system, which serves as an instrument of the precautionary principle and of sustainable development, providing for state of the environment reports, also identifying development aims and objectives to land use planning. At the state level, landscape programmes are prepared, at the city and community levels, landscape plans are prepared, and at the level of the binding master plans, open space master plans are prepared.

Different administrative levels focus on different assessment issues in spatial/land use planning. While there are certain similarities in all 16 Federal states, each state has its own distinct planning system in place. Subsequently, only those features that are common to all spatial/land use planning systems in the 16 states are addressed here. At the national level, the Federal Spatial Planning Act (*Bundesraumordnungs-gesetz*) provides for the overall framework within which spatial/land use planning happens. This outlines processes and basic rules for sustainable spatial development. Furthermore, at the national level, a federation-wide spatial orientation framework is prepared, providing for an overall national spatial development concept. In this context, SEA is currently not required.

The implementation of land use planning below the federal level is the responsibility of the 16 states and of the municipalities and is achieved through the preparation of a range of formal planning documents, as follows (all involving preparation of SEA):

- State level – State Spatial Development Plans (*Landesentwicklungspläne/-programme*); these identify basic aims and objectives for spatial/land use planning in the various states, and need to take some basic rules, defined within state spatial acts, into account (scales of maps 1:100,000 to 1:300,000).

- Regional level – regional plans (*regionale Raumordnungskonzepte*); and, at Kreis (county) level – informal – county development plans (*Kreisentwicklungspläne*); these identify spatially concrete aims and objectives (scales of maps 1:50,000 to 1:100,000).

- Local level:
  - Preparatory Land Use Plan (*Flächennutzungsplan – FNP*); these set out land use rules for municipalities and are binding for the planning authorities (scales of maps 1:5,000 to 1:50,000);
  - Binding Land Use Plans (*B-Plan*); these are prepared for small areas of a municipality (scales of maps 1:1,000 to 1:5,000) and are the only planning documents in the planning system that are binding for everyone.

The German spatial/land use planning system is not organized in a strictly top-down manner. Instead, the so-called 'counter-current principle' is applied, according to which decisions of all administrative levels need to take PPPs prepared at other levels into account. Furthermore, there is institutional backing for the subsidiarity principle in planning. The different administrative units at different decision-making levels need to fully cooperate and coordinate their activities. As decision-making is supposed to be 'administration consensus-based' (Fischer, 2002a), normally all units participate in 'important' administrative decisions. Direct public participation takes place in project developments. Furthermore, the public is also involved in PPP preparation at the local level. Figure 3.11 summarizes the spatial/land use planning hierarchy in Germany and indicates where SEA needs to be applied.

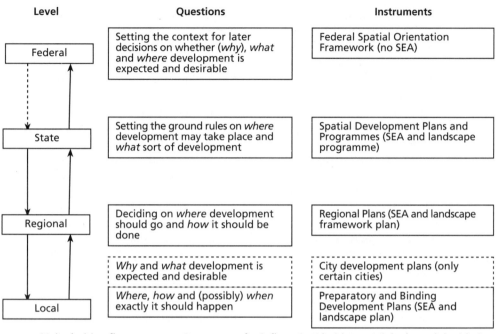

Level	Questions	Instruments
Federal	Setting the context for later decisions on whether (*why*), *what* and *where* development is expected and desirable	Federal Spatial Orientation Framework (no SEA)
State	Setting the ground rules on *where* development may take place and *what* sort of development	Spatial Development Plans and Programmes (SEA and landscape programme)
Regional	Deciding on *where* development should go and *how* it should be done	Regional Plans (SEA and landscape framework plan)
Local	*Why* and *what* development is expected and desirable	City development plans (only certain cities)
	Where, *how* and (possibly) *when* exactly it should happen	Preparatory and Binding Development Plans (SEA and landscape plan)

——►Main decision flow   - - - - - -►Some scope for influencing decisions, mainly through legislation

Source: Thomas Fischer

Figure 3.11 *Spatial/land use planning hierarchy in Germany*

Possible barriers to effective tiering

How appropriate issues and alternatives may be identified in SEA has been explained above, based on a tiered approach to SEA. Transport planning, energy transmission planning and spatial/land use planning were considered. While this has shown that tiering can potentially be beneficial, there are barriers to effective tiering that assessors need to be aware of and which are subsequently discussed. First though, the question of what can be understood by effective tiering is addressed.

Effective tiering cannot be understood simply in terms of a one-to-one implementation of what is said in a policy, plan or programme. Policies, for example, may at times be somewhat vague and need interpretation in order to be implementable. Furthermore, a strictly top-down approach that does not allow for any flexibility or feedback mechanisms would imply a rationality that is not normally observed in real practice and that would run counter to current understanding of how decision-making works. In order to establish how effective SEA tiering can be understood, Wallagh's (1988, pp122–123, in Faludi, 2000, p.310) definition of strategic plan making effectiveness provides for a suitable starting point. He suggests that strategic plan making can be considered effective, if:

- *an operational decision conforms to the plan and explicit reference is being made to it, demonstrating that conformance has not been accidental*
- *arguments are being derived from the plan for taking non-conforming decisions, i.e.* departures are deliberate
- *the plan provides the basis for* analysing consequences of an incidental decision which happens to contravene the plan, *thus bringing that decision under the umbrella of the plan*
- *if and when departures become too frequent and the plan must be reviewed, the original plan may still be said to have worked for as long as the review takes that* plan as its point of departure.

Translating this to SEA, tiering can be considered to function effectively as long as explicit reference is made to it in PPPs and projects, even if subsequently there is – deliberate – deviation from it. In this context, Hironaka and Schofer (2002) suggest that characterizing a policy as 'failed if there is no tight causal link between policy and outcome is simplistic and unhelpful', and that other outcomes such as clear agenda setting for environmental protection and an increased environmental awareness resulting from environmental assessment are just as important.

Barriers to effective tiering have been identified by a range of authors (for planning in general, see de Roo, 2000, 2003; for SEA, see Valve, 1999; Tomlinson and Fry, 2002; Hilden et al,

2004; Fischer, 2006a). These barriers are summarized by Arts et al (2005) to include:

- An implicit assumption of tiering as a linear planning process that does not appear to fit well with the dynamic nature of decision-making in practice (namely, projects may precede strategic plans and projects may not have previously been included in PPPs);
- Limited shelf life of the information provided by SEA; particularly in fast moving topics, assessments may be out of date quickly;
- The time lag between PPPs and projects, which is problematic, particularly when considering political election cycles;
- Competencies and influencing power of government bodies is limited; PPPs may be self-binding for governments but not for private persons;
- The subsidiarity principle in planning.

A problem for effective SEA tiering that is particularly difficult to overcome is the time gap between PPP preparation and actual implementation at the project level. This is most relevant at the level of policies, as it may take many years before any implementation may occur, for example, through concrete projects. In this context, of particular importance is that policy objectives may change quite substantially over a few years. This was shown by the author (Fischer, 2004a) looking at the development of transport policy in Merseyside (city region of Liverpool), the regional body of Amsterdam and Berlin.

Comparing the main transport policy documents in these places in 1997 and 2002, some considerable changes were identified over five years, particularly in terms of the overall objectives pursued, the potential implementation measures

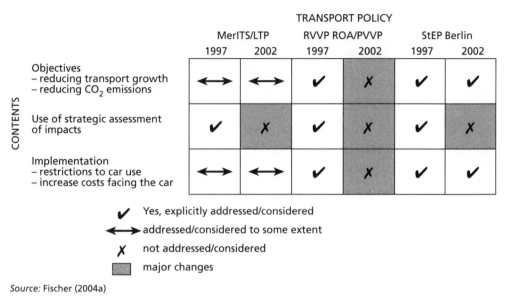

	TRANSPORT POLICY					
	MerITS/LTP		RVVP ROA/PVVP		StEP Berlin	
CONTENTS	1997	2002	1997	2002	1997	2002
Objectives – reducing transport growth – reducing CO_2 emissions	↔	↔	✔	✗	✔	✔
Use of strategic assessment of impacts	✔	✗	✔	✗	✔	✗
Implementation – restrictions to car use – increase costs facing the car	↔	↔	✔	✗	✔	✔

✔ Yes, explicitly addressed/considered

↔ addressed/considered to some extent

✗ not addressed/considered

▒ major changes

Source: Fischer (2004a)

Figure 3.12 *Transport policy in Merseyside, Amsterdam and Berlin – 1997 and 2002*

considered and the assessment of different policy options. This is shown in Figure 3.12, which indicates that changes were particularly dramatic in the Amsterdam region. Here, some fundamental political changes had occurred between 1997 and 2002. At the national level, in 2002 a centre-right government was in place with markedly different attitudes towards transport policy making than the previous social-democrat government of 1997. While the latter had put an emphasis on meeting overall transport reduction objectives, the former did not consider reduction targets to be feasible, but rather saw transport as a 'right' and 'fun'. Furthermore, at the provincial level, a new government was also elected in 1999. Changes in Liverpool and Berlin were less dramatic, and there were fewer political changes in these two city regions.

Summary and conclusions

In this chapter, ways to identify appropriate alternatives for use in SEA were discussed. A tiered approach to SEA was shown to play a crucial role. Based on the evidence provided by transport planning in northern and western European countries, a systematically tiered transport SEA framework was designed, consisting of four main strategic levels of decision-making: policy, network plan, corridor plan and programme.

The underlying assumption of a tiered approach to SEA, as reflected in the generic transport SEA framework, is that any decision to construct a concrete transport infrastructure project is associated with other policy, plan and programme decisions. In this context, it is acknowledged that transport planning may not necessarily happen in a strictly hierarchical manner, and that project ideas may be developed, for example, based on an *ad hoc* basis or in a more bottom-up manner. While critics may argue that the application of a hierarchical framework was unsuitable in such systems, there is evidence that, even here, evaluation of potential projects is still necessary, based on what has been specified in other previous relevant transport PPPs. Therefore, higher tiers can be understood to provide a framework for evaluation at lower tiers. Furthermore, while the framework implies that higher tier decisions should be considered in subsequent SEAs, PPPs, projects and EIAs, it is not suggested that there may not be changes or derivations to what was originally intended. While derivations are likely to happen in most PPP situations, they should occur in a conscious manner. In this context, feedback to subsequent PPP making and assessment practice is of particular importance.

How the conceptual transport SEA framework can be used to evaluate existing practice was shown, using the example of the German transport planning system. From this example and reflections on practice elsewhere, it is clear that while any of the strategic transport planning documents that are currently prepared can be allocated to a specific systematic tier, no known planning system currently appears to cover all tiers systematically, therefore leaving certain gaps.

Practice examples of electricity transmission planning and spatial/land use planning also showed that tiered frameworks play a crucial role when attempting to establish appropriate issues and alternatives in SEA in areas of application other than transport. The case study of ScottishPower showed that SEA and a tiered approach to planning and assessment can be beneficial for the private sector. However, it also indicated that tiering is likely to be more complicated in situations where different tiers fall into different responsibilities. Energy policy is frequently the responsibility of national governments and can only be influenced indirectly by an electricity company. The ScottishPower example also showed how an SEA framework can be adapted to existing practice, for example, to accommodate an existing line routeing methodology. In spatial/land use planning, tiering may be happening differently from other sectors, as systematic tiering normally appears to be synonymous with administrative tiering. The two spatial/land use planning systems introduced here, from England and Germany, demonstrated that there is currently an important gap, with the national level not being subject to SEA. That there may not just be tiering between administrative levels in spatial/land use planning, but also systematic differences between different spatial/land use SEAs is shown in Chapter 6, looking at five case studies representing different levels of strategicness. Finally, barriers to effective tiering were found to be connected in particular with the time gap between the formulation of policies and actual implementation.

Notes

1   This section draws on Fischer, 2006a.
2   In this context, the boundaries between different SEA tiers as well as between SEA and EIA may not always be as clear-cut as is suggested here for reasons of simplification. In some countries (for example, in The Netherlands and Germany), uni-modal corridor assessments have been conducted as part of EIA for many years, before SEA requirements were introduced.
3   To date, the new Prodi government has not pursued further this project of the former Berlusconi government.
4   Pricing/administrative measures include an increase of petrol prices, vehicle taxes based on CO_2 emissions, reduction of petrol use, alternative transport of bulky goods, increase in lorry taxation, cutting subsidies for home–work trips according to kilometres driven, increase in penalties, more traffic monitoring, road pricing, speed limits, parking management, increase in parking fees, residential parking only areas, restrictions on lorry access and 'job tickets'.

Infrastructure development measures include the extension of waterways, railways (regional), roads, the (re)introduction of trams, more bus lanes, increase in bus speeds, location of new housing areas, improvements of the cycle network, park and ride/bike and ride, goods transport hubs and city logistics.

Organizational measures include more frequent public transport, better public transport to Hamburg harbour, better information for public transport users, public campaigns, improvement of the city rail network, a regional public transport tariff system, public transport safety and cleanliness, a shopping storage service, car sharing and traffic management systems.

5   This section draws on Marshall and Fischer, 2006.

Comparative Review of 11 Established Strategic Environmental Assessment Systems

Chapter 4 provides for a comparative review and evaluation of 11 established SEA systems from ten countries worldwide, based on SEA context, procedural and wider methodological factors, as introduced in Chapters 1 and 2. These include systems in five EU and five non-EU countries. An important aim of the chapter is to help those looking for experiences from elsewhere to find systems that may be similar to their own. SEA is likely to be fully effective only in the long term, particularly through changing established routines and attitudes of those involved in PPP making (see Chapter 1). Therefore, only systems are considered where SEA has been applied routinely for some considerable time, normally for at least over a decade. Regarding EU examples, only member states are considered that had pre-Directive SEA practice in place.

SEA requirements are not static. Therefore, it is likely that specific requirements within the systems portrayed here will be subject to continuous change. However, with the main purpose of the chapter being to evaluate systems from a follow-up perspective in order to learn about systems' effectiveness, the review is of practical value that goes beyond any specific requirements at a particular point in time, that is, the evidence brought forward is not going to be outdated simply because of a few changes to requirements. First, the chapter provides an overview of formal requirements worldwide in countries outside the EU (transformation and implementation status of the SEA Directive in EU member states are described in Chapter 5). This is followed by a description of the review methodology. The 11 SEA systems are then described, evaluated and discussed. Finally, conclusions are drawn.

Formal SEA requirements in countries outside the EU

Many countries worldwide have shown an interest in SEA, with some having conducted SEA case studies, others having released guidance and still others having put formal requirements into place. Currently, the number of countries with formal SEA requirements is still limited, albeit clearly increasing. In this context, it is difficult to give an exact account of formal SEA systems globally because:

- terminology varies and not all systems explicitly refer to the term SEA; this even includes the SEA Directive, which only refers to 'environmental assessment of certain plans and programmes';

- as a consequence of different terminology used, systems not represented by authors who publish in the international SEA literature may remain unmentioned and, as a consequence, unnoticed.

When trying to decide on what systems to consider, it is crucial not to simply look out for systems that explicitly use the term SEA, but rather to explore decision-making support mechanisms and instruments that share SEA's main aim, namely to ensure that environmental and possibly other sustainability aspects are considered effectively in PPP making.

Formal requirements should mean more than simply mentioning the possibility of SEA. Rather, either legislative or administrative requirements should be in place that clearly explain when SEA is required and what it should involve, if conducted. The systems from outside the EU with formal requirements listed in this section were identified from the international SEA literature, particularly Dalal-Clayton and Sadler (2005), Jones et al (2005) and Schmidt et al (2005). Three non-EU systems with legislation requiring SEA are reviewed and evaluated later in this chapter, namely:

1 *California* – programmatic environmental impact report (PEIR), following the California Environmental Quality Act of 1970 (federal requirements in the US are based on NEPA);
2 *Western Australia* – SEA of land use plans, following the Western Australia Protection Act from 1986 (federal requirements are based on the Australia Environmental Protection and Biodiversity Conservation Act of 1999);

3 *New Zealand* – integrated regional land transport strategies, following the Land Transport Management Act of 2003 (general national requirements are based on the Resource Management Act of 1991).

Other countries with SEA-type requirements formulated in legislation but that are not discussed further in this book also include:

1 *China* – EIA for plans, following the Environmental Protection Law from 1979, as supplemented by the Environmental Protection Management Ordinance for Construction Projects from 1998 (see, for example, Tang Tao et al, forthcoming);
   - in addition, for the special administrative region of Hong Kong, following the EIA Ordinance from 1998, pursuant to the then Governor's Policy Address in 1992 (see Au and Hui, 2004; Environmental Protection Department, 2004);
2 *Korea* – prior environmental review system under the Environmental Policy Act from 1999 (see, for example, Song Young-Il, 2006); since 2007 there are also general SEA requirements, based on the Framework Act on Environmental Policy revision from 2005;
3 *Bulgaria* – EIA for national development programmes, territorial development and urban development plans, following the Environmental Protection Act from 1991 (see, for example, Dalal-Clayton and Sadler, 2005); on 1 January 2007, Bulgaria also became a EU member state (with Romania);
4 *Norway* – instructions for consequence assessment, submission and

review procedures in connection with official studies, regulations, propositions and reports to the Storting (national parliament), issued by Royal Decree on 18 February 2000 (see, for example, Hanssen, 2003);

5 *Newly Independent States* (NIS) (former Soviet Republics, including Russia, Belarus, Ukraine, Kazakhstan, Turkmenistan, Armenia, Georgia, Moldova, Azerbaijan, Kyrgyzstan, Tajikistan, Uzbekistan, following Cherp, 2001); all of them have EIA-type frameworks in place that include SEA elements, based on the system of the State Environmental Review (SER) established in the former Soviet Union in the mid-1980s; assessment of environmental impact requirements (OVOS) were established alongside SER. However, judging by a World Bank study (Klees et al, 2002), only

Ukraine shows a high compatibility with internationally accepted standards.

In addition to SEA based on legal requirements, there are other systems where SEA is regulated through administrative provisions. Outside the EU member states, these include *Canada*, where SEA is applied to cabinet submissions, following the Cabinet Directive on Environmental Assessment of Policy, Plan and Programme Proposals from 1999 (see below). Finally, there are now also a growing number of experiences with SEA in developing countries. Currently, these are closely connected with the activities of development banks, international aid organizations and other donor agencies. An account of the experiences to date in over 30 developing countries is provided by Dalal-Clayton and Sadler (2005).

Review methodology

Eleven SEA systems from ten countries are reviewed, five of which are EU member states. As stated above, while a number of case studies are now available following the introduction of the Directive, it is clearly too early to evaluate systems connected with the Directive regarding their performance. However, in all five member states presented here, emerging post-SEA Directive practice is closely connected with existing pre-Directive practice, with certain new elements being introduced.

The systems under review are from Canada, South Africa, California (US), Western Australia, New Zealand, the UK, The Netherlands (two systems), Germany, Finland and Italy. While nine of the systems are applied in a national context, two are state systems (California and Western Australia). These were chosen,

based on advice of experts that they provide for better examples than national systems. Systems represent different SEA categories, as introduced in Chapter 1:

1   Administration-led SEAs:
    –   EIA-based SEAs to plans and programmes:
        •   California's programmatic environmental impact report (PEIR),
        •   Western Australia's SEA (including aspects of policy plan SEA),
        •   South Africa's SEA,
        •   The Netherlands' SEA,
        •   Italy's SEA,
        •   Germany's landscape planning,
        •   Finland's SEA;
    –   Policy plan SEAs (see also Chapter

3):
- New Zealand's regional land transport strategies;
- Environmental/sustainability appraisal in England.
2   Cabinet SEAs:
  - Canada's SEA,
  - The Netherlands' e-test.

While nine of the ten countries have formal SEA requirements in place, South Africa does not. However, this country also has some substantial SEA experiences and its inclusion was considered useful, particularly in order to learn from an established informal system. All countries included here are from the Western developed world, with South Africa being what may be called a transitional economy. While all chosen countries are democracies with elected governments at various decision-making levels (national, regional and local), they all have different political, institutional and planning traditions. It was not the intention here to evaluate all SEA systems in the ten countries. Rather, a selection was made based on availability of data and the available experts being comfortable talking about their specific systems.

The only category introduced in Chapter 1 not included in the systems' review is administration-led policy (vision) SEA, for two main reasons. First, while policy SEA was applied in several countries in the 1990s, particularly in the context of vision making in Europe (Fischer, 2002a), more recently, SEA-type elements in these visions appear to have very much disappeared. It is unclear why exactly this is the case and there is a need for further research. However, there is some indication that this may be connected with the focus of the SEA Directive on plan and programmes, and not policies. Second, in visions, assess-ments are fully integrated with the policy-making process and practitioners often do not recognize it as SEA. This makes it difficult to obtain information on these systems, for example, through interviews. A vision-based policy-SEA case study is, however, presented in Chapter 6: the Development Vision for Noord-Holland.

Evaluation of the systems is based on context criteria for enabling effective SEA, as introduced in Chapter 1. These consist of a total of 18 elements. Furthermore, some procedural and wider methodological factors are also considered. Factors for evaluating SEA systems are shown in Box 4.1. The empirical basis for the review was generated through:

- Interviews with 16 international SEA experts representing the different systems, which were conducted in March and April 2005 either by phone or in person. A structured questionnaire was used, which was based on the elements introduced in Box 4.1. For all questions, possible replies included 'yes, fully effective', 'partially effective' and 'no, not effective'. International SEA experts were chosen from the membership database of the IAIA. In this context, only academics and consultants were included. Government officials were thought to be potentially biased in favour of their SEA system and were therefore not contacted. Interview results were then sent to other experts from the respective countries for verification.
- A review of the international professional literature to verify results and to fill any possible gaps. A wide range of publications is now available in the form of journal articles, books and book chapters, which provide a good basis for evaluation.

Box 4.1 Factors for evaluating SEA systems

Context factors

a   Formal requirements and clear provisions to conduct and effectively consider SEA:
  - Are there requirements, based on legislation, regulations or directive?
  - Is there any specific or general SEA guidance available?
  - Are competences/responsibilities clear?
  - Is there enforcement through an agency, legal threats or independent review?
  - Is SEA actually considered in PPP making?
  - Is there compliance with SEA requirements?

b   Clear goals for assessment:
  - Are there clear and compatible (substantive) goals for assessment in place?
  - Is SEA succeeding in changing established thinking?

c   Appropriate funding, time and support:
  - Is appropriate funding, time and support being made available?

d   Achieving a willingness to cooperate – considering and influencing traditional decision-making approaches:
  - Is there a developed environmental consciousness in the population and among stakeholders in the system within which SEA is applied?
  - Do SEA results get considered in other PPPs and projects?
  - Is there a sound public, legal, administrative and political support base?
  - Is there a tradition of transparency and cooperation?

e   Setting clear boundaries – addressing the right issues at the right time/defining roles of assessors:
  - Is there a clear, effectively tiered planning hierarchy in place?
  - Is there a clear focus of assessment?
  - Are the roles of assessors clearly defined?
  - Is there an effective project EIA system in place?

f   Acknowledging and dealing with uncertainties:
  - Are uncertainties acknowledged and dealt with?

Procedural factors

g   A systematic SEA process:
  - Are there requirements for screening, scoping, report preparation (reporting/documentation), review, preparation of a clear summary, monitoring and integration with underlying PPP process?

h   Adequate consultation and participation:
  - Is consultation with experts and other administrations conducted?
  - Is there public participation?

Wider methodological factors

i   Adequate impact prediction and consideration of alternatives:
  - Are appropriate alternatives considered?
  - Does assessment come with clear predictions, whenever possible quantitatively?
  - Does assessment consider measures for avoiding, minimizing, mitigating or compensating impacts?

California

In California, SEA is called programmatic environmental impact report – PEIR – and is applied based on the formal requirements formulated by the California Environmental Quality Act of 1970 (see, for example, Shepherd and Ortolano, 1996). There is therefore over 35 years of practical experiences with environmental assessment. PEIR is used whenever land use changes caused by plans and programmes are expected to have significant environmental effects. Opposite to the NEPA-based US federal system, private plans and programmes with significant environmental effects also require SEA. Californian SEA is EIA based and is applied in a very similar manner for different sectors. Between tens and hundreds of SEAs are prepared annually. A long tradition of public involvement in decision-making, coupled with case law,

have played a crucial role for the development of PEIR. Support and guidance for assessors is provided by the California Governor's Office of Planning and Research (COPR). The SEA process itself is conducted by the agency responsible for the plan or programme under consideration.

In California, there is a well-developed planning hierarchy in place, within which all those actions that can potentially lead to significant environmental impacts are covered by environmental assessment. Californian society has been said to have a high environmental consciousness and a highly developed culture of participation. Furthermore, generally speaking, there is a preference in US assessment culture for quantitative technical solutions. The application of state-of-the-art and scientifically robust

---

BOX 4.2 KEY ASPECTS OF THE CALIFORNIAN SEA SYSTEM AND CURRENT WEAKNESSES

Key aspects of the Californian SEA system:

- Clear legislative requirements,
- Strong enforcement through legal system based on case law,
- Both public and private action covered,
- Support by COPR,
- Structured and clear EIA-based process,
- High environmental consciousness in Californian society,
- High technical assessment standards (data, methods, techniques),
- Highly developed culture of participation,
- Well-developed planning hierarchy.

Current weaknesses:

- Overall effectiveness dependent on interests of lead agency conducting SEA; plan or programme lead agency also responsible for approval,
- Reactive nature,
- SEA only applied to plans and programmes, but not to policies,
- Weak follow-up and monitoring.

techniques and methodologies that provide for clear and quantifiable results are seen as preferable, not least because of the threat of possible legal action.

A weakness of the Californian SEA system is its rather reactive nature and the interviewed expert stated that a more proactive approach would clearly be preferable. Clear environmental objectives are not always readily available, apart from technical standards, as only few communities have sustainable develop-

ment strategies in place. Furthermore, follow-up and monitoring are not currently easily enforceable. Another weakness of the Californian SEA system is that the lead agency for a particular plan or programme is also responsible for approval. The overall effectiveness of SEA therefore depends on the interests of the agency conducting SEA. Box 4.2 summarizes those aspects that are at the heart of the Californian SEA system and shows current weaknesses.

Western Australia

In Western Australia, SEA is conducted for local land use plans ('planning strategies' or policy plans), drilling programmes and satellite mining developments, prepared by public planning authorities and based on the Western Australia Environmental Protection Act from 1986 (last amended 2003) and Town and Country Planning legislation. There is about 20 years of practical experiences with SEA, which is applied in an objectives-led, EIA process-based manner. There is an integrated approach to planning and assessment procedures. There are also other, less extensive SEA experiences at the national level based on the Environmental Protection and Biodiversity Conservation Act (1999) and the National Environment Protection Council Act (1994), most of which stem from the fishery sector and some offshore petroleum exploitation and major military exercises (Marsden and Ashe, 2006). About 20 SEAs are prepared annually in Western Australia.

Generally speaking, the Environmental Protection Agency (EPA) of Western Australia is an important enforcement institution and plays a crucial support role for effective SEA application, providing clear guidance and

watching over SEA processes. Furthermore, the EPA defines the environmental objectives to be used in SEA and has released land use specific *Environmental Guidance for Planning and Development* (EPA, 2005). There is a highly developed participative and cooperative culture in planning and decision-making in place in Western Australia, with planners and assessors normally cooperating well. There is also a highly developed environmental consciousness. In this context, it is interesting to note that more environmental officers have been employed, following the introduction of SEA requirements. Other PPPs take SEA results into account when being drawn up, through advice bulletins released by EPA. There is a well-developed planning hierarchy in place with an allocation of different tasks at state, regional and community levels, leading to a reduction in the need for project EIA, which is required based on the Environmental Protection and Assessment Act (1979, 1993). Furthermore, the system is intended to adapt to changes, meaning that in case of unforeseen effects, there is the possibility of remedial action, in other words, adaptive environmental management is

---

BOX 4.3 KEY ASPECTS OF THE WESTERN AUSTRALIA SEA SYSTEM AND CURRENT WEAKNESSES

Key aspects of the Western Australia SEA system:

- Clear legislative requirements,
- Objectives-led EIA process-based policy plan appraisal approach,
- Highly developed participative and cooperative culture,
- Integrated land use and SEA process,
- Highly developed environmental consciousness of Western Australian society,
- Effective approach to uncertainties through adaptive environmental management,
- An effectively tiered planning system means SEA reduces the need for EIAs,
- Strong enforcement and support role of Western Australia EPA,
- More environmental officers employed since the formal introduction of SEA.

Current weaknesses:

- Negotiation right of minister reduces transparency,
- Consideration of alternatives weak,
- Weak follow-up and monitoring.

---

conducted.

A current weakness is that decision-making is not fully transparent, mainly because of the need for the land use plans to be confirmed by the responsible minister, who can negotiate on whatever issues he/she wishes. This 'negotiation right' is the main reason why SEA results may not always be fully reflected in the final plan.

Also, the consideration of alternatives is not well developed because an assessment approach is followed that aims at optimizing development policies (that is, statements of intent). Furthermore, follow-up and monitoring arrangements are currently weak. Box 4.3 summarizes key aspects of the Western Australia SEA system and current weaknesses.

Canada

Canadian SEA practice is different from all other countries considered in this chapter in that experiences come almost entirely from federal cabinet decision processes (based on the 1999 Cabinet Directive on Environmental Assessment of Policy, Plan and Programme Proposals; see, for example, Noble, 2002). Practice follows *The Environmental Assessment Process for Policy and Programme Proposals* guidance by the Federal Environmental Assessment Review Office (FEARO) (FEARO, 1993), which later became the Canadian Environmental Assessment Agency (CEAA), and other sector specific guidelines. There are now over 10 years of practical experiences of cabinet SEA. There is no legislative basis for SEA, mainly because cabinet decision-making processes are not regulated. While there are some other SEA-related experiences, based on EIA requirements in the provinces and territories (Dalal-Clayton and Sadler, 2005), currently most sector and land use plans and programmes that are not cabinet submissions are not subject to SEA. Approximately 80 SEAs are conducted annually.

In line with what has been explained in Chapter 1, the cabinet SEA process is organized in a flexible manner. No direct consultation or public participation takes place. Instead, public and stakeholder opinions are said to be taken into account indirectly through political lobbying. Regarding effective implementation and enforcement of SEA, government agencies need to verify whether practice complies with cabinet decisions (for example the development agencies for Atlantic Canada or Western Quebec). Due to its unregulated nature, there are various ways for conducting the SEA process.

SEA-related enforcement is largely the responsibility of those federal departments/agencies conducting it. At times, enforcement is rather weak. The Commissioner of the Environment and Sustainable Development (CESD) is supposed to oversee SEA processes and monitor performance of the SEA system on an annual basis. She/he is also supposed to monitor the general federal government's environmental performance. Furthermore, support for those conducting SEA is provided by the CEAA.

While there is administrative and political support for SEA, the absence of legal support mechanisms makes enforcement difficult. Furthermore, there are currently no clear environmental goals available for conducting SEA to cabinet submissions and there appears to be very little funding available for SEA. Practical support by the CEAA is currently somewhat limited with only four people working on SEA. Box 4.4 summarizes the key aspects of the Canadian SEA system and current weaknesses.

BOX 4.4 KEY ASPECTS OF THE CANADIAN SEA SYSTEM AND CURRENT WEAKNESSES

Key aspects of the Canadian SEA system:

- SEA in cabinet decision-making,
- Requirements based on a directive,
- Support by both the CEAA and the CESD,
- Generic SEA guidance,
- Enforcement largely the responsibility of individual federal departments or agencies,
- Participation through political lobbying,
- Flexible procedural approach.

Current weaknesses:

- Enforcement weak (no legislative SEA requirements),
- Documentation not publicly available and no public participation,
- Absence of clear environmental goals,
- Funding and time for conducting SEA not fully satisfactory,
- Only cabinet SEA system in place.

New Zealand

In New Zealand, SEA elements are reflected in the integrated approach to land use and resource planning, based on the Resource Management Act of 1991. The country has about 15 years of SEA experience. Furthermore, regional land transport strategies include important SEA elements. More recently, the Land Transport Management Act of 2003 has strengthened the position of the environment in transport planning (Ward et al, 2005). Generally speaking, New Zealand can be said to subscribe to overall SEA objectives and principles, without conducting separate SEA processes. An integrated policy plan SEA approach is followed.

The focus here is on regional land transport strategies (RLTSs), as practice coming out of the Resource Management Act has mainly revolved around project rather than strategic assessment. In this context, integrated RLTS SEAs are prepared for the transport strategies of the 16 New Zealand regions by responsible transport administrations every three years (that is, about five per year on average in New Zealand). There is currently no guidance available for regional land transport strategies on how to consider environmental aspects.

Generally speaking, New Zealand has a tradition of transparent and cooperative planning. Consultations and public participation are important elements of public decision-making processes. Furthermore, there is a high degree of environmental consciousness in New Zealand's society, which is said to be connected with New Zealand's economy being largely based on natural resources. A well developed and effective project EIA system is also in

---

BOX 4.5 KEY ASPECTS OF THE NEW ZEALAND SEA SYSTEM AND CURRENT WEAKNESSES

Key aspects of the New Zealand SEA system:

- Policy plan SEA approach followed,
- Highly developed environmental consciousness in society,
- Objectives-led approach to integrated environmental management with clear sets of goals,
- Tradition of transparency, participation and cooperation in public decision-making,
- Integrated transport and SEA process,
- High potential for changing attitudes of those involved in the strategy process.

Current weaknesses:

- No guidance,
- Only indirect enforcement,
- No distinguishable environmental section in strategies, no separate environmental report,
- Weak consideration of alternatives, impact mitigation and compensation,
- Poor connectedness of transport strategies with land use plans,
- SEA somewhat reactive,
- Dominance of traffic engineers.

---

place. There is a fairly clear, but incompletely implemented, planning hierarchy, with national policy statements feeding into regional and district management plans. As is the case with transport planning systems in most countries, there is a dominance of traffic engineers involved in plan making. However, there is said to be a high potential for changing the attitudes of those involved in strategic processes.

Somewhat surprisingly, there is currently no guidance available for RLTSs on how to integrate and assess environmental aspects. Furthermore, enforcement only takes place in an indirect way, namely through funding decisions by the Land Transport New Zealand Government Agency (LTNZGA). Decisions are supported by an evaluation checklist that includes environmental aspects. In this context, if checklist aspects are not covered in a transport strategy, LTNZGA might decide not to approve funding. Currently, transport strategies are poorly connected with land use plans. Also, the consideration of alternatives, impact mitigation and compensation is weak. Box 4.5 summarizes the key aspects of the New Zealand approach and current weaknesses.

South Africa

South Africa's SEA experiences have frequently been reported on in the literature (see, for example, Roussow and Wiseman, 2004). However, while there are a range of examples (Dalal-Clayton and Sadler (2005) showed that around 50 SEA were conducted in South Africa between 1996 and 2003, and there are about 10 years of SEA experiences), there are currently no formal SEA requirements and SEAs are prepared on a voluntary basis. South Africa is therefore the only system considered in this chapter that does not have any formal SEA requirements. In South Africa, SEA is seen as an emerging process with draft enabling legislation in place. Most experiences stem from EIA-based SEA in land use and sector planning, and by mid-2005, up to 15 SEAs had been prepared annually.

Public consultation and participation and a highly developed environmental consciousness in society are key features of the South African SEA system. While monitoring is very weak in practice, it features strongly in draft national guidance documents. SEA is currently largely private-sector driven. There are no national environmental or sustainability objectives for South Africa, although state of the environment reporting (SOER) has been widely developed at national, provincial and local levels. The lack of nationally agreed sustainability objectives hampers the application of SEA and its ability to deal with the concept of sustainability, especially in relation to the so-called objectives-led approach to SEA. In addition, strategic planning in South Africa is not well developed.

The majority of SEA consultants see their role purely as technical experts, responsible for providing objective information. This view reflects the widespread technical perception by the planning and assessment communities that more comprehensive information will lead to better decision-making. Most assessors also argue that because they do not have a mandate to negotiate political priorities, they merely focus on providing information, in other words, they do not see themselves as proactive. Generally speaking, SEA consultants seem to be struggling

---

BOX 4.6 KEY ASPECTS OF THE SOUTH AFRICAN SEA SYSTEM AND CURRENT WEAKNESSES

Key aspects of the South African SEA system:

- No legal requirements,
- SEA currently largely private-sector driven,
- Draft guidance,
- Highly developed environmental consciousness in society,
- Long tradition of participation and consultation.

Current weaknesses:

- Weak EIA system; EIA perceived as an obstacle to development; too many unnecessary EIAs,
- Weak political and administrative support,
- Insufficient funding of both SEA and EIA,
- No system of environmental or sustainability objectives in place,
- Strategic planning not well developed,
- SEA practitioners and assessors see themselves only as technicians, not as proactive actors.

---

to cope with the vagueness and lack of detail typical of strategic information, and the subsequent uncertainties associated with such data. SEA is sometimes seen as being superficial and lacking real 'science' because there is a perception that funding is insufficient. Finally, a current problem also is that EIA is perceived as an obstacle to development, and that there are too many unnecessary EIAs. Box 4.6 summarizes the key aspects of the South African approach to SEA and describes current weaknesses.

The Netherlands

Until the SEA Directive became relevant in 2004 (formally transposed into national legislation in July 2006, see Chapter 5), in The Netherlands, SEA had been applied based on the national EIA Act from 1987 (amended 1994), mainly in the context of land use changes caused by plans and programmes ('big project EIA-based SEA system'; Thissen and Van der Hijden, 2005). This means there are almost 20 years of experience of SEA. In this context, a project EIA approach has been consistently applied. Furthermore, draft regulations and other policy intentions sent to the national cabinet have also been subject to an e-test since 1995 (last amended 2003), based on a cabinet order, that is, SEA is also applied in cabinet decision processes. In addition to these practices, informal SEAs in the form of integrated assessments have been conducted for integrated transport and other sectoral policies (visions and programmes) and for spatial visions since the beginning of the 1990s. Examples include the Second Transport Structure Plan (Ministerie van verkeer en waterstaat, 1989), regional transport plans and local spatial development visions (see Fischer, 2002a). This section focuses on the formal EIA-based system and on the e-test. On average, tens of SEAs were prepared annually in each of these systems prior to the SEA Directive coming into force.

The EIA-based SEA system is based on legal requirements and clear guidance, with competences and responsibilities of the various bodies involved in the process, including assessors, being well defined. The EIA Commission provides for some solid professional support and to date, it has played an important role in enforcing quality. Generally speaking, EIA-based SEA has been described as being effective in leading to a better consideration of the environment. Also, funding and time for assessment are normally portrayed to have been satisfactory. There is a well-developed decision hierarchy and tiering has tended to work well in The

Netherlands, with SEA being able to reduce the number of project EIAs.

Regarding the e-test, until 2003, minimum procedural requirements had been in place, consisting of screening and scoping, impact analysis, documentation, review and submission for decision-making. However, the first five-year review of experiences with the e-test found that the instrument had a negligible effect on decision-making, one of the main reasons being that it was applied too late (Verheem, 2005). It was recommended that assessment would be more effective if applied to strategic proposals prior to or separate from the legislative process. Since 2003, a quick scan has been used prior to conducting a proper test for substantiating the need for draft regulation to be e-tested. Box 4.7 summarizes key aspects of the Dutch approach and its current weaknesses.

BOX 4.7 KEY ASPECTS OF THE DUTCH SEA SYSTEM AND CURRENT WEAKNESSES

Key aspects of the Dutch SEA system:

- Comprehensive approach to SEA, applying it in different forms to a wide range of strategic actions (formal EIA-based, cabinet e-test and informal policy SEA in visions),
- Traditionally there is a proactive environmental management approach to EIA and SEA,
- Clear and enforceable legal requirements for EIA-based SEA,
- In EIA-based SEA, generally speaking, compliance with requirements,
- In EIAbased SEA, clear guidance,
- In EIA-based SEA, a high degree of participation and cooperation,
- In EIA-based SEA, EIA Commission plays a strong supporting role,
- Established planning hierarchy with a clear focus,
- In EIA-based SEA, appropriate consideration of alternatives, clear/transparent predictions,
- In EIA-based SEA, satisfactory funding, time and support,
- Effective project EIA.

Current weaknesses:

- E-test has had a rather weak impact on decision-making,
- Monitoring weak.

United Kingdom

Prior to the SEA Directive coming into force, in the UK, objectives-led 'environmental appraisal' had been applied within land use, resource and waste development planning since the early 1990s, based on *Planning Policy Guidance Note 12* (DoE, 1992; see also Chapter 3 and Fischer, 2004b). There are therefore about 15 years of experience with SEA, mainly in terms of SEA being applied to policy plans. Furthermore, informal SEAs (taking various shapes and forms) have also been conducted since the early 1990s in various sectors, including transport, oil and gas licensing and wind energy generation (DTI, 2001). While there has also been appraisal guidance for central government policy making ('Policy Appraisal and the Environment') (DoE, 1991), practice in this area has remained limited. More recently, regulatory impact assessment (RIA) has been applied in cabinet decision-making, however, its main focus is on economic appraisal and so cannot be considered an SEA equivalent. The policy plan SEA system for development plans is evaluated here, of which around one hundred were prepared every year until mid-2004, that is, before SEA Directive requirements came into force.

One of the main strengths of the UK's SEA system is the various published guidance documents that are available to support good practice. However, due to the lack of formal requirements and no

---

BOX 4.8 KEY ASPECTS OF THE UK'S SEA SYSTEM AND CURRENT WEAKNESSES

Key aspects of the UK's SEA system:

- Long experience of informal non-EIA-based policy plan SEA (environmental and sustainability appraisal),
- Informal SEA type practices at various levels and in various PPP and project situations,
- Extensive guidance available,
- In development plan practice, policy plan SEAs were observed to be able to effectively influence plan making when the appraisal team was able to actively participate in plan making processes,
- Clear focus of assessment.

Current weaknesses:

- Lack of proper enforcement,
- Lack of consideration of baseline data (even in post-SEA Directive practice, this appears to pose a problem; while baseline data are listed, at times to quite a large extent, it normally remains unclear how these are subsequently used in assessment),
- No consideration of alternatives (now changing due to SEA Directive requirements),
- Insufficient consultation and participation in pre-SEA Directive practice (changing in post-Directive practice).

---

practical support, for example, by an environment agency or ministry, enforcement has been weak and the quality of the assessments prepared has varied widely, prior to SEA Directive requirements coming into force. Appraisal in development plan making has not focused on an evaluation of different alternatives, but on a 'policy-optimization' approach (that is, development policies are optimized, based on environmental and sustainability objectives). However, current post-SEA Directive practice is strengthening the requirement to consider alternatives.

Furthermore, in pre-Directive practice, a purely qualitative approach to assessment had been pursued, marked by an absence of baseline data. While there was only a little wider public consultation and participation in pre-SEA Directive practice, this has now changed due to the requirements formulated in the new guidance, *Sustainability Appraisal of Regional Spatial Strategies and Local Development Documents* (ODPM, 2005a). Box 4.8 summarizes key aspects of the UK's SEA approach and shows its current weaknesses.

Italy

In Italy, planning has traditionally been heavily dominated by political negotiations 'behind the scenes'. As a consequence, planning processes have been described as being 'weak' (Gazzola et al, 2004). Furthermore, neither a national EIA law nor EIA guidance have been put in place. However, prior to the SEA Directive being transposed in mid-2006, there had been some formal SEA requirements, particularly at the regional level. In this context, some regions introduced SEA through regional planning laws, making it part of the planning process. These include the Emilia Romagna, Tuscany and Liguria regions. Prior to SEA Directive requirements coming into force, other regions had also introduced SEA as an extension of project EIA, for example the Valle d'Aosta region. In addition, SEA had been formally introduced for specific purposes, such as the 2006 Turin Winter Olympic Games.

Those SEA systems that had been in place in Italy prior to the Directive being transposed tended to have clear procedural and substantive requirements. In this context, generally speaking, those

actors that needed to prepare SEAs in certain PPP making situations were clearly identified. Importantly, requirements normally specified that those actors preparing SEA should be different from those responsible for the preparation of the underlying plan or programme.

This section briefly reflects on experiences in the Emilia Romagna region, where formal SEA requirements had been introduced through Regional Planning Law No 20/2000. There are just over five years of SEA experience in this region, making it the only system considered in this chapter with less than 10 years of SEA practice. Italy is included here because its planning tradition differs markedly to all other systems considered, and its practice is rarely presented in the professional literature.

In Emilia Romagna, a few SEAs were prepared each year. A structured EIA-based process was followed, with requirements for public involvement. There was an implementation deficit, relating to both, planning and environmental assessment. Effective SEA application appeared to be difficult to

---

**BOX 4.9 KEY ASPECTS OF THE ITALIAN
SEA SYSTEM AND CURRENT WEAKNESSES**

Key aspects of the Italian SEA system:

- In pre-SEA Directive times, formal and compulsory requirements for applying SEA in certain regions,
- EIA-based SEA approach,
- Clear substantive and procedural SEA requirements,
- SEA team should be separate from the plan/programme proponent.

Current weaknesses:

- Vulnerability to political influences,
- Poor environmental consciousness among politicians and the public,
- Implementation deficit relating to both, planning and environmental assessment practices,
- Lack of coordinating guidance and of a framework law at the national level (this is changing due to SEA Directive requirements; see Chapter 5),
- Poor institutional support.

---

achieve, not least due to poor environmental consciousness, not just among politicians, but also among the general public. Institutional support was also poor, with no agency or commission being in place to help those conducting SEA. Box 4.9 summarizes key aspects of the Italian approach to SEA and describes its weaknesses.

Germany

Germany has had extensive environmental assessment-related experience, even before the transposition of the European SEA Directive. In spatial/land use planning, this has been particularly related to the formal landscape planning system, based on the Federal Environmental Protection Act of 1976 (last amended 2002) and to EIA-based assessments of master plans for smaller areas, for example, of a municipality. In total, there are over two decades of experiences with assessment practice at PPP levels of decision-making. Various authors have reported on the relationship between SEA and landscape planning (see Jacoby, 2000; Scholles et al, 2003).

Landscape plans and programmes are prepared in order to protect and develop the natural environment and landscapes. They include an extensive baseline description and the development of environmental aims and objectives. In some states, since the mid-1990s, landscape plans have also been prepared in parallel to local land use plans, assessing the impacts of different development alternatives. In this context, Fischer (2002a) reports on experiences in the state of Brandenburg, which is the basis for this section. Guidance for landscape planning had been released in various states by planning/environment ministries. Furthermore, there was professional support provided through state ministries.

In addition to spatial/land use planning, there are other SEA-type experiences in various sectors, particularly in the transport sector, where comprehensive multi-criteria-based assessment practice of transport plans and programmes exists (see, for example, Wende et al, 2004). Furthermore, EIA has been observed to include transport corridor considerations that are often portrayed as being part of SEA (see Chapter 3). Overall, there is a high technical standard regarding field surveys, preparation of maps and impact prediction. There is normally a clear sequence in place for avoiding, minimizing, mitigating and compensating impacts.

This section focuses on the experiences of the landscape planning system, with a focus on the state of Brandenburg.

Several hundreds of local and regional landscape plans and programmes were prepared each year prior to formal SEA requirements coming into force in mid-2004 (the example of the Landscape Plan Ketzin is presented in Chapter 6). There is scope for improving the way in which the public is enabled to participate in the process. While there is a well-developed planning hierarchy in place, this is frequently described as being overly complicated and in need of streamlining (Fischer, 2002a). There is a highly developed environmental consciousness in German society. Generally speaking, the consideration of uncertainties is weak. Box 4.10 summarizes key aspects of the German approach and lists current weaknesses.

BOX 4.10 KEY ASPECTS OF THE GERMAN LANDSCAPE PLAN-BASED SEA SYSTEM AND CURRENT WEAKNESSES (BASED ON PRACTICE IN THE STATE OF BRANDENBURG)

Key aspects of the German landscape plan-based SEA system:

- Formal and enforceable EIA-based landscape plan/programme SEA requirements,
- Area wide SEA, parallel to land use planning,
- SEA does not only identify impacts but is also supposed to enhance and develop the biophysical environment,
- Clear sequence in terms of avoiding, minimizing, mitigating and compensating impacts,
- Guidance through state ministries,
- Professional support through state environment agencies,
- High technical standard of surveys, preparation of maps and impact prediction techniques.

Current weaknesses:

- Poor public participation (this is now changing based on SEA Directive requirements),
- Planning system somewhat overcomplicated,
- Consideration of uncertainties weak.

Finland

In Finland, both EIA-based SEA for public authorities' plans and programmes and SEA of government bills (cabinet SEA) have been conducted for many years. Whereas EIA-based SEA has been applied to plans and programmes since 1994 (that is, there are over 10 years of SEA experience; see Hilden and Jalonen, 2005), mostly in land use planning (based on the Building and Planning Act of 1999 and the EIA Act of 1990 – last amended 2005), SEA of government bills has been in place since a decision-in-principle by the Finnish government in 1998. Tens of SEAs were prepared annually prior to the implementation of the SEA Directive. Apart from general guidance, there is also theme specific guidance, for example, on biodiversity.

Institutional support for SEA is provided by regional environment centres, which are regional offices of the national Ministry of the Environment. Further support, for example, on how to use methods and techniques is provided by the Finish Environment Institute. A set of national land use objectives is available that provides for some guiding principles based on which situation-specific environmental objectives can be designed. Generally speaking, SEA appears to have led to a greater environmental awareness of those involved in SEA and plan making processes and there is also a tradition of extensive public involvement and transparency in public decision-making, with requirements formulated in the Finish constitution. Furthermore, there is a good record of enforcement in the Finnish EIA-based SEA system.

Process integration is said to normally function well, with SEA being conducted as a separate process that connects with plan making and other assessment

---

BOX 4.11 KEY ASPECTS OF THE FINNISH SEA SYSTEM AND CURRENT WEAKNESSES

Key aspects of the Finish SEA system:

- EIA-based SEA system in land use-related planning,
- Requirements for cabinet SEA,
- High environmental consciousness in Finnish society, pressure on public authorities to consider the environment,
- Highly developed participative and cooperative culture due to constitutional right to transparency,
- Good record of enforcement,
- Clear guidance,
- Solid institutional support base through regional environment centres and the Finish Environment Institute,
- Well-developed planning hierarchy,
- Well-developed monitoring.

Current weaknesses:

- Consideration of alternatives, impact mitigation and compensation measures somewhat weak (may now change due to SEA Directive requirements).

processes (economic, social) at regular intervals. There is a well-developed planning and decision-making hierarchy in place. Environmental consciousness is highly developed in Finnish society with pressure coming from the general public to take environmental aspects into account in PPP making. In contrast to most other systems globally, monitoring in Finland is developed well.

Weaknesses include an insufficient consideration of alternatives. Furthermore, the interviewed expert said that impact mitigation and compensation are weak. Box 4.11 summarizes key aspects of the Finnish approach and current weaknesses. Only the EIA-based SEA system is evaluated in Table 4.1 because the author was not able to receive sufficient information on the government bills (cabinet) SEA system.

Evaluation and discussion of different systems' experiences

Table 4.1 provides an evaluation of the 11 SEA systems in terms of the context, procedural and wider methodological factors introduced in Box 4.1. This is based on a distinction of factors in terms of whether they were fully, near fully, partly or not met. Out of the 11 SEA systems, ten were based on formal requirements, with eight being legally regulated. Nine systems were of an administration-led SEA type. The two cabinet SEA systems of Canada and The Netherlands were based on a cabinet directive and a cabinet order, respectively. The only country where SEA had been applied voluntarily is South Africa. In ten systems, SEA was a separate, clearly distinguishable process, with only New Zealand having had a fully integrated SEA and plan/programme making system in place. In five systems, there was strong institutional support by an independent environmental agency, institute or EIA Commission, namely Western Australia (EPA), Canada (CEAA), Finland (Finnish Environmental Institute), Germany (state environment agencies) and the Dutch EIA-based SEA system (EIA Commission). Furthermore, in California, institutional support was provided by the COPR. Ten of the 11 systems had practical experiences with SEA application for at least a decade. Only in Italy was practice restricted to roughly five years.

Table 4.2 summarizes results for the 11 SEA systems in terms of the extent to which context and procedural factors were in place. Furthermore, opinions of experts are shown (as identified in interviews; see above) on whether SEA was able to lead to a better consideration of the environment. In this context, SEA systems that received a yes/explicit mark for at least two thirds of the factors are distinguished from those that received a yes/explicit mark for between one third and two thirds of the factors, and from those that received a yes/explicit mark for less than one third of the factors. Wider methodological factors are not summarized in this way, as there are only three.

Presence of context factors and the likelihood of SEA leading to a better consideration of the environment

In five SEA systems, at least two thirds of the context factors obtained a yes/explicit mark. These are all EIA-based SEA

Table 4.1 *Evaluation of 11 SEA systems*
(EU systems based on pre-SEA Directive practice)

Country or state in which system is based	Coverage of SEA	SEA approach (underlined approach is evaluated)	Requirements ✔ = legislative ⇔ = regulation, directive ✗ = no requirements	Guidance ✔ = clear guidance ⇔ = guidance, but not fully clear/not covering all sectors ✗ = no guidance	Competences/ responsibilities clear	Enforcement ✔ = agency, legal threat ⇔ = indirectly through independent review ✗ = no real enforcement
California	Every land use, including private (ie administration planning related) several 10s to 100s of SEAs/year	Formal EIA based	✔	⇔	✔⇔	✔
W Australia	Land use plans (ie administration planning related), approx 20/year	Formal EIA based	✔	✔⇔	✔	✔
Canada	Decisions of Can Parliament (ie cabinet SEA), approx 80/year	Policy SEA (cabinet)	⇔	⇔	✔	✗
New Zealand	Regional Land Transport Strategies (transport planning), all regions, every 3 years (ie 5/year on average)	Formal policy plan SEA (integration planning)	✔	✗	(✔⇔) Expectation based on recent requirements, too early to comment	⇔
South Africa	Voluntary only (all levels, sectors), in planning (up to 15/year)	Mostly EIA based (informal)	✗	⇔	✗	✗
Netherlands	(1) land use changes (several/year), (2) government bills, (10/year), (3) transport and otehr visions (10s/year)	(1) Formal EIA based (2) Political SEA (3) informal policy SEA	✔ / ⇔	✔ / ⇔	✔ / ✔	✔ / ✗
UK	(1) regional and local development plans (100s/year), (2) transport plans, (3) government policies	(1) Formal policy plan based, (2) informal para SEA, (3) policy SEA	⇔	✔	✔⇔	✗
Italy	Land use changes, with main focus on Emilia Romagna region	Formal EIA based	✔ not very clear	✗	✗	✗
Germany	(1) State, regional, local spatial and land use planning (100s/year), (2) transport policies and programmes (10s/year)	(1) Formal SEA, (2) informal SEA	✔	✔	✔	✔
Finland	(1) Land use plans, transport and other sectors (10s/year), (2) government bills and proposals	(1) Formal EIA based and (2) policy SEA	✔	✔	✔	✔

KEY

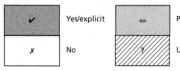

✔	Yes/explicit	⇔	Partially/explicit	
✗	No	?	Unclear	

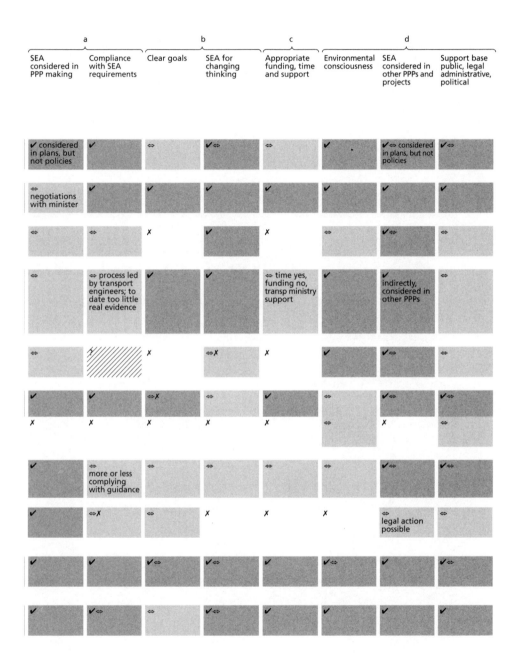

Column group headers:

a		b		c		d	
SEA considered in PPP making	Compliance with SEA requirements	Clear goals	SEA for changing thinking	Appropriate funding, time and support	Environmental consciousness	SEA considered in other PPPs and projects	Support base public, legal administrative, political

Table 4.1 *continued*

Country or state in which system is based	d — Tradition of transparency and co-operation	Planning hierarchy ✔ = effective PPP hierarchy in place, covered by SEA ⇔ = hierarchy in place, but not covered fully by SEA ✗ = no hierarchy in place	Clear focus	e — Roles of assessor clearly defined?	Effective project EIA	f — Uncertainties	Screening	Scoping
California	✔	✔	✔⇔	✔⇔	✔⇔	✔	✔	✔
W Australia	✔	✔⇔	✔	✔⇔	✔	✔	✔	✔
Canada	⇔	⇔✗	✔	⇔	⇔	⇔	✔	✔
New Zealand	⇔	✔	✔	⇔	✔	⇔	?	✔
South Africa	⇔	✔	✗	⇔	⇔	✗	?	✔
Netherlands	✔⇔	✔	✔	✔	✔	⇔	✔	✔
	⇔	✔	⇔	⇔	✔	✗	✔	✔
UK	✔⇔	✔⇔	✔	⇔	⇔	⇔	⇔	✔
Italy	⇔✗	⇔	✗	⇔	✗	✗	⇔	⇔
Germany	✔⇔	✔⇔	✔	✔⇔	⇔	⇔	✔	✔
Finland	✔	✔	⇔✗	✔	⇔	⇔	✔	✔

KEY

✔ Yes/explicit	⇔ Partially/explicit
✗ No	? Unclear

...eport	Review	Summary	Monitoring	Process integration	Consultation	Public participation	Consideration of appropriate alternatives	Clear prediction, if possible quantitative	Avoid, minimize, mitigate, compensate
	✔	✔	⇔	✔	✔	✔	✔	✔	✔
	✔	✔	⇔	✔	✔	⇔	⇔✗	⇔	✔
...ut not ...blicly ...ailable	✗	✗	⇔	⇔	✗	✗	⇔	✔	✔
...no ...vironmental ...port of ...stinguish-...le section	⇔	✗	✔	✔	✔	✔	⇔	✔	⇔
	⇔	✔	(hatched)	⇔	✔	✔	⇔	⇔	⇔
	✔	✔	✔	✔	✔	✔	✔	✔	✔
	✗	✗	⇔	✗	✗	✗	⇔	✗	⇔
	⇔	⇔	⇔	✔⇔	⇔	⇔	⇔	⇔	⇔
	⇔	✗	⇔	⇔	✔	⇔	✗	⇔	⇔
	✔	⇔	⇔	✔⇔	✔	⇔	✔⇔	✔⇔	✔
	✔	⇔	✔	✔	✔	✔	⇔	✔⇔	⇔

Table 4.2 *SEA systems' performance and existence of context and procedural factors*

	Context factors in place	Procedural factors in place	Is SEA likely to lead to a better consideration of the environment? (expert opinions)
Administration-led SEA			
EIA-based SEA			
California	✔	✔	✔
Western Australia	✔	✔	✔
South Africa	✗	⇔	⇔
The Netherlands	✔	✔	✔
Italy	✗	⇔	⇔
Finland	✔	✔	✔
Germany	✔	✔	✔
Non EIA-based SEA			
UK	⇔	⇔	⇔
New Zealand	⇔	⇔	⇔
Cabinet SEA			
Canada	✗	⇔	✔⇔
The Netherlands	✗	✗	✗

Notes:
✔ =   at least two thirds of factors received a yes or explicit mark/SEA perceived as leading to a more effective consideration of the environment;
⇔ =   in between one third to two thirds of factors received a yes or explicit mark/SEA perceived as only occasionally leading to a more effective consideration of the environment;
✗ =   less than one third of factors received a yes or explicit mark/SEA perceived as not leading to a more effective consideration of the environment;
✔⇔ = varied performance record; some effective, some partially effective.

systems, and include California, The Netherlands, Finland, Germany and Western Australia. In the non-EIA-based administration-led SEA systems from the UK and New Zealand, at least one third and two thirds of the factors obtained a yes/explicit mark. In four systems, finally, less than one third of the factors obtained a yes/explicit mark. These include the remaining two EIA-based SEA systems, from South Africa and Italy, and the two cabinet SEA systems from Canada and The Netherlands.

Generally speaking, the extent to which context factors obtained a yes/explicit mark was closely correlated with positive perceptions of interviewees. Thus, the five systems that were perceived

to be leading to a more effective consideration of the environment obtained a yes/explicit mark for more than two thirds of the factors. The UK and New Zealand systems were said to be partially effective in leading to a better consideration of the environment in strategic decision-making, and both obtained a yes/explicit mark for between one third and two thirds of the factors. Whereas the South African voluntary EIA-based SEA system and the Italian EIA-based SEA system obtained a yes/explicit mark for less than one third of the context factors, they were still perceived as being able to at least occasionally lead to a better consideration of the environment. Only the Dutch cabinet SEA system (the e-test) was not

---

4.12 CONTEXT-RELATED ENABLING FACTORS WITH PARTICULAR IMPORTANCE FOR EFFECTIVE SEA

- Legal requirements for SEA;
- A well-developed legal, political and administrative support base;
- Strong enforcement mechanisms, leading to practice complying with requirements;
- An independent support environment agency/institute/commission;
- Appropriate funding, time and support for SEA;
- Clearly defined responsibilities.

---

perceived as being able to lead to a more effective consideration of the environment at all. Here, a yes/explicit mark was obtained for less than one third of the factors. Judging from the interview results with national SEA experts, certain context-related enabling factors appeared to be particularly important for making SEA effective, which should always be considered when introducing SEA requirements into any system. These are summarized in Box 4.12.

There are indications that an existing culture of transparency and cooperation helps SEA to support a more effective consideration of the environment. Generally speaking, planning systems with a culture of extensive political negotiations 'behind the scenes' (some can be considered normal in any system) are going to be faced with some serious problems when attempting to introduce SEA, particularly if no effective enforcement mechanisms are in place. Finally, a well-developed societal environmental consciousness also appears to support the effective application of SEA.

Presence of procedural factors and the likelihood of SEA leading to a better consideration of the environment

For 10 of the 11 systems, there was a perfect correlation of the extent to which procedural factors were in place and the perceived likelihood of SEA leading to a better consideration of the environment. Only in the Canadian case was there a slight difference between the two. In Canada, between one third and two thirds of procedural factors received a yes or explicit mark, yet there was still a perception that SEA was, at least occasionally, leading to a better consideration of the environment. Based on the evaluation of the 11 SEA systems, therefore, the extent to which EIA-based procedural stages are in place is correlated with a perceived effectiveness of SEA. This also appears to be the case in cabinet SEA. There is, therefore, at least some scope to challenge the claim that a high degree of procedural flexibility (in terms of individually determining assessment stages) is always required in cabinet SEA.

Presence of wider methodological factors and the likelihood of SEA leading to a better consideration of the environment

Only three wider methodological factors were considered in the evaluation. Therefore, results are interpreted here only qualitatively. While there are some indications that these factors are also related to the perceived effectiveness of

SEA, this relationship is not as strong as in the case of context and procedural factors. Those with a perceived high effectiveness were normally considering alternatives explicitly. Furthermore, they were predicting impacts, if possible quantitatively, and were following a sequence of avoiding, minimizing, mitigating and compensating for impacts.

Observations on cabinet SEA

Based on the evaluation of the 11 SEA systems, it may be suggested that, overall, the extent to which context and procedural factors are present within a particular system does indeed have an impact on the extent to which environmental aspects are considered in strategic decision-making. However, while there is a very close fit of procedural performance and perceived effectiveness of SEA for both administration-led and cabinet SEA, there are indications that context criteria may not be entirely suitable for describing cabinet SEA performance. In both cabinet SEA systems, context factors were found to obtain a yes/explicit reply for less than one third of the enabling elements. However, while the Dutch e-test was indeed perceived as not being effective in leading to a better consideration of the environment in decision-making, in the Canadian case, SEA was perceived to be able to do so at least partially. Understanding the differences between the Canadian and Dutch cabinet SEA systems can therefore potentially provide for a starting point to understand cabinet SEA better and help to design suitable context factors for SEA applied at this level of decision-making. In this context, institutional support appears to be particularly crucial. Whereas in Canada, the Commissioner of the Environment and Sustainable Development oversees the SEA process and monitors performance of the SEA system on an annual basis, there is no similar body in place in The Netherlands. Furthermore, while in Canada support is provided by the CEAA, in The Netherlands, only an advisory body is in place that is administered by the ministries of trade and of the environment. In this context, it is important that institutional support in Canada for cabinet SEA appears to be stronger than in The Netherlands. There are, therefore, indications that SEA's effectiveness in leading to a better consideration of environmental aspects is related to the will of those involved in cabinet decision-making to take environmental aspects into account. Furthermore, if the environment is to become a permanent feature in cabinet decision-making, support by an institutional body and proper enforcement is likely to be of crucial importance.

Conclusions

This chapter provided a comparative review of 11 developed SEA systems from ten countries worldwide. Using the SEA categories introduced in Chapter 1, nine systems were found to apply an administration-led SEA approach (seven EIA-based and two non-EIA-based). Furthermore, two cabinet SEA systems were considered. Evaluation of SEA systems was based on context, procedural and wider methodological factors.

One of the main aims of the evaluation provided here is to help those attempting to learn from experiences in other systems to better understand and appreciate the specific circumstances of those systems and be able to focus on systems that may have similarities with their own systems. This is important particularly when trying to understand, for example, what the underlying factors for producing good SEAs may be. To date, in the professional literature, SEA systems have frequently been presented without explaining whether they were performing well. In this context, the chapter aimed to contribute towards a better understanding of different systems.

Systems were chosen on the basis of whether SEA had been applied routinely for at least a decade, with the exception of Italy, where there has been only five years of SEA experience to date. Systems were from five European and five non-European countries. As SEA systems are said to need some time to be fully effective and to change attitudes and values of those involved in PPP making (see Chapter 1), the review did not include emerging EU systems, following the requirements of the SEA Directive. Experiences gained in this context have been too recent to allow for an evaluation of systems' performance, particularly as some systems only transposed the Directive as recently as mid-2006, with three systems not having transposed at all to date (see Chapter 5).

The perceived ability of SEA to lead to a better consideration of the environment appears to be closely connected with the extent to which SEA (enabling) context factors are in place. In administration-led SEA, in five of the seven EIA-based systems, SEA was perceived to lead to a more effective consideration of the environment in plan and programme making. In these systems, at least two thirds of the context factors received a yes/explicit mark. These included the

Californian PEIR, the Dutch, Finnish and Australian EIA-based SEA systems and the German local landscape plan-related SEA systems. In those two systems, where SEA was perceived to be able to only occasionally lead to a more effective consideration of the environment, less than one third of the context factors received a yes/explicit mark. These included South Africa, the only system considered here that is not based on formal SEA requirements, and Italy, a system marked by a culture of extensive behind the scenes political negotiations. The two policy plan SEA systems of New Zealand and the UK, finally, led to a better consideration in policy plan making occasionally. In these two systems, between one third and two thirds of the enabling factors received a yes/explicit mark. Finally, in the two cabinet SEA systems considered in this chapter, Canada and The Netherlands (e-test), less than one third of the context factors received a yes/explicit mark. However, while the Dutch e-test was not perceived to being able to lead to a better consideration of the environment in cabinet PPP making, the Canadian system was said to have a varied performance record, with some SEAs being effective and others only being partially effective. This appears to be connected with institutional support that in certain instances was said to be strong in Canada.

There was a perfect fit in the extent to which EIA-based procedural factors were in place and the perceived effectiveness of SEA, not just for administration-led SEA, but also for cabinet SEA. This raises some questions regarding the quest for SEA procedural flexibility at this level of decision-making. Therefore, until further empirical evidence has been obtained, a cautious approach should be applied, possibly meeting as many EIA procedural stages as possible in any SEA.

Finally, as a word of caution, it needs to be added that the evaluation conducted in this chapter relied on a limited database. Nevertheless, findings appear to be largely in line with those of other, similar studies, of which, however, there are currently only very few. Therefore, there is clearly a need for further research.

The European SEA Directive:
Its Transposition and Implementation
in the Member States

Chapter 5 deals with recent changes to SEA systems in the EU and provides for a mid-2006 update of the transposition and implementation status of the Directive 2001/42/EC (the SEA Directive) in the 25 EU member states (since 1 January 2007, there are 27 member states, with Romania and Bulgaria having joined the EU). Member states were supposed to have transposed the Directive by 21 July 2004 at the latest. The focus is on emerging legal requirements and guidelines.[1]

The main purpose of the chapter is to raise awareness of the different ways in which administration-led SEA for plans and programmes may be implemented. The fact that different approaches are taken within one policy framework (that is, they follow a directive within a quasi federal system that aims at standardizing SEA), supports the suggestion that SEA needs to be implemented in a tailor-made manner.

First a brief description of the main requirements laid out in the SEA Directive is provided. Furthermore, a summary of the transposition and implementation status of the Directive in the member states is given. Finally, legal requirements and guidelines released within each of the member states are listed. In this context, lists of mostly web-based references to legislation and guidance documents are provided. Case studies are also listed in Annex 2.

This chapter is based on two sources of information: first, a questionnaire survey with national experts from each country, which was conducted in July 2006; and second, a review of documents in mid-2006, released in the various member states relating to the SEA Directive transposition and implementation status, focusing on spatial/land use planning.

The European SEA Directive

This section provides a brief introduction of the scope and content of the European Directive 2001/42/EC 'on the assessment of the effects of certain plans and programmes on the environment'. Under the Directive, environmental assessments are to be conducted for certain plans and programmes (see Box 2.5). Policies and

cabinet decision processes are not mentioned. However, it is worth noting that based on the so-called 'Cardiff process' (following an agreement reached at a European Council meeting in Cardiff in 1998), the environment is also supposed to be integrated into policy making.

Article 3.2 of the Directive specifies plans and programmes that should be subject to SEA. These include plans and programmes prepared for:

agriculture, forestry, fisheries, energy, industry, transport, waste management, telecommunications, tourism, town and country planning or land use and which set the framework for future development of projects listed in Annexes I and II to [the EIA] Directive 85/337/EEC, or which, in view of the likely effects on sites, have been determined to require an assessment pursuant to Article 6 or 7 of [the Habitat – areas with special EU protection status] Directive 92/43/EEC.

The European SEA Directive requirements can be summarized by six overall themes, four of which are explicitly listed in Article 2(b) of the SEA Directive. In addition, tiering and monitoring are also included here because these are formally required and currently appear to pose some particular problems in emerging SEA practice in most EU member states. The six themes are:

1 Effective *tiering*;
2 Preparation of an *environmental report* on the likely significant effects of the draft plan or programme;
3 Carrying out *consultations* on the draft plan or programme and the accompanying environmental report;
4 Taking into account the environmental report and the results of consultation in *decision-making*;
5 Providing *information* when the plan or programme is adopted and showing how the results of the environmental assessment have been taken into account;

6 Effective *monitoring*.

Generally speaking, the SEA Directive formulates procedural requirements, asking for an EIA-type assessment process to be conducted. This consists of screening, scoping, assessment, environmental report preparation, consideration of assessment results in decision-making, monitoring/follow-up, consultation and participation (see Figure 1.1). While, theoretically, a review of the quality of the environmental report is not explicitly required by the Directive, in practice, administrations and those that are consulted on the report are likely to evaluate the completeness and quality of the information provided in the report. In this context, an evaluation checklist/review table is likely to be essential. Annex 1 introduces a review table based on SEA Directive requirements. This is organized in terms of six environmental report review themes, as follows:

1 Plan/programme and environmental baseline description; plan/programme and SEA process integration;
2 Identification and evaluation of key issues/options;
3 Determination of impact significance;
4 Consultation process;
5 Presentation of information and results;
6 Recommendations on preferred options and monitoring.

Some other more recent directives in the EU are closely related with the SEA Directive and there may be implications in certain situations for SEA (see, for example, Marsden and de Mulder, 2005). Most importantly, these include the Water Framework Directive (European Commission, 2000; see also Gullon, 2004) and the Habitats Directive (European Commission, 1992). The

Habitats Directive requires an assessment to be conducted for policies, plans, programmes and projects that may have significant impacts on areas protected under the Directive. In the UK, associated assessments are referred to as 'appropriate assessments' (see Levett-Therivel et al, 2006).

The SEA Directive in 25 EU member states: A summary[2]

Table 5.1 summarizes SEA Directive transposition and implementation status, as of July 2006, making reference to five aspects of emerging SEA practice:

1   Legislation transposing the SEA Directive;
2   Guidance released to support authorities conducting SEA following the SEA Directive;
3   Extent of SEA application;
4   The existence of any other (statutory, formal, informal) management instruments/methods that aim to ensure the environment is given due consideration in spatial/land use and sector planning;
5   The existence of pre-Directive SEA practice (practice in five member states has already been reviewed in Chapter 4, including The Netherlands, UK, Germany, Finland and Italy).

A summary of the performance of the 25 pre-2007 EU members states in terms of these five aspects is provided below.

Transposition status

Most EU member states had transposed the SEA Directive by mid-2006. Only three states were identified that did not yet have SEA legislation: Portugal, Greece and Luxembourg. References to all the main pieces of legislation are provided below. Two states, Germany and Italy, had national SEA framework legislation in place, however, with Germany being a federal state and with Italy having strong regional powers, legislation still needed to be released for most of the 16 German *Länder* and for Italy's 20 regions and two autonomous provinces. In Slovenia, only draft legislation on SEA was in place. In The Netherlands, finally, legislation transposing the SEA Directive had only been released in 2006. However, in spatial/land use and other sector planning, formal SEAs had been conducted for many years based on the national EIA Act. Overall, in EU member states, requirements for SEA were formulated through:

*   Explicit SEA (framework) laws: UK, Denmark, Spain, Ireland, Malta, Cyprus, Finland and Hungary; the latter two in combination with sector/land use planning regulations/environment codes;
*   Amendments to existing EIA regulation: Belgium, Estonia, Latvia, Czech Republic, Slovakia, Poland and Germany; the latter two in combination with amendments to sector/land use acts/environment codes;
*   Amendments to an environment code: The Netherlands, Slovenia, Italy, Sweden, Lithuania and France; the latter three in combination with amendments to sector/land use planning legislation;
*   Amendments to land use planning/sector legislation: Austria.

Table 5.1 *SEA Directive transposition and implementation status in 25 EU member states*

SEA aspects Member states (alphabetical order)	(1) Transposition status of the SEA Directive	(2) Guidance	(3) Extent of SEA application	(4) Other management instruments?	(5) SEA started based on Directive
1 Austria	✔	(✔)/?	✔	⇔	Prior
2 Belgium	✔	✔[1]	⇔	⇔	Prior
3 Cyprus	✔	⇔	✗	⇔	Post
4 Czech Republic	✔	✔[2]	✔	⇔	Prior
5 Denmark	✔	✔	✔	⇔	Prior
6 Estonia	✔	⇔	✔	⇔	Prior
7 Finland	✔	✔	✔✔	⇔	Prior
8 France	✔	✔/?	✔✔	⇔	Prior
9 Germany	(✔)	(✔)/?	✔✔[5]	✔[7]	Prior
10 Greece	✗	✗	⇔	✔[8]	Post
11 Hungary	✔	✔	⇔	⇔	Prior
12 Ireland	✔	✔	✔	⇔	Post
13 Italy	(✔)	⇔	⇔	⇔	Post
14 Latvia	✔	✗(✔)	✔	⇔	Post
15 Lithuania	✔	✗(✔)	⇔[6]	⇔	Prior
16 Luxembourg	✗	✗	✗	?	Post
17 Malta	✔	✗[3]	⇔	⇔	Post
18 The Netherlands	✔	✔	✔✔	✔[9]	Prior
19 Poland	✔	✔	✔✔	✔[10]	Prior
20 Portugal	✗	⇔	⇔	⇔	Post
21 Slovakia	✔	✗	⇔	⇔	Prior
22 Slovenia	⇔	✗	⇔	✔[11]	Prior
23 Spain	✔	✔[4]	✔	⇔	Prior[12]
24 Sweden	✔	✔	✔✔	⇔	Prior
25 UK	✔	✔	✔✔	⇔	Prior

Status: July 2006

✔ = fully transposed (ie legal requirements are in place)	✔ = guidance available	✔✔ = over 100	✔ = other instrument in place	Prior: Prior to the SEA Directive
⇔ = partly transposed/ transposed shortly	⇔ = draft / general guidance (may only mention SEA)	✔ = quite a few	⇔ = general requirement to consider	coming into force
✗ = not yet transposed	⇔ = one or very few / pilot studies	⇔ = general requirement to consider environment in	Post = started based on SEA
(✔) = transposed at national level,; states/regions need to follow (have been given extensions by the EC)	✗ = no guidance (✔) = state guidance partly available/ partly under preparation	✗ = none	spatial planning	Directive

Notes:

1 EIA/SEA website by provincial ministry, www.mervlaanderen.be
2 deemed outdated
3 foreign guidance
4 regional guidance
5 practice mainly coming from the level of small scale binding land use plans and local landscape plans in certain states
6 all currently under preparation
7 landscape planning
8 EIA for certain land use plans
9 comprehensive EIA based SEA has been in place since the late 1980s
10 eco-physiographic studies
11 EIA for physical plans since 1993 according to the Environmental Protection Act
12 for EC structural funds
Source: Fischer, 2006c.

SEA guidance

In total, over 40 guidelines/guidance documents were identified through the questionnaire survey and literature review (see references in the next section). Only five states had no guidelines at all, namely Greece, Luxembourg, Slovakia, Slovenia and Malta (even though the expert from Malta referred to guidance documents from other states). In two states, Latvia and Lithuania, SEA guidance was said to be due for release shortly. Four states had general or sector/land use planning specific guidelines in place that mentioned SEA, namely Estonia, Italy, Cyprus and Portugal (Portugal being on strategic integrated assessment, rather than SEA). Furthermore, a number of states had released guidelines that only covered certain sectors or regions. These included Germany, Spain, Austria and France. Comprehensive guidance for certain sector and spatial/land use plan making, finally, had been released in the UK, Sweden, Finland, Denmark, Poland, Ireland and Hungary. While guidelines were also in place in the Czech Republic, by mid-2006 these needed updating. Furthermore, in Flanders (Belgium), a website provided for some SEA guidance (www.mervlaanderen.be). In The Netherlands, while SEA Directive-based guidelines were said to be due for release, comprehensive guidance had been available since the end of the 1980s for EIA-based SEA by the national EIA Commission (www.commissiemer.nl). Finally, it should be added here that the EC had also released general guidelines on SEA, available in 11 languages (http://ec.europa.eu/environment/eia/).

Extent of SEA application

By July 2006, there was a wealth of practical experience with SEA in many EU member states. Judging from the experts' replies, there were likely to be over a thousand SEAs/SEA-type assessments conducted by mid-2006, most of which, however, predated the SEA Directive. States with the most extensive SEA application included those with numerous pre-Directive SEA experiences, namely the UK, The Netherlands, Germany, Sweden and Finland. Furthermore, and somewhat surprisingly when considering the very limited information available in the professional literature, Poland and France also appear to have had some extensive SEA experience. In all of these states, SEA had been routinely applied in more than a hundred or several hundred cases. Other states with some substantial case/pilot study experiences included Austria, Denmark and, again somewhat surprisingly, Estonia, Spain, Latvia and the Czech Republic. Most of the other states were said to have had at least a few SEAs (either routinely prepared or pilot studies). Only in Cyprus had no SEA been prepared by July 2006.

Other environmental management instruments/pre-Directive SEA practice

Regarding the existence of other environmental management instruments within planning systems, most states had systems in place before having had to transpose the SEA Directive, aiming at integrating environmental with other aspects. This was particularly extensive in spatial/land use planning. In this context, some states have had more informal SEA systems, including, for example, the UK (environmental/sustainability appraisal) and Sweden (integrated land use planning). Many questionnaire respondents said that environment ministries/departments had always been supposed to ensure environmental aspects were adequately considered in planning. In The Netherlands, Greece and Slovenia, EIA had been applied to small-scale land use plans for many years. Furthermore, two states had other environmental management instruments in place, namely Germany and Poland. In Germany, landscape plans were prepared at various administrative levels, acting as state of the environment reports and also defining environmental development objectives. In certain *Länder* (for example Brandenburg), since the mid-1990s, landscape plans had been prepared in parallel to local land use plans, identifying potential impacts and supporting impact avoidance, reduction, mitigation and compensation (see Chapters 4 and 6). In Poland, 'ecophysiographic' studies were prepared for each local and regional draft land use plan. These were supposed to characterize natural environmental elements in a specific plan area and potential interactions with future anticipated land use.

Most states had started working on SEA prior to Directive requirements coming into force. This was connected with the above mentioned need of most planning systems to duly consider environmental aspects. Only in seven states was the Directive perceived as the explicit trigger for applying SEA, including Italy, Portugal, Ireland, Latvia, Malta, Greece and Cyprus.

Legal documents and guidelines in 25 EU members states

In this section, legal documents and guidelines for SEA in the 25 EU member states are presented. In this context, extensive web-based references are provided that allow the reader to access documentation for most of the 25 member states. It is important to note that most documents are only available in the national language. Case studies from the different countries are listed in Annex 2. Please note that whenever full references are provided, these are not be repeated in the Bibliography at the end of the book.

Austria

By mid-2006, legal documents transposing the SEA Directive in Austria had been released at the federal level and at the level of the nine states (*Länder*). At the federal level, these include (most of the information accessible via www.anidea.at/aktu.html):

- Federal Act on Waste Management (waste management regarding federal competencies);
- Federal Act on Strategic Assessment into the Transport Sector (transport regarding federal competencies);
- Federal Act on Environmental Noise (noise issues regarding federal competencies);
- Federal Act on Air Quality (air quality issues regarding federal competencies);
- Federal Act on Water Management (water management issues regarding federal competencies).

There was also guidance on how to conduct SEA within local land use planning published by certain provincial governments. These include Lower Austria (www.raumordnung-noe.at/dynamisch/showinfostand.php?id=87) and Styria.

Belgium

It was only possible to obtain information for the region of Flanders (and not for the other two regions of Belgium, Wallonia and Brussels). In Flanders, the SEA Directive was transposed, based on the EIA and SEA Decree (Decree of the Flemish Government of 18 December 2002), to complete the Decree of 5 April 1995, with a title concerning environmental safety reporting: Belgisch Staatsblad/Le Moniteur Belge – B.S. 13/02/2003. A website of the Flemish Environment Ministry also provides guidance on how to do SEA (see www.mervlaanderen.be). This relies mainly on SEA case studies.

Cyprus (south)

The Directive was fully transposed through the Law No. 102(I)/2005, which entered into force on 29 July 2005. A booklet was prepared by the Environment Service in November 2005, and was disseminated to all the authorities, consultancies and people involved. The booklet can be found on the web page of the Environment Service (www.moa.gov.cy, follow the links to 'environment service', 'environmental impacts' and 'SEA').

Czech Republic

The SEA Directive was transposed in 2004 through amendments to the new Czech EIA Act (no. 100/2001 Coll.). SEA of land use plans had a special place in this system. There was a slightly different procedure for SEA of land use plans and for SEA of all other 'concepts'. Framework SEA requirements for land use plans will be further developed in the revision of the Law on Construction and Land Use Planning, which was expected to be adopted in 2007. Guidance for SEA of land use plans (produced in 1995) and

a 2nd update of the general guidance on SEA, issued in 2004, was available in mid-2006. However, at the time, they were likely to be replaced by new SEA guidelines for all types of land use plans.

Denmark

The SEA Directive was transposed by the Act on Environmental Assessment of Plans and Programmes (Act nr. 316 of 5 May 2004; www.skovognatur.dk/Lovgivning/Love/miljoevurdering.htm). Guidance was written in 2005 and published in June 2006, covering all plans and programmes (see www.skovognatur.dk/NR/rdonlyres/DD63EB1B-F0E6-4ABB-97447336B1C9C98E/22773/Samlet_SMV_vejledning_juni06.pdf).

Estonia

The SEA Directive was transposed by the Environmental Impact Assessment and Environmental Management System Act (SEA Act) on 3 April 2005 (www.envir.ee/92022). However, there was no SEA guidance published by mid-2006.

Finland

The SEA Directive was transposed through the Act and Decree on the Assessment of the Impacts of the Authorities' Plans, Programmes and Policies on the Environment and by amendments to the Land Use and Building Act and Decree, which entered into force on 1 June 2005 (www.ymparisto.fi/default.asp?contentid=65699&lan=en and www.ymparisto.fi/default.asp?node=17876&lan=en).

There was a range of land use specific guidelines:

- Public Participation and Impact Assessment in Regional Land Use Planning (2000);
- Shoreline Land Use Planning (2005);
- Biodiversity Impact Assessment in Regional Planning, EIA and Natura 2000 Assessment (2003);
- Social Impact Assessment in Land Use Planning (2005);
- Assessment of the Impacts of Hypermarkets and Shopping Centres in Land Use Planning (2001).

In addition, there was an ongoing development project, called 'Impact Assessment in Land Use Planning – KASEVA', which was supposed to result in general guidelines concerning both the process and content of SEA.

France

Transposition of the SEA Directive at the legislative level took place in the '*ordonnance*' (a special law) of 3 June 2004. This had two separate parts: one general and one specifically related to spatial planning. There were two different texts defining the precise rules of assessment: one relating to spatial planning, Decree of 27 May 2004, modifying the Town and Country Planning Code, and a second relating to other plans and programmes, Decree of 27 May 2004, modifying the Environment Code (www.ecologie.gouv.fr/article.php3?id_article=5737). There were also two different general guidelines (*Circulaires*): one relating to spatial planning, *Circulaire* of the Ministry in Charge of Town and Country Planning of 6 March 2006, and a second relating to other plans and programmes, *Circulaire* of the Ministry in Charge of Environment of 12 April 2006.

There was also one sectoral guideline for waste management. Furthermore, in mid-2006, guidance for water management was under preparation. Guidelines for land use plans at the regional level were also prepared in mid-2006.

Germany

In order to comply with SEA Directive requirements, the EIA Act (UVPG) was amended by the German Parliament on 12 May 12 2005 and by the *Bundesrat* (Chamber of the *Länder*) on 27 May 2005. Amendments came into force on 25 June 2005 through the 'Act for Introducing SEA' (see www.uvp.de). The 16 *Länder* had to implement SEA through their own laws, since the EIA Act and the Federal Spatial Planning Act only constitute overall frameworks. In order to do so by mid-2006, bills had been prepared in most of the *Länder*.

For spatial/land use planning SEA, the Act to Accommodate EU requirements (including the SEA Directive) within the Federal Construction Law (*EAG Bau*) came into force on 21 July 2004. The Federal Building Code and the Federal Spatial Planning Act were amended (http://bundesrecht.juris.de/bundesrecht/b baug/index.html). Draft guidelines have been released for transport planning (FGSV, 2004). Further guidance documents include:

- Guidance on how to adapt the Federal Construction Act with new EU Directives (www.uvp.de/merkblat/ Erlass_EAG_Bau_1207_2004.pdf);
- Recommendations of the Federal Ministry for the Environment, Nature Protection and Nuclear Safety of 2 August 2004 for direct implementation of the SEA Directive through the *Länder* (www.uvp.de/aktuell/ empfehlung_suprl.pdf);
- The Environmental Report in Practice (Bavarian Ministry of the Environment, Health and Consumer

Protection), covering statutory local land use plans and master plans (www.stmi.bayern.de/bauen/baurecht/staedtebau/15463).

Greece

By mid-2006, the SEA Directive had not been transposed and no guidance was available.

Hungary

The SEA Directive had been transposed based on amendments to the Environment Act in 2004 and a Government Decree on the Environmental Assessment of Certain Plans and Programmes in 2005. Two guidance documents were available: the 'Methodological Questions of the Socio-economic and Environmental Impact Assessments Associated with Regional Development Programmes' guidelines by the Hungarian Agency for Regional Development and Country Planning 2003, Budapest; and the 'Strategic Environmental Assessment' guidelines by the Hungarian Association of Nature Conservation 2003, Budapest.

Ireland

The SEA Directive was transposed through the European Communities (Environmental Assessment of Certain Plans and Programmes) Regulations 2004 (Statutory Instrument Number (SI No.) 435 of 2004), and the Planning and Development (Strategic Environmental Assessment) Regulations 2004 (SI No. 436 of 2004). Both sets of regulations became operational on 21 July 2004 (see www.environ.ie).

Guidance at the national level for regional authorities and planning authorities was released in 2004 (Department of the Environment, Heritage and Local Government, 2004; Implementation of SEA Directive (2001/42/EC): Assessment of the Effects of Certain Plans and Programmes on the Environment (www.environ.ie/DOEI/DOEIPol.nsf/0/18 29f4edf25b12b380256f5d004dd108/ $FILE/SEA%20Guidelines%20-%20 Final%20Text.pdf).

Italy

The SEA Directive was transposed by the Act on Environmental Matters D. lgs. n. 152, on 3 April 2006 (www.parla mento.it/leggi/deleghe/06152dl.htm).

There was also a Legislative Decree Framework in place (precursor to D. lgs. n. 152), the text of which was approved by the Council of Ministers on 10 February 2006 (www.apgw.net/ delega%20ambientale/2006-02-10/ decreto2006-02-10.pdf and annexes www.apgw.net/delega%20ambientale/ 2006-02-10/decreto2006-02-10_allegati. pdf).

Italy consists of 20 regions and two autonomous provinces, Trento and Bolzano, which all need to release their own legislation. Guidance documents that were available by mid-2006 included an Italian translation of the EU Guidance (http://ec.europa.eu/environment/eia/0309 23_sea_guidance_it.pdf), and guidelines developed on the basis of the ENPLAN project (www.interreg-enplan.org).

Latvia

The SEA Directive was transposed by the Environmental Impact Assessment (EIA) Act on 26 February 2004 and 15 September 2005 and by new secondary legislation (for example, Cabinet of Ministers Regulations) on 23 March 2004 (www.vidm.gov.lv/ivnvb/Esivn.htm). No guidance had been released by mid-2006, however, there were plans to prepare guidance documents by the end of 2006.

Lithuania

The SEA Directive was transposed by umbrella legislation, the 'Law on Environmental Protection of the Republic of Lithuania' (Žin., 1992, Nr. 5-75; 2004, Nr. 36-1179) and the 'Law on Territorial Planning' (Žin., 1995, Nr. 107-2391; 2004, Nr. 21-617). Detailed requirements of the Directive were also reflected in several orders. The Manual for SEA in Lithuania was under preparation in mid-2006. It is available on www.am.lt. The manual for EIA is also available on this website.

Luxembourg

The SEA Directive had not been transposed and no guidance was available by mid-2006.

Malta

SEA legislation transposing the SEA Directive was put into place at the end of 2005. The legal notice transposing the EU Directive into the local legislation (LN 418 of 2005) can be accessed on www.mepa.org.mt/environment/legislatio n/LN_418_2005_E.pdf. The commencement notice for the above mentioned legislation was published later (LN 32 of 2006, www.mepa.org.mt/environment/ legislation/LN_32_2006.pdf). No guidance had been prepared by mid-2006.

The Netherlands

The Environmental Management Act was revised in July 2006 (www.vrom.nl/ get.asp?file=Docs/milieu/MER_Samenvatt ingwetsvoorstel190304.pdf), incorporating the requirements of the SEA Directive.

Guidelines for Directive-based SEA included: Guidance for Strategic Environmental Assessment, Ministry of Transport, Water Management and Public Works (forthcoming), and plan environmental assessement within the Ministry of Transport, Water Management and Public Works, EIA/Transportation Centre, Delft (forthcoming).

Poland

The SEA Directive was transposed by an act of 9 November 2000 on 'Access to Information about the Environment and its Protection and on the Environmental Impact Assessment' (EIA Act 2000) and the Environmental Protection Law of 1 October 2001 (www.mos.gov.pl/1akty _prawne/ustawy/ochrona_srodowiska/ and http://isip.sejm.gov.pl/servlet/Search? todo=open&id=WDU20010620627).

Furthermore, for spatial/land use planning, the Land Use Planning and Management Act of June 2003 (http://isip.sejm.gov.pl/servlet/Search?todo =open&id=WDU20030800717) and the Order of the Minister of Environmental Protection of 14 November 2002 on detailed criteria of the prognosis of the environmental impact for local land use plans were relevant (www.mos.gov.pl/ 1akty_prawne/rozporzadzenia_ms/02.197 .1667.shtml). In mid-2006, available guidelines included: a methodological approach for SEA in spatial planning, Institute Rozwoju Miast, Kraków (www.mos.gov.pl/1materialy_informacyjn e/raporty_opracowania/podstawy.pdf), and analysis of EIA for plans and programmes – strategic documents, Eko-Konsult, Gdansk (www.mos.gov.pl/ 1materialy_informacyjne/raporty_opraco wania/analiza.pdf).

Portugal

In Portugal, the legislation that would transpose the Directive was still under preparation in mid-2006. The only guidance available in Portugal was on strategic impact assessment of land use/spatial plans (regional, inter-municipal, municipal, urban plans, coastal areas plans, natural protected areas plans and water reservoir plans). This guidance was issued in 2003 by the National Directorate General for Land Use Planning and Urban Development.

Slovakia

The EIA Act (No. 24/2006 Coll.) transposing the SEA Directive came into force on 1 February 2006, covering land use/spatial planning and any 'substantial development policy' in the areas of energy supply, mining, industry, transport, agriculture, forestry and water management, waste management and tourism. Furthermore, the Act on Right to Access on Information (law No. 211/2000 Z.z.), and the act on the list of authorized experts in the field of EIA (No. 52/1995) were of importance. Further information on SEA in Slovakia can be obtained at www.enviro.gov.sk. There was no guidance available in mid-2006.

Slovenia

The SEA Directive was yet to be transposed within the Environmental Protection Act. In mid-2006, no guidance was available.

Spain

The SEA Directive was transposed by the SEA Law of April 2006 (www.juridicas.com/base_datos/Admin/l9 -2006.html or www.coccineti.info/ evaluacion%20de%20planes%20y%20 programas.pdf). Regional laws that include certain SEA requirements have been in place since the late 1980s/early 1990s in Valencia, Cantabria, Canarias, Andalucía, the Basque Country, Castilla y Leon and Cataluña.

There were no guidelines at the national level. At the regional level, however, the Basque Country had released two guidance documents. In addition, there were also ENPLAN Guidelines with case studies from Cataluña, Andalucía, Baleares and Murcia (www.carm.es/ siga/europa/interreg/enplan.htm).

Sweden

SEA Directive requirements were incorporated into the Environmental Code in July 2004 (www.sweden.gov.se/sb/d/2023/a/ 22847). Various guidance documents for SEA in land use planning had also been published, all by The National Board of Housing Building and Planning (Boverket). For documents on detailed development plans, see www.bover ket.se/shopping/ShowItem.aspx?id=1402 and id=773. For guidance on SEA in general, see www.boverket.se/mondo search/search.aspx?id=723&searchQuery =smb.

UK

The SEA Directive was transposed through the Environmental Assessment of Plans and Programmes Regulations 2004 (of which there were four sets for each nation, England, Scotland, Wales and Northern Ireland, following normal UK practice) (see www.opsi.gov.uk/si/ si2004/20041633.htm). In Scotland, the Environment Assessment (Scotland) Bill extended SEA to all public sector plans and programmes and to strategies, subject to screening for significant environmental effects. In England and Wales, the Planning and Compulsory Purchase Act of 2004 required sustainability appraisal to be conducted in spatial planning (www.opsi.gov.uk/acts/acts2004/2004000 5.htm). Here, SEA in spatial/land use planning was applied within the context of SA. Guidelines included:

- ODPM (2005a), *Sustainability Appraisal of Regional Spatial Strategies and Local Development Documents* (www.odpm.gov.uk/ index.asp?id=1161341);
- ODPM (2005b), *Local Development Framework Monitoring: A Good Practice Guide* (www.odpm.gov.uk/ index.asp?id=1143905);

- SEA Guidance for Transport Plans and Programmes (2004) (www.webtag.org.uk/webdocuments/ 2_Project_Manager/11_SEA/index. htm);
- Countryside Council for Wales, English Nature, Environment Agency, Royal Society for the Protection of Birds (2004), SEA and biodiversity, Guidance for Practitioners, (www.rspb.org.uk/policy/planning policy/s_e_a.asp);
- Environment Agency (2004), Strategic Environmental Assessment and Climate Change (www.environment-agency.gov.uk/commondata/105385/s ea_climate_change_905671.pdf).

Notes

1   Publications dealing with transposition, implementation and application of the SEA Directive were all somewhat outdated by mid-2006. These include a report by the European Environment Bureau in 2005 (www.eeb.org/activities/ biodiversity/Final-SEA-report-271205. pdf), which identified 14 member states that had final SEA laws in place and two states that had released draft laws. This report neither provided any legal/guidance references, nor did it further investigate the situation in the other nine member states. National legal implementation measures for the SEA Directive are also listed at the Eur-Lex website (http://eur-lex.europa.eu). However, the various measures are not explained, that is, it is unclear what legal requirements cover and whether the Directive has been fully or only partly transposed.

2   This section draws on Fischer, 2006c.

Spatial and Land Use Case Studies

Chapter 6 introduces five spatial/land use SEAs from The Netherlands, UK, Germany and Austria, representing different administration-led SEA approaches. Transport and electricity transmission planning SEA examples were already discussed in Chapter 3. In this chapter, the five SEAs represent EIA-based as well as flexible assessment processes:

- Flexible assessment processes (non-EIA based):
  1 Development Vision Noord-Holland, The Netherlands – a policy/vision SEA approach (provincial level) (Provincie Noord-Holland, 1997);
  2 SEA of the unitary development plan of Oldham, UK – a policy plan SEA approach (local level) (Oldham Metropolitan Borough Council, 2001; Fischer, 2003b; see also Chapter 3);
- EIA-based process:
  3 Landscape plan for the local land use plan of the municipality of Ketzin in Brandenburg, Germany – an area-wide plan SEA approach (local level) (Amt Ketzin, 1996);
  4 SEA for the local land use plan of Weiz, Austria – a programme SEA approach (local level) (Aschemann, 1999);
  5 SEA for new housing and business development areas in Rotterdam-

Leiden, The Netherlands – a big project SEA approach (regional level) (VROM, 1996).

The main purpose of this chapter is to make the reader aware of different approaches to SEA for spatial/land use PPPs. Cases were chosen according to their ability to reveal differences and to allow for follow-up evaluation. Therefore, only examples were included that had been completed and for which follow-up evidence was available. While all five examples are from pre-SEA Directive practice, possible changes to the approaches presented here in emerging post-SEA Directive practice are also commented on whenever possible. In this context, it is of particular importance to note that the programme SEA approach represented by the Austrian example appears to become preferred post-Directive practice, not just in Austria, but in other member states as well.

The five SEAs are described below with regard to their overall spatial/land use planning and SEA context. The SEA process and the methods/techniques used are introduced. The case studies are also evaluated in terms of whether they are leading to the benefits that are thought to result from SEA application, as introduced in Chapter 1, Box 1.2.

Development Vision Noord-Holland

As explained in Chapter 4, in The Netherlands various types of SEA are applied. These include formal EIA-based SEA, e-test-based policy SEA and various other forms of informal SEA. In this section, an informal policy SEA example is introduced, namely the SEA for the provincial Development Vision Noord Holland. The SEA Directive does not cover this level of decision-making and has therefore no direct impact on the approach presented here.

Spatial/land use planning and SEA context

There are three main planning levels in The Netherlands: national, regional and municipal (with over 630 municipalities in the country). While national and local levels are synonymous with the levels of democratically elected bodies, the regional level may represent a province (there are 12 provinces in The Netherlands), parts of a province or may be inter-provincial. At each of the three levels of decision-making, formal spatial/land use PPPs are prepared but there is no strict planning hierarchy, however, PPPs of a higher hierarchical level do set the context for those of a lower hierarchical level. Municipalities traditionally have had some considerable autonomy in decision-making. Table 6.1 summarizes spatial/land use planning instruments in

The Netherlands, consisting of statutory instruments and non-statutory visions.

Visions started to be prepared in the early 1990s. They were a reaction to what was then perceived as an inflexible and technocratic planning system, thought to be ill-equipped to deal with the challenges of a globalizing world. Visions were also a reaction to the economic crisis in The Netherlands in the mid-1980s, which had brought a loss of jobs and high unemployment. In connection with an increasing interest in sustainable development, there was a desire to be able to better anticipate possible future developments and scenarios. In this context, there was also a growing interest in assessing public opinion on the way in which society should develop.

One of the main reasons for conducting visions is a desire to solve problems of traditional regulated planning systems. This is why visions serve as dynamic and flexible instruments. Visions are not just prepared in spatial/land use planning but in other sectors as well. In The Netherlands, their use has been particularly widespread in transport planning, where their application became quasi-formalized through the requirements of the Second National Infrastructure Plan (SVVII) (MVW, 1989), and subsequently the national Transport Act of 1998.

While there is no formalized standard format for development visions, normally

Table 6.1 *Spatial/land use planning instruments in The Netherlands*

Administrative Levels	Statutory	Non-statutory
National	National spatial plan (*Nota Ruimtelijke Ordening*)	Visions (*visies*)
Provincial	Regional plans (*Streekplannen*)	Visions (*visies*)
Municipal	• Local plans (*Structuurplannen*) • Master plans (*Bestemmingsplannen*)	Visions (*visies*)

they tend to be procedurally flexible, comparing different scenarios and development options. Furthermore, most of them have a time horizon of roughly 30 years. Visions are highly participative, with extensive use of internet-based fora, workshops, exhibitions and at times also round tables (see also Chapter 2). Spatial development visions have been prepared at a range of formal and informal decision-making levels, including national, inter-provincial, provincial, regional, inter-regional, municipal, inter-municipal and other local levels (for example, for inner city areas).

The case study: An introduction

Noord-Holland is one of the 12 Dutch provinces, with about 2.5 million inhabitants living in an area of 2667km², 30 per cent of which (750,000) are in the city of Amsterdam. With a population density of 926 inhabitants per km², this is a densely populated province (the average population density in The Netherlands is 455/km²). The provincial capital is Haarlem with 150,000 inhabitants (see Figure 6.1).

Whereas the southern part of the province is heavily urbanized and home to one of Europe's largest airports (Schiphol), the northern part has some extensively used agricultural land. Currently, the province's population and economy are growing.

The SEA process and methods/techniques

The Development Vision was prepared over a two-year period from 1996 to 1998. While it did not follow any formal process, three main preparation stages can be distinguished: first, agenda setting (establishing the baseline and the important issues to be considered in the Vision);

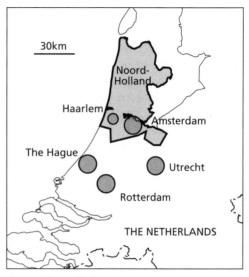

Source: Thomas Fischer

Figure 6.1 *The province of Noord-Holland*

second, identification of possible development scenarios and options; and third, approval. The first and second stages were subject to some considerable external involvement.

Within the development vision, impacts were outlined for four themes:

- Main transport infrastructure;
- Main development areas;
- Main environmental and recreational 'open/green' areas;
- Ground and surface waters.

Furthermore, possible future economic development scenarios were identified:

- The continuation of current trends;
- A 'divided Europe' scenario, with the EU putting market protection measures into force;
- A 'European coordination scenario', with a general openness in the EU towards globalization.

119

For all three scenarios, first, impacts on population growth, development of residential and business areas and the number of jobs were estimated. Second, three main development options were assessed: one where development would only be allowed within existing settlement structures; a second representing unlimited urban sprawl; and a third option representing an in-between scenario where some sprawl around existing settlements would be permitted. Figure 6.2 shows how the urban sprawl option was translated onto a map, which was used as the basis for the prediction of impacts. The new developments shown on the map are those anticipated by the experts involved in the development visioning process should urban sprawl be allowed to go ahead without any restrictions.

During the preparation process of the Development Vision, other PPPs, either existing or under preparation, were also considered. These included other visions, for example, the forthcoming National Vision for The Netherlands and various municipal visions prepared in the province.

Within the preparation process of the vision, impacts on CO_2 emissions, nature and biodiversity, waste management and natural resources, as well as water and the urban environment were considered. Furthermore, impacts on agriculture, air traffic, accessibility and public administration were assessed. Impact predictions were made based on maps (see Figure 6.2), computer simulations, workshops and expert consultations.

Based on the visioning process, it became clear that the in-between option was favoured by most of those involved in the process, meaning that future development should not be restricted within existing urban structures. However, unlimited urban sprawl should be avoided.

Evaluation of the SEA

The Development Vision Noord-Holland represents an example where SEA and policy were fully integrated. As explained above, it represents a policy SEA for which currently no formal SEA requirements exist in the EU. The four potential benefits that result from SEA, as presented in Box 1.2, are now discussed with reference to the Development Vision case study.

More systematic and effective consideration of wider environmental impacts/alternatives

The integrated approach of the development vision allowed for a consideration of

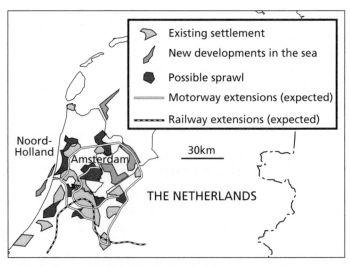

Source: following ontwikkelingsvisie Noord-Holland

Figure 6.2 *Development option urban sprawl*

wider environmental impacts and alternatives. However, if a separate SEA had been
prepared, this might have also allowed for
a more systematic approach. Full integration of SEA into the vision-making
process meant that environmental aspects
were somewhat hidden in the document
and that the choice of options was very
much determined by economic considerations.

Proactive formulation of strategic action for sustainable development

The approach taken can be said to have
had both proactive and reactive elements.
The starting question was not how certain
aims or objectives could be achieved, but
rather what development scenarios were
possible, likely and preferred.
Subsequently, when comparing different
development options, no set thresholds
were used in order to decide what would
be a preferred option. This led to some
uncertainty due to a lack of rigour and
clarity.

Increased efficiency of tiered decision-making, strengthening of project EIA

There is no formal requirement for
authorities and their PPPs and projects to
take the Development Vision into
account. Environmental impacts considered in the vision are of a general nature
and no recommendations were given on
how impacts may be reduced or offset.
Therefore, there is no logical link with the
project-level EIA. Finally, an internet
search in 2006 found that the
Development Vision was not accessible
anymore, only eight years after its
completion and 24 years before the
vision's date of reference, 2030. This
means that at this point in time, those
wishing to use and refer to the vision for

their own PPP endeavours will have some
problems obtaining relevant information.

More effective involvement in strategic decision-making

The vision-making process was highly
transparent and participative.
Documentation regarding the various
stages of the process was freely accessible
on the internet. However, it is important
to add that visions/policies like the one
discussed here are often perceived by the
general public as being too abstract and
the number of lay people actually taking
an interest may be low.

Success factors, problems, shortcomings and outlook

The Development Vision preparation
process was fully open and flexible
without having had any limitations in
terms of, for example, predefined aims
and objectives that should be achieved.
Within the process, different economic
and population growth scenarios were
considered and different options were
assessed for how spatial development
could take place and may potentially be
influenced. The vision can be said to have
raised awareness among a large audience
of what future development in the
province may look like and how it could
potentially be influenced.

Some problems and shortcomings are
also evident. First, while the vision
resulted in the propagation of a development option that was preferred by most of
those involved in the process (the option
in-between unrestricted sprawl and strict
adherence to existing settlements), it did
not elaborate on this option further.
Rather, this was left to other subsequent
PPPs. Not to examine the preferred option
further was a missed opportunity to get a
better understanding of the impacts and

possible mechanisms to reduce or offset them. Furthermore, as the vision is non-statutory, there are no formal requirements that other PPPs, projects and administrations consider its results. It can therefore be said to have a somewhat weak status. Probably the most serious shortcoming (for those wanting to refer to the vision) is the fact that in 2006, only eight years after its completion, the vision was no longer accessible on the internet.

Sustainability appraisal of the Oldham Unitary Development Plan

SEA practice in the UK has already been discussed in the previous three chapters, mostly focusing on requirements and practice in England. With devolution of certain powers to the four constituent parts of the UK (England, Scotland and Wales and Northern Ireland), planning and SEA practice has recently started to differ within the UK. The case introduced here is a typical example for assessments conducted since the mid-1990s in England at the unitary development plan (UDP) level (see also Chapter 3), based on which current post-SEA Directive practice is developing.

After the introduction of formal SEA Directive requirements, the basic approach to policy and plan SEA making, as portrayed in this section, has remained the same in England and Wales. This may best be described as a 'matrix-based, participative and qualitative impact estimation approach', aimed at optimizing planning policies. The SEA Directive requires changes to established practice, particularly in terms of the portrayal and evaluation of baseline data, the assessment of options, as well as wider participation. Regarding Directive-based practice, to date mainly scoping documents have been prepared. While it is therefore too early to provide any reliable account of complete SEA processes, it is possible to comment on emerging practice, particularly regarding the presentation of baseline data and the generation and assessment of options (Fischer and Gazzola, 2006b). Currently, many SEAs involve the collection of large amounts of data (particularly in the form of other PPPs that may be relevant), without then using these data for assessment in any meaningful way. The consideration and assessment of options still appears to be problematic. Only for 'core strategies' of the recently introduced local development frameworks (see Chapter 3) does the author know of SEA examples in which this appears to have been logical and clear. These include, for example, site alternatives for potential new housing or business areas. By contrast, the development of options is not effectively pursued in supplementary planning documents (see Chapter 3). Most SEAs of SPDs known to the author only appear to consider options of the type 'SPD' vs. 'no SPD', which cannot be considered a real option. For development plan policies, which are at the core of LDFs, options generation is frequently somewhat confusing. Thus, in many cases, different options are identified for each of the policies, meaning that in effect tens or hundreds of options are generated. In this context, a participative qualitative impact estimation matrix-based approach is normally used.

Spatial/land use planning and SEA context

England's planning system is discretionary, allowing for a high degree of flexibility. The main purpose of the discretionary approach is the achievement of a balance between public and private interests. Another key feature of the planning system in England is the strong position of local governments. Furthermore, the regional level has recently been substantially strengthened owing to UK devolution policy.

In England, SEA in spatial planning is applied within the context of sustainability appraisal. One of the main objectives of SA is to test the consistency and performance of plans and their objectives against sustainability objectives. Prior to 2004, the planning system looked somewhat different from the one described in Chapter 3, with central

government releasing planning policy guidance (PPG) notes and RPG for the regions (RPG 13 in the North West). Furthermore, at the subregional level, planning documents were prepared either at county and local levels (structure and local plans) or at unitary levels (unitary development plans). The UDP of Oldham falls into the last category (see Figure 1.2). In the new planning system, the two-tier structure at the local level, consisting of structure and local plans, has been abolished.

The case study: An introduction

Oldham is one of the 10 metropolitan boroughs that form Greater Manchester. It is situated in the north-west region of England (see Figure 6.3). Oldham has a total population of about 217,000 inhabitants. The borough was one of the cradles of the industrial revolution in the 19th

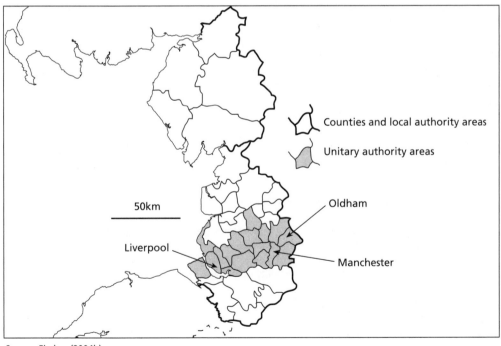

Source: Fischer (2004b)

Figure 6.3 *Location of Oldham within north-west England*

century. During much of the second half of the 20th century it experienced economic and population decline. Over the past 10 years, however, this has been reversed and the borough is currently witnessing economic and population growth. While there are still many derelict areas, there is now also a considerable amount of regeneration taking place.

The UDP sets out policies that need to be taken into account when considering applications from prospective developers. The main aim is to balance different types of development within a planning horizon of about 10 years.

The SEA process and methods/techniques

The SEA was conducted for a replacement UDP. The consistency and performance of the plan and its objectives were tested against overall sustainability objectives. This exercise is normally done by preparing a 'compatibility matrix'. The assessment was prepared in parallel with the formulation of plan policies. Plan making and SEA were therefore integrated exercises. The objectives of the UDP were defined by the Oldham Partnership, which is constituted by the council and by public, private and voluntary sector organizations active within the borough. The SEA/SA team was composed of the

Oldham Borough Environment Forum, the planning committee, a 'critical friend' (in this case a consultant who accompanied the process), the Government Office of the North West of England (GONW), Oldham Chamber of Commerce, Oldham Groundwork, the Environment Agency and members of Oldham council. The SEA team was split into two groups: the 'sustainability appraisal group' (with the purpose of carrying out a detailed appraisal at each stage of plan preparation); and the 'sustainability appraisal sounding board' (consisting primarily of elected members and aiming to provide for a greater degree of thoroughness and an ongoing political input). According to government regulations, the UDP review process must be subjected to public participation at regular intervals throughout.

Within the SEA/SA, all UDP policies and proposals were assessed in a qualitative way through expert judgements. This was done based on key sustainability objectives taken from the north west's strategy for sustainable development, 'Action for Sustainability' (AfS) (NWRA, 2003). The SEA process consisted of nine steps, as shown in Table 6.2.

The assessment consisted of the sustainability appraisal team discussing proposed policies in terms of their sustainability impacts. In this context, matrices were used to support the appraisal,

Table 6.2 *Main procedural steps of the UDP sustainability appraisal*

Step 1	Screening, using the regional AfS as a starting point for the appraisal
Step 2	Appraisal of the 'issues paper' (document that sets out, topic by topic, the current policy approach, the drivers for policy change and key issues) against the AfS
Step 3	Development of local sustainability objectives, indicators and targets
Step 4	Appraisal of site selection criteria
Step 5	Appraisal of the first draft policies
Step 6	Appraisal of second draft policies
Step 7	Appraisal on the future use of difficult sites
Step 8	Consultation strategy
Step 9	Future appraisal stages

showing anticipated impacts of proposed policies on sustainability objectives.

Evaluation

Overall within north-west England, the Oldham UDP sustainability appraisal is widely perceived as a good practice example (Fischer, 2003b). The widespread involvement of different institutions is seen as especially positive. Below, the case is evaluated in terms of the four benefits that are thought to result from SEA application, as introduced in Box 1.2.

More systematic and effective consideration of wider environmental impacts/alternatives

While the SEA is said to have brought many changes to the UDP, it is unclear to what extent environmental impacts were systematically considered. It is important to note that the UK government is promoting the use of SA because it assumes that there is a balance to be stuck between different aspects within PPP making, that is, environmental aspects do not have special status. Furthermore, due to the specific policy plan appraisal approach that aimed at optimizing policies, no alternatives were considered.

Proactive formulation of strategic action for sustainable development

The SEA ran in parallel to the plan making process and is said to have influenced the UDP on various occasions. It was set up as a proactive instrument and that achieved a considerable level of impact, according to opinions expressed by representatives of the appraisal group and sounding board. As an outsider, however, it is somewhat difficult to verify this claim because the publicly available documentation is far from systematic and results are not transparent.

Increased efficiency of tiered decision-making, strengthening of project EIA

Regarding substantive assessment issues, no clear connection can be made with other decision-making levels because the publicly available documentation is unclear about any follow-up action. While central and regional policy documents were taken into account when conducting the SEA/SA, it is unclear how the project level can ultimately be influenced, particularly because the available documentation focuses on describing the process rather than outcomes.

More effective involvement in strategic decision-making

The SEA acted as a learning process for those involved, namely 19 representatives of public administration, the council, governmental and non-governmental organizations and the 'critical friend'. In this context, the SEA contributed to changing views of individuals as well as their respective organizations. However, while those involved in the appraisal group and sounding board were effectively involved, how outsiders were actually involved is unclear.

Success factors, problems, shortcomings and outlook

In north-west England, the SA for the Oldham UDP was widely perceived as a good practice case. This is mainly due to the positive opinions of those involved in the appraisal group and sounding board. Furthermore, information was made available to the general public.

A particular problem/shortcoming is that the available documentation almost entirely focuses on describing the process, rather than on dealing with assessment outcomes. Furthermore, some essential SEA stages and elements were missing in the process, including formal reporting of findings for all of the key stages of the process and the development and appraisal of options and mitigation measures.

Landscape plan for the Local Land Use Plan of the Municipality of Ketzin in Brandenburg

Chapters 3 and 4 introduced SEA in spatial/land use planning in Germany. The importance of the landscape planning system was underlined; this system covered many important SEA components, even before the SEA Directive came into force. Practice in the state of Brandenburg was highlighted, where, since the mid-1990s, local landscape plans had identified overall environmental objectives for local land use plans and assessed the effects of anticipated future land use, representing an area-wide plan SEA approach. In 2002 (two years before formal SEA requirements came into force), in a comparative study on spatial/land use and transport planning in England, The Netherlands and Germany (Fischer, 2002a), these landscape plans were found to meet the requirements of the then draft SEA Directive to the greatest extent of all the SEA type instruments examined in the three countries.

In order obtain a better understanding of what may be called an area-wide plan SEA approach, the landscape plan for the municipality of Ketzin, prepared in 1995–1996, is introduced below (see Buschke et al, 2002; Fischer, 2005c).

Spatial/land use planning and SEA context

As explained in Chapter 3, in Germany there are four main administrative levels at which spatial/land use PPPs are prepared: federal, state (*Länder*), regional and municipal. All levels have corresponding democratically elected bodies, with the exception of the regional.

Landscape plans and programmes are prepared in parallel to the various statutory spatial/land use PPPs. The main aim of the landscape planning system is the improvement of environmental quality by protecting areas that are of high value for nature and landscape, and by developing and optimizing parts of the landscape. An important function of landscape plans and programmes is the identification of areas that are suitable for certain developments and areas that are to be kept free from development. In the state of Brandenburg, since the mid-1990s, landscape plans and programmes have been prepared in parallel with statutory local land use plan making processes. In this context, mitigation and compensation measures are identified according to the Federal Intervention Rule for those anticipated impacts of future developments that cannot be mitigated. By mid-2006, over 400 landscape plans had been prepared for local land use plans in Brandenburg.

Table 6.3 summarizes the spatial/land use and associated landscape planning system in Germany. There are legal requirements for preparing state-wide landscape programmes, region-wide landscape framework plans and local landscape plans. There is no strict top-down approach in planning and, instead,

Table 6.3 *Land use and landscape plans and programmes in Germany*

Planning level		Spatial/land use planning	Landscape planning/SEA	Scale of landscape plan/programme maps
(1) Federal		Federal Spatial Orientation Framework	No requirement	
(2) State		State spatial development plan (*Landesentwicklungs-plan/-programm*)	Landscape programme (*Landschafts-programm*)	1:500,000 to 1:200,000
(3) Regional		Regional plan (*regionales Raumordnungskonzept*)	Landscape framework plan (*Landschafts-rahmenplan*)	1:100,000 to 1:25,000
(4) Local	Community, city	Land use plan (*Flächennutzungsplan*, §1 Federal Construction Law Book – BauGB)	Landscape plan (*Landschaftsplan*)	1:50,000 to 1:5,000
	City district (informal)	City district plan (*Bereichsentwicklungsplan*)	No requirement	Around 1:3,000
	Part of the community	Master Plan (B-Plan, §1 Federal Construction Law Book – BauGB)	Open space master plan (*Grünordnungs-plan*)	1:2,500 to 1:1,000

Source: Fischer (2005c)

the counter-current principle is applied, meaning that each level needs to take the PPPs prepared at other levels into account. Overall, decision-making can therefore be said to aim at being 'administration consensus-based'.

The case study: An introduction

Ketzin is a municipality located in the state of Brandenburg, about 40km west of the city centre of Berlin (see Figure 6.4). It has a population of 6400 inhabitants living in 93km². Large parts of the municipality are agricultural land, with small forested areas, as well as some surface waters, including rivers and lakes. Ketzin is part of the so-called core development area (which may also be called metropolitan region) around Berlin and lies between the two urban centres of Potsdam

(140,000 inhabitants) and Nauen (11,000 inhabitants). A stagnant population and economy is expected for the foreseeable future as there are currently no major development pressures.

Statutory local land use plans were prepared for the five administrative areas of the municipality of Ketzin. Their overall goal was to create the basis for positive future economic, social and environmental development. The landscape plan/SEA under consideration covered the whole area of Ketzin, that is, it was prepared in parallel with the five separate land use plans.

The SEA process and methods/techniques

The landscape plan/SEA was prepared between 1995 and 1996 at the same time

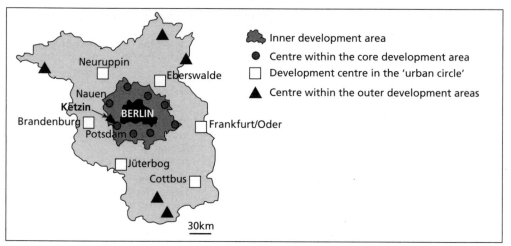

Source: based on MUNR (1995)

Figure 6.4 *Location of Ketzin within Brandenburg*

as the local land use plans. It involved the formulation of the environmental development objectives for these plans and the assessment of the potential environmental impacts of anticipated land use changes.

The planning authority of Ketzin was responsible for both the preparation of the local land use plans and the landscape plan. Documentation was prepared by a consultant. As a general rule, land use plans are approved by the State Building and Construction Authority, but SEAs are confirmed by the State Environment Agency. There is extensive consultation in land use plan making and SEA with both statutory and non-statutory bodies, including investors and other stakeholders. Furthermore, there is public participation within the formal land use plan making processes, during which the SEA is also made accessible to the general public.

Within the landscape plan making process, all main 'conventional' SEA stages were covered, either directly or, as in the case of monitoring and public participation, through the land use plan making process (general environmental

monitoring is carried out by the Lower Environmental Protection Agency). The landscape plan was conducted in a proactive manner, playing a vital role in setting the development agenda for the land use plans. Table 6.4 summarizes those procedural stages covered by the land use plans and landscape plan Ketzin.

In the SEA process, various suggestions for future land use were assessed. In this context, alternative sites were compared and evaluated. Evaluation was based on existing data, as well as data specifically generated for the SEA. Generally speaking, site alternatives with the least environmental impacts were identified, based on overlay mapping (while GIS could have been used, due to cost constraints maps were manually produced). These were later included in the land use plans. An environmental development concept was designed, mainly aiming to promote measures in the areas of environmental protection, agriculture, water management and settlements. This concept was developed based on area sensitivities identified through the overlay mapping exercise. Measures will

Table 6.4 *Main procedural stages of land use and landscape plan making*

	Screening	Scoping	Prediction/ Evaluation	Report preparation	Review	Monit- oring	Consult- ation	Public participation
Land use plan	✔	✔	✗	✔	✔	✔	✔	✔
Landscape plan (SEA)	✔	✔	✔	✔	✔	⇔	✔	⇔

Note: ✔ = yes; ⇔ = indirectly, through land use plan-based and general environmental monitoring by the Environmental Protection Agency; ✗ = no.

partly be implemented through compensation for project impacts, as identified in project EIA, following formal requirements of the Federal Impact Intervention Rule.

The landscape plan report consists of six sections. These are an introduction, a baseline description and evaluation (climate and air, geology and soils, water, flora and fauna, landscape and recreation), land use conflicts, a development concept, further action and a summary. Figure 6.5 shows the (simplified) area-wide environmental development concept.

Evaluation

Overall, the SEA for the land use plan of Ketzin can be considered a good practice SEA. Generally speaking, it was well received by all participating authorities/agencies and by those involved in the process (see Fischer, 2002a). Below, the case is evaluated in terms of the four benefits thought to result from SEA application introduced in Box 1.2.

More systematic and effective consideration of wider environmental impacts/alternatives

The landscape plan was indeed able to lead to a more systematic consideration of

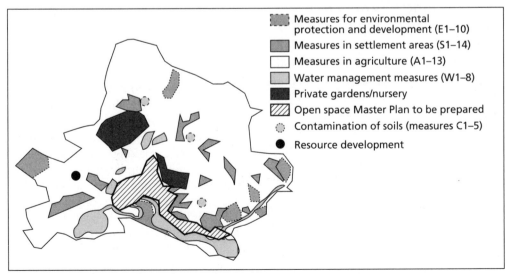

Measures for environmental protection and development (E1–10)
Measures in settlement areas (S1–14)
Measures in agriculture (A1–13)
Water management measures (W1–8)
Private gardens/nursery
Open space Master Plan to be prepared
Contamination of soils (measures C1–5)
Resource development

Source: following landscape plan Ketzin

Figure 6.5 *Development concept of landscape plan/SEA of Ketzin*

environmental impacts. The fact that the land use plans cannot be approved without completion and confirmation of the landscape plan is of particular importance. Suitability for certain uses in all municipal areas were identified, thus representing a proactive approach to SEA and to the consideration of alternatives. For example, areas were identified that are to be kept free from development, based on their value to the environment.

Proactive formulation of strategic action for sustainable development

The landscape plan proactively identified aims, objectives and alternatives for protecting areas that were of high value for nature and landscape. Furthermore, measures were identified for developing and optimizing parts of the landscape. The landscape plan was thus able to set the context for avoiding harmful environmental impacts, identifying environmental objectives, and for designing a development concept that will be the basis for future action.

Increased efficiency of tiered decision-making, strengthening of project EIA

The landscape plan was prepared within a tiered plan and programme making system, working in parallel to the spatial/land use PPP making system. Different spatial development options were considered and preferred areas for development were identified, thus setting the context for project EIA. In this context, mitigation measures were identified and compensation areas were designed that can subsequently be used in project EIA when impacts cannot be avoided or mitigated. Therefore, the landscape plan indeed led to increased efficiency of tiered decision-making,

strengthening project EIA.

More effective involvement in strategic decision-making

During the landscape plan making process, stakeholders were involved both formally and informally at various points. Furthermore, the general public was able to comment during the statutory land use planning public participation process, as is indicated in Table 6.4. Due to the extensive efforts regarding involvement of stakeholders, the landscape plan was very positively perceived.

Success factors, problems, shortcomings and outlook

Factors that were crucial for the overall perceived success of the SEA particularly include the consultant who proved to be an effective facilitator. Furthermore, the widespread consultations with various stakeholders throughout the SEA process led to the landscape plan being perceived very positively. Finally, the existence of formal and transparent plan making and SEA procedures, as well as the checks made and the support given by the state agencies, were important.

While the SEA can be considered an example of good practice, there are aspects related to the overall context within which the SEA was prepared that could be improved. First, one SEA was prepared for five land use plans (representing the five administrative areas of the municipality), making coordination of activities more complicated than if there had only been one land use plan. The planning system itself is rather complex and simplification could lead to greater clarity. Finally, no proper assessment of economic and social effects was done. As a consequence, potential trade-offs were difficult to establish.

In post-SEA Directive practice, landscape plans continue to play a very important role in the German spatial/land use PPP making system. In particular, they provide the necessary terms of reference for the assessment of impacts. Emerging post-SEA Directive practice appears to frequently follow a programme SEA approach, similar to the one described below for the municipality of Weiz, particularly regarding land use plan revisions. In Germany, this is connected with earlier SEA research studies (see, for example, Bunge, 1998).

SEA for the land use plan revision in the municipality of Weiz, Austria

Up until the introduction of SEA Directive-based requirements, there was neither a formal nor informal SEA-type system in place in spatial/land use planning in Austria. However, since the mid-1990s, a range of voluntary pilot studies has been implemented, several of which are in spatial/land use planning. According to Aschemann (2004), these include:

- The Regional Development Plan for the Danube Area in Lower Austria (unpublished);
- The Regional Programme of Tennengau (www.salzburg.gv.at/stra_tennengau);
- The Urban and Transport Development in the North-East of Vienna City (www.wien.gv.at/stadten twicklung/supernow/);
- The Local Land Use Plan of Weiz (discussed below).

In addition, the following sectoral pilot SEAs were prepared:

- The Local Energy Plan of Graz City (www.graz.at/umwelt/kek.htm);
- The Transport Demonstration Study Danube Corridor (www.bmvit.gv.at/sixcms_upload/med ia/231/band004.pdf);
- The Waste Management Plan of Vienna City (Arbter, 2005);
- The Waste Management Plan of Salzburg Province (www.salzburger abfall.at).

While Directive-based SEAs have now also started to be prepared, to date, no documents have been made publicly available that would allow a concrete description and evaluation of post-Directive SEA practice. This section reports on the pilot SEA for the Local Land Use Plan of Weiz, which was prepared between the end of 1997 and late summer of 1998. The SEA was sponsored by the Federal Ministry of Environment, Youth and Family. Its main focus was the future use of 27 potential development areas in the city, while a central objective was to test the feasibility of Directive-based SEA implementation in existing plan making. As a consequence, the SEA was based on a 1996 draft of the Directive. There are indications that the approach is developing into a preferred SEA approach, not only in Austria (Pröbstl et al, 2006), but also in other EU member states, for example Germany (see UVP, 2006), and at least in some cases, in a similar format for site-specific allocations of land in England (Fischer and Gazzola, 2006b). This is most likely connected with the comparative simplicity of this approach.

Spatial/land use planning and SEA context

There are four main levels of decision-making in Austrian spatial/land use planning, including national, state/*Länder* (which have the main responsibility for spatial planning), district/regional and municipal. Levels at which spatial/land use plans are prepared correspond to democratically elected bodies. A hierarchical land use planning principle is in place, that is, land use planning works in a top-down manner of decision-making. Table 6.5 summarizes spatial/land use planning instruments in Austria.

Since 21 July 2004, SEA Directive requirements cover all instruments listed in Table 6.4. At the time of writing this book in mid-2006, it was not possible to estimate the total number of Directive-based spatial/land use SEAs that had been started in Austria. However, for the state of Lower Austria, some detailed information was available on the internet regarding SEAs that were under preparation, including seven SEAs for local development plans (www.raumordnung-noe.at/dynamisch/showcontainer.php?id=110). Furthermore, the SEA handbook of the Akademie der Wissenschaften (2006) suggests that about 80 SEAs had been started by mid-2006.

The case study: An introduction

Weiz is a district capital in the state of Styria with about 9200 inhabitants. The municipality covers an area of roughly 5km². Weiz lies within the south-eastern Alps at about 500m above sea level in the valley of the Weizbach river. Apart from the main settlement, the municipality also has some extensive meadows and forested areas. Figure 6.6 shows the geographical location of the municipality of Weiz in Austria.

The existing urban plan of the municipality was to be revised and 27 areas with present or potential claims for new developments were identified. In order to support effective and efficient decisions on their best use, a decision was made to revise the land use plan and to conduct a voluntary SEA. The municipality of Weiz was responsible for the preparation of both urban plan revision and SEA, with the latter being sponsored by the Federal Ministry of Environment, Youth and Family. The time horizon of the plan was five years (2000–2005).

An SEA process was conducted which was in line with the 1996 draft of the SEA Directive. The development of a suitable SEA methodology and an effective communication strategy were key objectives of the exercise.

The SEA process and methods/techniques

The SEA process was conducted by the city council of the municipality of Weiz. The Styrian state government approved

Table 6.5 *Spatial/land use planning in Austria*

Planning level	Spatial/land use planning instrument
National	National spatial planning concept
State	State spatial planning programme
District (region)	Regional spatial planning programme
Municipal (local)	• Local development concept • Land use/zoning plan • Building (regulation) plan

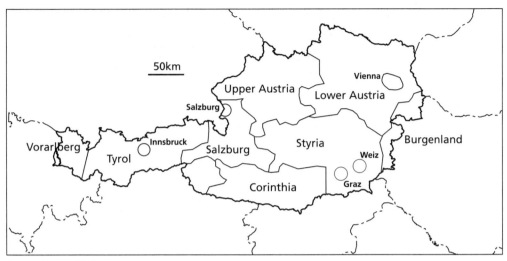

Source: Thomas Fischer

Figure 6.6 *Location of Weiz within Austria*

both the urban plan and SEA. Furthermore, the Styrian Environment Ministry was included in the SEA scoping exercise. There was public participation in both plan making and SEA. An interdisciplinary team, consisting of air, noise, climate, nature protection and spatial planning experts was present at a total of three SEA scoping meetings.

The main conventional SEA stages were covered, including screening, scoping, report preparation, review, consultations and public participation. Only monitoring was not considered in this pilot SEA. A scoping document was prepared, based on the draft revision plan. There was a high degree of process integration of plan making and SEA. Public participation for the plan and the SEA were integrated and conducted according to the requirements of the Austrian Spatial Planning Act. Information on plan revision and SEA was mainly given to the public through the *City Gazette*, a local newspaper, distributed to every household free of charge. A non-technical summary of the SEA was distributed to the general public in this way.

Each of the 27 potential development areas were assessed individually. In this context, three alternative development options were considered. Besides a 'no-action' alternative (within most spatial/land use plan making situations, 'no action' would not be considered a realistic option), an 'intentions of the municipality of Weiz' alternative and a 'most environmentally friendly' alternative were considered. Furthermore, for reference purposes, land use allocated by the existing urban plan was also included. Environmental and socio-economic criteria were used to evaluate different uses in each of the 27 development areas. Environmental criteria included quality of soils, fauna and flora, water, air, landscape and climate. Socio-economic criteria included economic performance and development, settlement areas, technical and social infrastructures and the population. Evaluation was conducted using a scoring system from one (very positive effect) to five (very negative

Table 6.6 *Impact matrix for SEA urban plan revision in Weiz*

Area no. (from 1 to 27)		ALTERNATIVES			
		Old land use plan	No action	Intentions of municipality	Best environmental option
INFORMATION PROVIDED	Environmental criteria				
	Socio-economic criteria				
	Weighting				
	Recommendations, mitigation measures and comments				

Source: following Aschemann (1999)

effect). If no data were available, a question mark was allocated. If criteria were not relevant in a certain situation, this was also noted. Table 6.6 shows how the alternatives were compared in terms of the evaluation criteria within an impact matrix. Furthermore, Figure 6.7 shows the locations of the development areas within the urban plan revision.

The environmental report consists of eight chapters. An introduction describes aims, methodology and approach taken. An outline of the plan revision, a description of the environmental baseline, aims and objectives and potential significant effects follows, before the choice of alternatives is explained, reasons for rejecting certain alternatives are given and mitigation and compensation measures are introduced. Finally, problems and data gaps are identified and a non-technical summary is provided. Appendices include the scoping document and a glossary.

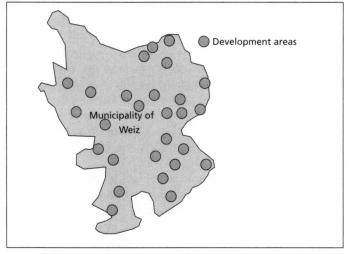

Source: following SEA Weiz

Figure 6.7 *Development areas assessed*

Evaluation

Overall, the SEA can be considered a successful case. The process was perceived positively and had a positive impact on a more environmentally sustainable revised urban plan. Below, the SEA is evaluated in terms of the four benefits that result from SEA application, as introduced in Box 1.2.

More systematic and effective consideration of wider environmental impacts/alternatives

The SEA led to a more systematic consideration of wider environmental impacts and alternatives than would have been the case in its absence. Due to the specific focus of the land use plan under consideration, only 27 selected sites within the municipality were considered that were anticipated for development. The consideration of the SEA results was not entirely effective and not all SEA recommendations were included in the plan due to investor interests and political pressures. This means that in certain instances, the final decision did not reflect the best possible environmental option.

Proactive formulation of strategic action for sustainable development

The SEA was proactive in the sense that it compared different uses for 27 potential development sites. However, reasons for the initial choice of the 27 sites were neither investigated nor shown. The SEA can therefore be said to have been less strategic and more project oriented. This is why the particular approach has been dubbed 'spatial land use programme SEA'.

Increased efficiency of tiered decision-making, strengthening of project EIA

There is a close link between the SEA and project implementation and thus project EIA. However, it remains unclear how the urban plan relates to and connects with higher tiers of decision-making. With the introduction of formal SEA following SEA

Directive requirements, however, higher tier plans (see Table 6.5) will also be subject to SEA. This can be expected to lead to increased efficiency of tiered decision-making.

More effective involvement in strategic decision-making

Due to the extensive information and consultation campaign conducted during the SEA process, more effective involvement can be said to have been reached in the plan/SEA making processes. Information leaflets were distributed to all households through a free newspaper.

Success factors, problems, shortcomings and outlook

Factors that were crucial for overall success of the SEA particularly include the effective cooperation of experts from different subject areas. The SEA was perceived as not having delayed the plan making process and as having raised its acceptance among those involved. Effective communication and coordination processes were considered to be of particular importance in achieving an effective SEA process.

While the SEA itself was positively perceived, there were also a few problems and shortcomings. Most importantly, the SEA started much later than the initial informal meeting on the plan revision. Furthermore, very few members of the general public actively participated in the plan making/SEA processes, despite the wide distribution of relevant information. Finally, according to those involved in the SEA, it appears that the municipal government did not always take the findings of SEA into account in subsequent action, particularly when SEA recommendations were contrary to local government intentions.

SEA for new housing and business development areas in Rotterdam and Leiden, The Netherlands

As explained in Chapter 4, SEA for major developments has been a formal requirement in The Netherlands since the 1987 EIA Act. The SEA for new housing and business development areas in Rotterdam and Leiden is an example conducted by the Dutch Ministry for Spatial and Environmental Planning between 1995 and 1997. The SEA was started because a range of development areas proposed by the two municipalities were in conflict with national spatial and environmental policy, mainly because they impacted on protected sites. The type of approach portrayed here is unlikely to change in post-SEA Directive practice.

Spatial/land use planning and SEA context

The Dutch planning and SEA systems were introduced above, so this section focuses on SEA applied to a major development project plan. Formal SEA Directive-based requirements only came into force in 2006 (see Chapter 5). These will apply to all formal spatial/land use plans.

The case study: An introduction

The cities of Rotterdam and Leiden are part of the Randstad, the main metropolitan region of The Netherlands, an area of economic and population growth. The Randstad lies within the perimeter of Amsterdam, Utrecht, Rotterdam and The Hague (see Figure 6.8). In 2005, Rotterdam had 600,000 inhabi-

tants, and Leiden had 115,000. Between 2005 and 2010, Leiden was predicted to need 4000 new homes and an additional 20ha of land for economic development. Rotterdam was expected to need 225ha for economic development. In between Rotterdam and Leiden lie the cities of The Hague (450,000 inhabitants), Delft (90,000 inhabitants) and Zoetermeer (105,000 inhabitants).

The city of Leiden wants to focus development activities in the 'Grote Polder' area, which is part of the Green Heart, a type of protected green belt between Amsterdam, The Hague, Rotterdam and Utrecht. Rotterdam wants to focus industrial development on the 'Hoeksche Waard' area, which is currently a protected 'open area'. Suggestions are not in line with development policy formulated in the VINEX Dutch National Spatial Plan (VROM, 1993), which aims at avoiding impacts on these two areas.

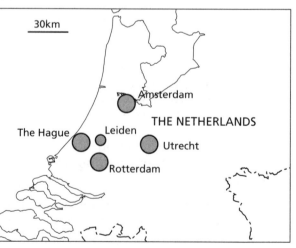

Source: Thomas Fischer

Figure 6.8 *Location of Leiden and Rotterdam within the Randstad*

The SEA process and methods/techniques

A formal SEA was prepared as part of a statutory 'core plan decision' process for national spatial policy. The decision to conduct an SEA was the outcome of some initial considerations on whether national spatial policy should be changed in order to accommodate the proposed developments in Rotterdam and Leiden. It was decided to not only consider environmental but also economic and social aspects. Various alternative development areas were selected as the basis for evaluation, including those preferred by the municipalities of Rotterdam and Leiden. A preparatory administrative 'core plan decision' process was conducted, which lasted for more than two and a half years from mid-1995 until the end of 1997, before the plan and the SEA were submitted to national parliament for approval. The SEA took into account national transport policy (based on the Second Transport Structure Plan), 'green spaces' policy (based on the Green Spaces Structure Plan), military areas (based on the Structure Plan of Military Areas), as well as the economically driven note 'Space for Regions' and the Development Plan for the main Dutch international airport of Schiphol, which lies adjacent to the Leiden region.

The SEA process was conducted by the national Ministry of Public Housing, Physical Planning and Environmental Affairs (VROM). Various national ministries, the two affected provinces (North (*Noord*) and South (*Zuid*) Holland), the city regions of Rotterdam, The Hague and Amsterdam and the Association of Communities in the Leiden region were part of the main working group. Institutional support was provided by the national EIA Commission, the Commissioner for Environmental

Hygiene, and the Spatial Planning Advice Council. The process included public participation and was concluded by a national parliamentary decision.

All main EIA-based SEA stages were covered in accordance with national EIA regulations. These included screening, scoping, report preparation, review, consultations and public participation. Monitoring was done indirectly through national spatial and environmental monitoring.

In the SEA process, various alternative suggestions for development areas were assessed. Evaluation was based on existing data. Most and least favourable development alternatives were identified in terms of five aspects, in other words, a multi-criteria analysis was conducted. The five aspects included liveability (local environmental quality), environment, sustainability (global environmental effects, that is, CO_2), economy and development costs. Various subelements to these aspects were evaluated in order to generate an overall impact score.

Visualization of the impacts was achieved through an impact matrix, identifying 'good' (+), 'mediocre' (0) and 'poor' (−) scores. In addition, other opportunities for future development were verbally discussed. Based on the results of the SEA, preferred development alternatives were formulated from the view of the national government. Whereas in the Leiden case, the 'Grote Polder' area was not confirmed as a preferred alternative, in the Rotterdam case, the 'Hoeksche Waard' was supported. Figure 6.9 shows the development alternatives for the Leiden region as an example. Table 6.7 shows the most and least favourable alternatives for the five evaluation aspects, indicating an economy–environmental dilemma, with the best environmental alternative being the least economically favourable and vice versa.

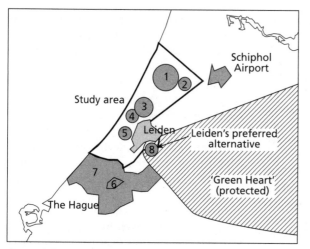

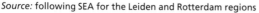

Source: following SEA for the Leiden and Rotterdam regions

Figure 6.9 *Development alternatives*

The environmental report consists of two main parts. Part A presents the overall assessment results in four chapters, including an introduction, an explanation of the background to the assessment and a comparison of alternatives for the two regions. Part B provides some background information, with a general explanation of how scoring was done, the presentation of the baseline for the two regions and a summary of knowledge and data gaps. Part B also includes an annex, a list of workgroup participants, sources and terminology used, as well as a glossary.

Table 6.7 *Final results for different alternatives*

	Most favourable alternative	Least favourable alternative
Liveability	5	3
Environment	2, 7	8
Sustainability	1	8
Economy	2, 8	1, 3
Costs	3	5

Evaluation

The SEA was conducted as a formalized process. The case is evaluated below in terms of the four benefits that are thought to result from SEA application, as presented in Box 1.2.

More systematic and effective consideration of wider environmental impacts/alternatives

The SEA led to a more effective consideration of wider environmental impacts and alternatives. It was conducted in order to broaden the views of the municipalities of Rotterdam and Leiden, ultimately in order to get them to consider other alternatives not in conflict with national environmental policy goals. This was done in a systematic way within a process that followed national EIA regulations.

Proactive formulation of strategic action for sustainable development

The process was proactive in that additional alternatives to those originally considered were identified. A number of possible site alternatives were then evaluated based on a range of environmental, economic and social aspects.

Increased efficiency of tiered decision-making, strengthening of project EIA

Overall, the SEA led to more efficient tiering, taking policies, plans and programmes from different administrative levels into account. The SEA aimed at replacing project EIA. The case provides for an interesting example regarding the long-term acceptance of planning decisions. In mid-2006, an internet search by the author found that the municipality of Leiden was still attempting to push forward development in the Green Heart, despite of the significant environmental impacts and the SEA conducted 10 years earlier. This was based on the perceived economic benefits.

More effective involvement in strategic decision-making

By applying a formalized EIA process, there was involvement at scoping and reporting stages of statutory and non-statutory bodies and the general public. The process can be said to have raised transparency and to have improved communication.

Success factors, problems, shortcomings and outlook

Factors that were crucial for perceived success include the existence of a formalized and participatory EIA-based process. The supporting role of the EIA Commission was of particular importance, as well as the involvement of all major stakeholders.

The SEA itself can be considered a good practice case. It is an example of an effective inter-municipal approach to plan making and assessment. However, as mentioned above, it also provides for an insight into the problems that may arise if a planning decision is not in line with the interests of the main economic stakeholders. Thus, political lobbying for Leiden's preferred development alternative (Grote Polder) was still ongoing in 2006, seemingly unperturbed by the SEA outcomes from a decade earlier.

Conclusions

This chapter introduced five case studies representing different administration-led SEA approaches used in spatial/land use PPP making. The cases represent two flexible assessment processes and three EIA-based processes. The five examples have different levels of 'strategicness', as is shown in Table 6.8.

Of all approaches introduced in this chapter, the Development Vision Noord-Holland represents the most strategic approach, identifying guidance for action for subsequent decision tiers. The policy plan approach of the Oldham example is representative of the UK matrix-based appraisal approach, which has been frequently described and advocated in the professional literature. It is likely to be most usefully applied whenever general development intentions need to be assessed. The Ketzin area-wide landscape plan represents an example of how comprehensive state of the environment reporting and the identification of development objectives for the biophysical environment may be approached within SEA, with an emphasis on the preparation of comprehensive baseline data. The Weiz programme SEA only focused on those areas within a defined geographical region that are potentially subject to future development. The approach is most likely to be used within plan revisions. In emerging SEA Directive-based practice, this approach appears to gain some popularity, not just in Austria, but also in other countries. The 'big project' SEA approach, finally, represented by the Leiden-Rotterdam case, allows for the identification of cumulative effects of major developments. Here, the differences with project EIA are minimal.

Table 6.8 *The five spatial/land use SEAs and their main focus*

SEA	Focus
Vision Noord-Holland (policy SEA approach)	– Long time horizon (30 years) – Focus on development scenarios
Oldham UDP (policy plan SEA approach)	– Long to medium time horizon – Statements of development intent are assessed qualitatively
Ketzin landscape plan (plan SEA approach)	– Long to medium time horizon – Identification of desired area-wide development and development objectives
Weiz land use plan (programme SEA approach)	– Medium to short time horizon – Future use of potential development sites
Leiden–Rotterdam development areas ('big project' SEA approach)	– Short time horizon – Focus on large development projects

Strategic ↕ Project

7

Summary and Conclusions

In Chapter 7 the main elements of the book are summarized. Furthermore, conclusions are drawn and recommendations for practice and further research are provided. The chapter is divided into four sections. In the first, the reader is reminded of the starting point for the book and an overview of current SEA understanding and application is provided. There is also an explanation of how the book attempted to provide a more systematic approach to SEA and its aim, objectives and underlying assumptions are summarized. In the second section, a review of current SEA practice is provided. Third is an explanation of how the book attempted to advance SEA theory and how, as a consequence, a more systematic approach to SEA is possible. Finally, some concluding remarks are made and recommendations for improving practice and for further SEA development and research are given.

Starting point of the book

The book was written for an international audience, aimed particularly at students and practitioners who are new to SEA or who wish to refresh their knowledge of the subject. It is based on the evidence and conceptual ideas brought forward in the professional literature to date, backed up by the author's own empirical research results. For teaching and training purposes, suggestions for exercise questions emerging from each chapter are provided in Annex 3.

Current SEA understanding and extent of SEA application

Since the term first emerged about two decades ago, SEA has developed into a global key environmental management instrument for public, and increasingly private, PPP making. It is now a formal requirement in all EU member states based on the EU SEA Directive (42/EC/2001) and is also advocated for use in other UNECE countries through the Kiev Protocol to the Espoo Convention on environmental assessment in a transboundary context. SEA is formally applied in a range of other countries outside the EU, for example, Canada, Australia, China and Korea. Furthermore, several countries have formal requirements for the application of SEA-type instruments, for example, New Zealand (Resource Management Act-based practice) and the US (NEPA-based practice). Informal requirements based on, for example, guidance documents, exist in a third group of countries. The best-known example is probably South Africa. Besides country-specific requirements and applications, SEA is also advocated by international development organizations and banks, for example, the World Bank, UNDP and others.

Initially, particularly at the end of the 1980s and beginning of the 1990s, SEA was mainly perceived as an extension of project EIA, applying the same process and using very similar methods and techniques in public planning authorities' plan and programme making. Currently, it is understood to also comprise more flexible approaches, particularly in public authorities' policy making and in cabinet decision-making. In the EU, SEA is most frequently perceived in terms of a systematic, objectives-led and participative assessment process coming out of the SEA Directive. Furthermore, SEA is increasingly used by private bodies. In addition to being a process, SEA is also an evidence-based instrument that aims at adding scientific rigour to decision-making by applying suitable methods and techniques. Finally, in order to be effective, SEA is advocated as a decision-making framework, within which distinct tasks are fulfilled at different decision tiers and levels.

Enabling a more systematic approach to SEA

While it has become widely accepted that SEA may be applied in different ways, depending on the specific situation within which it is used, the different types of SEA application have remained poorly explained to date. Furthermore, SEA theory remains fragmented. While various theoretical elements and aspects have been described in the professional literature, this has mostly happened in a somewhat isolated way. With this in mind, the book attempted to support the development of a more systematic approach, drawing on the evidence provided in the professional literature on SEA systems and case studies

worldwide, backed up by the results of new empirical research.

In the book, it was suggested that in order for SEA to be effective in supporting more environmentally sustainable PPP making, it needs to be applied in a normative and systematic manner. Furthermore, it needs to be tailor-made and adapted to the planning system it is applied in, therefore requiring an initial analysis of that system. It was argued that the effectiveness of SEA is enhanced by the presence of certain enabling factors. These include a range of context-related factors as well as the SEA process, methods and techniques.

Aim, objectives and underlying assumptions of the book

The overall aim of the book was to develop and promote a more systematic approach to SEA. In this context, four objectives were pursued:

- To portray current conceptual ideas and to develop them further;
- To provide for an overview of the fundamental principles and rules of SEA;
- To report on international SEA practice in a systematic manner;
- To advance SEA theory.

An underlying assumption of the book was that there is scope to develop SEA theory further, based on the empirical evidence provided to date, and taking into account the various conceptual ideas brought forward in the professional literature over the past two decades. Another assumption was that due to the highly diverse and complex nature of SEA, there is not one but a range of different ways in which SEA may be appropriately applied. However, there are also certain core principles that underlie any SEA.

Structure of the book

In order to meet the aim and objectives of the book, Chapters 1, 2 and to some extent 3 set the background for developing SEA theory further, explaining various conceptual aspects of SEA, as portrayed in the professional literature. Chapter 1 focused on the role of the SEA process, current understanding and perceived benefits from SEA, differences with project EIA, the rationale for applying SEA and the capability of SEA to act as an instrument of integration in decision-making for sustainable development. Furthermore, Chapter 1 presented those aspects that make SEA effective and identified different types of SEA. Chapter 2 provided an in-depth discussion of the SEA process, not just in public planning authorities and increasingly private bodies, but also in cabinet decision-making. In addition, methods and techniques used in SEA were introduced

and discussed. Chapter 3 dealt with issues and alternatives to be addressed in SEA, introducing a generic SEA framework for transport planning consisting of various systematic decision tiers. Chapters 3, 4, 5 and 6 then reviewed practice in terms of the various conceptual aspects previously introduced. Chapter 3 focused on various practical examples of systematic tiering in decision-making and SEA, looking at transport planning, electricity transmission planning by the private company ScottishPower and spatial/land use planning. Chapter 4 provided a comparative review of 11 established SEA systems, covering the different types of SEA introduced in Chapter 1. Chapter 5 reported on the transposition and implementation status of the SEA Directive in the EU member states and Chapter 6 evaluated five spatial/land use SEA case studies, representing different levels of strategic-ness.

Review of current SEA practice

This section summarizes those chapters within which practical SEA experiences were reviewed and evaluated based on the various conceptual aspects introduced in Chapters 1 to 3. SEA tiering in transport, electricity transmission and spatial/land use planning are covered. Furthermore, the comparative review of the 11 SEA systems, the transposition status of the SEA Directive in EU member states, and the review of the five spatial/land use SEA case studies are summarized.

The development and practical application of a tiered SEA framework

In Chapter 3, the possible integration of SEA into the existing transport planning

system of Germany was discussed. A generic transport SEA framework was designed based on systematic decision-making tiers and consisting of policies/visions, network plans, corridor plans, programmes and projects. The framework was established on the basis of evidence derived from transport planning systems in northern and western European countries. It defined tasks and alternatives to be considered in a specific situation in terms of systematic decision tiers. Furthermore, the different types of impacts to be considered were also established, for example, energy-related CO_2 emissions, severance, noise and visual impacts. The roles different administrative levels may play were explained, ranging from full inter-administrative cooperation to one administration being the main actor. Finally, possible methods and techniques to be used were also identified (see Figure 3.3).

In Chapter 3, tiered SEA application was also discussed in a private sector application, namely electricity transmission planning by ScottishPower. Three SEA tiers were described:

- The preliminary establishment of need SEA tier;
- The regional transmission network SEA tier;
- The overhead line routeing SEA tier.

Finally, what a tiered SEA framework in spatial planning may look like was discussed for a unitary system (England) and a federal system (Germany). In this context, and opposite to sectoral planning, systematic tiers were found to be reflected by the different administrative levels (national, regional, local).

Reviewing 11 established SEA systems

Within Chapter 4 a comparative review of 11 established SEA systems from ten countries was provided. Only systems were considered in which SEA had been applied for some considerable time, normally for at least 10 years, in order to be able to look at the systems from a follow-up perspective and to learn from established experiences. The evidence base was provided by the existing professional literature and by interviews with experts. The systems' evaluation framework consisted of the contextal, procedural and wider methodological factors introduced in Chapters 1 and 2. Nine administration-led SEA systems were reviewed, seven of which were EIA-based (from California, Western Australia, South Africa, The Netherlands, Italy, Finland and Germany)

and two of which were non-EIA-based (from the UK and New Zealand). Furthermore, two cabinet SEA systems were also reviewed (Canadian SEA and The Netherlands' e-test).

Overall, there was a near perfect fit of experts' perceptions on whether the SEA were likely to lead to a better consideration of the environment and the extent to which EIA-based procedural stages were in place. EIA-based systems were perceived as being more effective at improving the consideration of environmental and possibly other sustainability aspects in PPP making. Furthermore, the positive perceptions of interviewees were also related to the extent to which contextual factors were in place (formal requirements, established goals, appropriate funding, time and support, willingness to cooperate, clear boundaries for assessment, acknowledging and dealing with uncertainties). An important outcome of the evaluation of the 11 systems was that while there are indications that EIA-based SEA application may be difficult in cabinet decision-making, a systematic process is important in any assessment situation.

The transposition status of the SEA Directive

Chapter 5 provided an overview of the transposition status of the SEA Directive in the EU member states. This was mainly based on a questionnaire survey with national SEA experts in July 2006, as well as the professional literature available at that time and represented the then 25 EU member states. Two years after the Directive came into force, only three countries had not formally transposed it (Greece, Luxembourg and Portugal). All other countries had either put explicit SEA legislation into force, extended their existing EIA or spatial/sector legislation, or had amended environmental codes. In total, over 40 guidance documents were identified, with only five member states not having any guidelines in place at all. By July 2006, all 25 member states together had produced several thousand SEA-type assessments, most of which, however, predated the Directive. In July 2006, while several hundred post-Directive SEAs had been started, very few had been completed.

Evaluation of five spatial/land use SEAs

In Chapter 6, five spatial/land use SEAs were reviewed, representing different levels of strategicness, ranging from policy/vision orientation to project orientation. The choice of case studies was driven by an ability to judge performance from a follow-up perspective. This is why the SEAs had all been prepared from the mid- to the end of the 1990s. Case studies included the SEAs of the Development Vision Noord-Holland (The Netherlands; a policy/vision SEA approach), the Oldham unitary development plan (UK; a policy plan SEA approach), the Ketzin land use plan (Germany; a plan SEA approach), the Weiz land use plan (Austria; a programme SEA approach), and the Rotterdam-Leiden main development areas (The Netherlands; a 'big project' SEA approach).

Policy SEA for the Development Vision Noord-Holland

The SEA for the Development Vision Noord-Holland was fully integrated with the vision-making process, representing an informal policy SEA approach. It revolved entirely around discussing different options for possible future spatial developments, considering different economic and population growth scenarios. Recommendations for a preferred spatial development option were made, which was a compromise between unrestricted urban sprawl and limited development to existing areas only.

Policy plan SEA for the Oldham UDP

The SEA for the Oldham UDP (a sustainability appraisal) represents the 'traditional' UK qualitative matrix-based policy plan appraisal approach, aiming to optimize statements of development intent (policies). The appraisal was a team effort and was conducted in a participative and qualitative way. It was based entirely on experts' opinions. The appraisal team consisted of a selected number of people from a range of administrations and statutory bodies.

Plan SEA for the Ketzin land use plan

The plan SEA for the Ketzin land use plan was prepared within the context of the landscape plan making process for the municipality of Ketzin. It identified overall environmental objectives for further use in subsequent planning tiers and was based on a comprehensive database and the extensive use of overlay maps. Furthermore, environmental and landscape impacts of anticipated future developments of the local land use plan were assessed, and suggestions were made for impact mitigation and compensation. Land use and landscape plan making processes were conducted in parallel.

Programme SEA for the Weiz land use plan

The programme SEA for the Weiz land use plan represents an approach that appears to be gaining popularity in post-SEA Directive practice, not just in Austria but also in other countries. Within the SEA, 27 anticipated development sites of the municipality were assessed in terms of four development options: objectives of the old land use plan; no action; intentions of the municipality; and the best environmental option. An impact matrix was used to compare the different options.

'Big project' SEA for the main development areas in Leiden and Rotterdam

The 'big project' SEA for the main development areas in Leiden and Rotterdam represents an SEA approach adhering to EIA requirements that have been followed in The Netherlands since the introduction of project EIA requirements in 1987. The focus was on identifying the spatial impacts of large defined areas that were supposed to be developed for specific uses (housing or industry). Multi-criteria analysis was used to compare different spatial options.

Advancing SEA theory: Towards a more systematic approach

Within the book, conceptual and practical aspects of SEA were presented that were subsequently used to evaluate practice. The main elements of a theory of SEA include:

- The rationale for SEA;
- The characteristics of SEA, based on which benefits are thought to result;
- The reasons for why SEA is thought to be effective;
- The factors that make SEA effective.

Based on these elements, a more systematic approach to SEA is possible that revolves around:

- The choice of suitable processes;
- The consideration of appropriate issues and alternatives;
- The choice of appropriate methods and techniques.

The elements and aspects are described in further detail below.

Main elements of an SEA theory

The rationale for SEA (EREGoSum)

The rationale for SEA is a result of shortcomings in current PPP making, including the need for stronger representation of strategic Environmental thinking, more effective Reasoning, more Efficient decision-making, and the support of Good governance and Sustainable development. Whereas the first three of these elements explain why SEA is needed, the last element revolves around the question of how to apply SEA.

Need for a stronger representation of strategic environmental thinking in PPP making

In many planning systems, the environment is still largely considered in a reactive way and dealt with in an add-on manner, rather than being treated as a core element of strategic decision-making. Consideration of environmental aspects frequently happens too late to have any discernable effect on the decisions taken.

Furthermore, until recently, in most countries environmental aspects were systematically considered only at the project level (through EIA), and not at the level of PPPs.

Need for more effective reasoning

The need for SEA arises from a need for more effective reasoning. SEA can set the framework for tiered decision-making, and it may help decision-makers to ask the right questions at the right time. These questions may revolve around the 'whys', 'whats', 'wheres', 'hows' and 'whens' of PPP making. SEA may thus lead to greater transparency and may help to avoid unnecessary duplication.

More efficient decision-making

The need for SEA arises from a need for more efficient decision-making. SEA helps to design more structured decision-making frameworks and supports more systematic PPP processes. Systematic and structured processes have proven to be particularly beneficial.

Support for good governance and sustainable development

The need for SEA arises from a need to support good governance and sustainable development. In this context, SEA can act as an instrument for integrating environmental, social and economic aspects in order to achieve sustainable development.

Characteristics of SEA based on its preceived benefits (SyProTIn)

SEA has various characteristics based on its perceived benefits. Ultimately, all of the benefits arising from SEA are directly or indirectly connected with an ability to save time and money. Characteristics include:

- The more *Sy*stematic and effective

consideration of wider environmental impacts and alternatives at strategic tiers of decision-making;
- The ability of SEA to act as a *Pro*active tool that supports the formulation of strategic action for sustainable development;
- The capability of SEA to increase the efficiency of *T*iered decision-making, to strengthen project EIA and to help identify appropriate and timely alternatives, thus helping decision-makers to focus on the right issues at the right time and uncover potentially costly inconsistencies;
- The ability of SEA to enable a more effective *In*volvement in strategic decision-making, creating knowledge at low costs.

Reasons why SEA is thought to be effective (InChAR)

The reasons why SEA is thought to be effective are connected with three core SEA functions: to *In*form decision-makers, to *Ch*ange *A*ttitudes and to change established *R*outines. SEA aims at providing decision-makers with better and scientifically sound information. Furthermore, it enables attitudes and perceptions to change through participation and involvement. Finally, in the long term, SEA aims at changing established routines.

Factors that make SEA effective (ProMtext)

Factors shown to make SEA effective include the SEA *Pro*cess, *M*ethods, techniques and the overall con*text* within which SEA is applied:

- The SEA *Pro*cess (Chapters 2 and 6):
  - The SEA process in plan and programme situations is likely to particularly reflect aspects of instrumental rationality and looks

similar to a project EIA process, including the stages of screening, scoping, analysis, reporting, review, consultation, participation, impacting decision-making and follow-up;

– The SEA process in cabinet decision-making and policy making is likely to reflect more discursive approaches and may need more flexibility than SEA applied in plan and programme situations.

• SEA Methods and techniques (Chapters 2 and 6):

– A range of methods and techniques are available for use in SEA, some of which are more appropriate to apply in certain situations than others. The choice of appropriate methods and techniques is likely to depend on the sector, the decision-making level and the specific procedural stages at which SEA is applied.

• The overall con*text* within which SEA is applied:

– Formal requirements and clear provisions to conduct and effectively consider SEA;

– Clear goals for assessment;

– Appropriate funding, time and support;

– Considering and influencing traditional decision-making approaches and achieving a willingness to cooperate;

– Setting clear boundaries – addressing the right issues at the right time and defining roles of assessors:

• SEA can provide for a decision framework consisting of policy, plan and programme tiers. Within this overall framework, the specific tier decides on the types of

impacts to be considered, the alternatives to be addressed, and potentially the methods and techniques to be used and the roles of different administrations. The design of any such framework requires an initial analysis of the existing PPP making system;

• Awareness of uncertainties.

Establishing a more systematic approach: Towards tailor-made SEA

As explained at various points in the book, a tailor-made application of SEA is possible, particularly in terms of the choice of suitable processes, the consideration of appropriate issues and alternatives, and the application of appropriate methods and techniques in SEA.

Choice of suitable processes

Chapters 1 and 2 demonstrated that the SEA process may range from a structured and predefined project EIA-based process, reflecting ideas of instrumental rationality, to a flexible and communicative policy-type process, reflecting ideas of communicative rationality. The extent to which EIA procedural stages are covered was found to be correlated with perceived effectiveness to lead to better consideration of environmental aspects. EIA-based processes would normally be expected to be applied in public authorities' and private bodies' plan and programme situations. Flexible, policy-type processes would normally be expected to be applied in public authorities' policy making and cabinet decision-making. However, practical experiences with policy and cabinet SEA systems indicate that even here, in the interest of SEA effectiveness, processes should not be entirely unstructured and unsystematic. This was confirmed by the evaluation of SEA systems in Chapter 4.

Consideration of appropriate issues and alternatives

There is a wide range of issues and alternatives that may be considered in SEA. The specific systematic tier and the administrative level can help to decide what aspects may be appropriately considered in a particular SEA. In this context, the design of SEA frameworks for different systems and sectors is likely to be particularly useful. Within SEA frameworks, issues (including indicators) and alternatives can be allocated to different situations of SEA application. For transport planning, a generic framework was designed in Chapter 3 (Figure 3.3), consisting of policies, network plans, corridor plans and programmes. At the policy level, all options may be considered that might lead to meeting overall policy objectives and targets. At the network plan level, national or regional infrastructure development options are assessed, whereas at the corridor plan level, spatial alternatives within corridors are the main focus. Finally, at the programme level, priority projects are identified. Other

examples for possible SEA frameworks were introduced for electricity transmission planning (Figure 3.8), and at least partly for spatial/land use planning (Chapters 3 and 6).

Choice of appropriate methods and techniques

Appropriate methods and techniques may be identified depending on the issues to be addressed and the alternatives to be considered. Whether SEA is applied in administration-led plan and programme making or used in cabinet and policy decision-making is likely to steer the selection of suitable methods and techniques. Furthermore, the administrative level at which SEA is applied is likely to be important. In Chapter 2, those methods and techniques most frequently used in different systems were described. In Chapter 3, the use of methods and techniques at different systematic tiers and administrative levels was discussed. The specific tier and administrative level of decision-making and the use of associated methods and techniques were also highlighted in the evaluation of the five SEA case studies in Chapter 6.

Concluding remarks and recommendations for practice and further research

Strategic environmental assessment is now widely used in different formats in many countries and systems around the world. Practice is developing quickly, particularly since 2004 in Europe due to the requirements of the EU SEA Directive. While the professional SEA literature reports on various conceptual aspects of SEA, usually in a somewhat fragmented manner, and has introduced numerous SEA case

studies, it is far from systematic. Based on the evidence emerging from SEA case studies and on the conceptual ideas in the professional literature, the development of a more systematic approach was advocated in this book.

While there is now clearly a lot of practical SEA experience, there remains a lack of systematic research into practice. As a consequence, there is still comparatively little empirical evidence, for example, assessing how different systems compare, or evaluating what makes SEA effective. Furthermore, while the advantages of applying SEA are normally stressed by the proponents of the instrument, evidence supporting these claims remains thin. The current lack of evidence is clearly a barrier to convincing sceptics and to making SEA more effective.

Based on the evidence provided in the book and on recent debates in the professional literature, recommendations for the further development of SEA can be formulated:

- Don't just focus on process but also on substance! SEA *by definition* has a substantive focus, namely to support the more effective consideration of environmental and possibly other sustainability aspects in PPP making. However, many SEA commentators over recent years have focused on procedural aspects only, particularly in the context of advocating an SEA approach based on communicative rationality.
- Use processes that are appropriate to the specific situation of application! While recently many authors have advocated procedural flexibility for SEA, there are many situations in which structured and rigorous processes are appropriately applied, particularly at the plan and programme level.
- Analyse PPP systems before applying SEA! In order to be able to apply SEA effectively, the system to which it is applied needs to be understood as fully as possible; how decisions are made and what issues are addressed at what point in the system are particularly important to establish.
- Design system-specific SEA frameworks! SEA needs to address the

'whys', 'whats', 'wheres', 'hows' and 'whens' of PPP making; SEA should encourage PPP makers to consider issues and alternatives that otherwise would have been left out; SEA should cover all levels and tiers of decision-making in order to be effective.
- Expert skills are important! SEA should support scientifically sound decision-making; expert knowledge is important and needs to be advanced, particularly in terms of supporting the SEA process in an optimal way (by mediation, advocacy or technical approaches) and by using appropriate and sound methods and techniques in a transparent and effective manner.
- Monitor and evaluate SEA systems! This is of crucial importance in order to be able to learn from past practice and improve systems.

Considering the importance SEA has achieved globally, there is an urgent need for more research, particularly regarding the following aspects of SEA:

- What makes SEA effective? While SEA effectiveness aspects have been presented in the book, these need to be supported by more evidence, particularly regarding non-EIA-based SEA; it will be particularly important to examine policy SEA systems further.
- What is the best format for applying SEA in a specific situation, particularly in terms of process, methods and techniques? It is important to identify those issues that should be addressed in existing PPP making systems; aspects of effective tiering are particularly crucial.
- To what extent can SEA be standardized, and to what extent does it need to be flexible? Research can focus on a range of aspects, including:

- Processes – examining the desired degree of strategicness and acting strategies for PPP makers and assessors;
- Methods and techniques;
- Indicators;
- Frameworks.
- Follow-up, covering issues such as:
  - Do subsequent PPPs make reference to SEA and do they conform to what the SEA established?
  - Have predictions proven to be right and is performance satisfactory?
  - Are results of SEA and follow-up distributed widely?
- To what extent can SEA be effective in the absence of certain contextual criteria that are thought to be essential? Whether and how SEA can be applied effectively even in the absence of contextal criteria is an important question, particularly in evolving planning systems.

Annexes

ANNEXES

Annex 1

EU SEA Directive-based environmental report quality review table

Reviewing the quality of an environmental report

In this annex, a table for reviewing the quality of an environmental report is introduced. It is based on the requirements laid out by Directive 2001/42/EC 'on the assessment of the effects of certain plans and programmes on the environment'. The review table has been developed for the web-based distance learning MA in spatial planning at the University of the West of England (www.built-environment.uwe.ac.uk/spatialplanning/catalogue.asp). It is based on mainstream approaches used in existing environmental assessment review packages, for example, the Lee et al (1999) Review Package (EIA Centre, University of Manchester) and the SEA Environmental Report Review Criteria (IEMA, 2005).

The purpose of the review table is to:

- Provide reviewers with a framework within which to evaluate the information provided in the environmental report;
- Enable reviewers to assess the quality and completeness of the information provided in the environmental report in a quick and easy-to-understand manner;

- Enable reviewers to make an overall judgement of the acceptability of the environmental report as a decision-informing document.

The review table consists of six main sections:

1 Plan/programme and environmental baseline description; plan/programme and SEA process integration;
2 Identification and evaluation of key issues/options;
3 Determination of impact significance;
4 Consultation process;
5 Presentation of information and results;
6 Recommendations on preferred options and monitoring.

Each section includes a range of questions that are the basis for evaluating the quality of the environmental report. All questions are graded, based on the reviewer's impression. Symbols are used, ranging from A (well performed) to G (task not attempted). Finally, the environmental report receives an overall grade (see end of review table). This is not strictly an average grade, but rather one that reflects the reviewer's overall impression. Thus, any significant shortcoming regarding one review question or section can lead to downgrading of the entire document.

Review procedure

The procedure for reviewing the environmental report consists of three stages:

1   Read through the environmental report quickly, identifying the layout and the whereabouts of essential information.
2   Read the review questions provided in the review table under the six main sections, use the appropriate grade symbols from A to G that are provided after the table and record a grade for each question.
3   Use the assessment grades awarded to each individual question within a particular review section in order to assess the review section as a whole.

When all review sections have been evaluated, the grades can be used to assign a grade to the environmental report as a whole (which is not necessarily an average grade). This overall judgement should be supplemented with a brief summary of the strengths and weaknesses of the environmental report and a consideration of whether it meets requirements. Ideally, review is done independently by various persons, results are compared and an agreement on report quality is achieved.

Table A1 *Environmental report review table*

(1) Plan/programme and environmental baseline description, plan/programme and SEA process integration	Grade	Comments
The environmental report:		
Outlines the contents and main objectives of the plan		
Outlines the relationship with other relevant plans and programmes		
Describes how the SEA was conducted		
Describes how SEA and plan making processes were integrated (i.e. SEA should take place during plan preparation and before plan adoption or submission to the legislative procedure)		
With a view to avoiding duplication of assessment, describes what issues are addressed in other assessments, i.e. at other levels/layers within a planning system/hierarchy		
Provides information on the relevant aspects of the current state of the environment, economy and social aspects likely to be significantly affected and the likely evolution thereof without implementation of the plan		
Provides information on any existing environmental/sustainability problems that are relevant to the plan including, in particular, those relating to any areas of particular environmental importance		
Provides information on environmental protection objectives, established at international, European or UK level, which are relevant to the plan and the way those objectives and any environmental considerations have been taken into account during its preparation		
Evaluation of section (1)		

(2) Identification and evaluation of key issues and options	Grade	Comments

The environmental report:
Describes how reasonable alternatives were identified, considering objectives and geographical scope of the plan

Lists the environmental issues considered in assessment

Describes how environmental issues considered in assessment were identified

Provides information on the likely significant effects of different options on:
• biodiversity
• population
• human health
• fauna
• flora
• soil
• water
• air
• climatic factors
• material assets
• cultural heritage, including architecture and archaeology
• landscape
• the interrelationship between the above factors

Lays out what matters are more appropriately assessed at other levels or layers of decision-making, with a view to avoiding duplication

Shows how state-of-the-art knowledge and methods of assessment were used

Evaluation of section (2)

(3) Determination of impact significance	Grade	Comments

The environmental report explains how impact significance was determined by:
Identifying the degree to which the plan sets a framework for project/other activities, either in terms of location, size, nature and operating conditions or by allocating resources

Identifying value and vulnerability of the area likely to be affected due to special natural characteristics or cultural heritage, exceeded environmental quality standards, exceeded limit values or intensive land use

Identifying the effects on areas or landscapes that have a recognized UK, European or international protection status of the various options

Identifying the probability, duration (short, medium and long term, permanent and temporary), frequency and reversibility of effects, both positive and negative, of the various options

Identifying the secondary, cumulative and synergistic nature of the effects of the various options

Identifying the trans-boundary nature of the effects of the various options

Identifying risks to human health and the environmental issues, e.g. due to accidents, of various options

Identifying the magnitude and spatial extent of the effects (geographical area and size of population affected) of the various options

Evaluation of section (3)

(4) Consultation process	Grade	Comments

The environmental report:

Describes how authorities were consulted when scope and level of detail of information in assessment were identified

Describes how the draft plan and environmental report were made available to authorities and the public likely to be affected or having an interest in the plan and were allowed to express their opinions within an appropriate time frame

Confirms that consultation results on plan and SEA are to be considered in decision-making

Evaluation of section (4)

(5) Presentation of information and results	Grade	Comments

The environmental report:

Includes a clearly distinguishable SEA section or separate environmental report, prepared according to SEA Directive requirements

Provides information on any difficulties (such as technical deficiencies or lack of know-how) and uncertainties encountered in compiling the required information

Once a decision has been made, is accompanied by a statement summarizing how environmental/sustainability considerations have been integrated into the plan or programme and how the environmental report and the results of the consultations have been taken into account and the reasons for choosing the plan as adopted in the light of the other reasonable alternatives dealt with

Evaluation of section (5)

(6) Recommendations on preferred options and monitoring	Grade	Comments

The environmental report:

Presents an outline of the reasons for selecting the alternatives dealt with, and a description of how the assessment leading to these reasons was undertaken

Provides information on the measures envisaged to prevent, reduce and as fully as possible offset any significant adverse effects on the environment of implementing the plan

Describes the measures envisaged concerning monitoring of the significant environmental effects of the plan implementation in order, *inter alia*, to identify at an early stage unforeseen adverse effects

Shall explain how monitoring is done, in order to be able to undertake appropriate remedial action

Shall explain how existing monitoring arrangements may be used, if appropriate, in order to avoid duplication

Evaluation of section (6)

Notes: Scoring system

Grade A – The work has generally been well performed with no important omissions.

Grade B – Is performed satisfactorily and complete with only minor omissions/ inadequacies.

Grade C – Is regarded as just satisfactory despite some omissions or inadequacies.

Grade D – Indicates that parts are well attempted but, on the whole, are unsatisfactory because of omissions or inadequacies.

Grade E – Is not satisfactory, revealing significant omissions or inadequacies.

Grade F – Is very unsatisfactory with important tasks poorly attempted.

Grade G – Task not attempted at all.

n/a – not applicable.

? – unclear.

OVERALL GRADE FOR ENVIRONMENTAL REPORT = –––––––––

Annex 2

Post-Directive SEA case studies in EU member states

This list has been compiled, based on information provided by national experts in mid-2006 (see Acknowledgements) in the context of the project 'Environmental Policy Advisory Service and Environmental Management', conducted for GTZ and SEPA of China.

Austria

Pilot SEAs included:

- SEA of land-use plan of Weiz, local level;
- SEA of regional programme of Tennengau/Salzburg, supra-local level.

While it is difficult to estimate the total number of SEAs all over Austria, on the government website of the state of Lower Austria, some detailed information is provided (www.raumordnung-noe.at/dynamisch/showcontainer.php?id=110). This says that there are seven SEAs for local development plans:

- Gemeinde Altenburg;
- Marktgemeinde Altlengbach;
- Gemeinde Jaidhof;
- Marktgemeinde Kirchstetten;
- Marktgemeinde Perchtoldsdorf;
- Stadtgemeinde Ybbs an der Donau;
- Gemeinde Weikersdorf am Steinfeld.

Although there are no exact numbers for other provinces, there are cases, for example, in Styria. According to the SEA

Handbook of the Academie der Wissenschaften (2006, http://hw.oeaw.ac.at/sup_collection?frames=yes), about 80 SEAs had been started/ prepared by mid-2006.

Belgium

According to the website of the EIA department of the Flemish Ministry of the Environment, by mid-2006 the following 19 SEAs had been prepared in Flemish Belgium (see www.mervlaanderen.be):

- Lange-termijnvisie Vlaamse Zeehavens;
- Masterplan Antwerpen;
- Actualisatie Sigmaplan;
- Ontwikkelingsschets 2010 Schelde estuarium;
- Ontwerp strategisch plan voor en de afbakening van de haven van Antwerpen in haar omgeving;
- Luchthaven Deurne;
- Integraal spoor Operationeel Programma Doelstelling 2;
- Integraal spoor Vlaams Programma voor Duurzame Plattelandsontwikkeling;
- Regionaal bedrijventerrein Zwartenhoek-Ham;
- Ontwikkeling van een hoogwaardig bedrijvenpark op de voormalige mijnsite van Waterschei;
- RUP Flanders X-po;
- Strategisch Masterplan Reconversie economische ontwikkeling Vilvoorde-Machelen (Integraal spoor);

- Ruilverkaveling Willebringen;
- Uitwerken van een strategisch luchthavenbeleid m.b.t. de ontwikkeling van de luchthaven van Zaventem en de luchthavenimpactregio;
- Strategisch Plan Haven van Oostende;
- Provinciaal RUP jachthaven Nieuwpoort;
- AWZ-plan Oostende;
- Ruilverkaveling in onderzoek Plateau van Izenberge. Ruilverkavelingsblok Sint-Rijkers;
- Aanleg AX tussen de N31 en de N49 te Westkapelle.

Cyprus

No SEA assessments had been prepared by mid-2006.

Czech Republic

SEA for land use plans (LUPs) are routinely prepared. Between 1992 and 2003, approximately 30 regional LUPs (perhaps more) were assessed through SEA. Since 2004, approximately 20 SEAs have been carried out under the new SEA regime. Examples include:

- SEA of Spatial Development Policy of the Czech Republic (main LUP document prepared for the Czech Ministry of Regional Development, 2005);
- SEA of the Land Use Plan of Karlovy Vary Region (for authority of Karlovy Vary Region, 2005 – very good SEA that examined a range of environmental impacts; also included detailed assessment of landscape fragmentation and impacts of proposed major windpower developments);
- SEA of the Land Use Plan for City of Chrast (this is a small but very interesting current SEA undertaken for the city of Pilsen, where the full integra-

tion of SEA into the elaboration of LUP and the framework for sustainability assessment was tested).

Denmark

In March 2006, a study was completed at Aalborg University, which found that 80 environmental reports (26 related to municipal plans and 54 to local plans) were compiled by 55 municipalities. In total there are 271 municipalities in Denmark.

Estonia

The SEA Act was enforced in 2005. By mid-2006 there were no completed SEAs, however, several were in the public consultation phase. Draft environmental reports and draft plans are accessible for the general public.

There were several (20–30) SEAs initiated for comprehensive municipalities (parishes), which had to adopt their plans by 2007. A study on the number of SEAs and their content, as well as the quality of environmental reports, will be prepared during 2007, two years after SEA Act was enforced.

Finland

Since the year 2001 (the year the Directive was published), hundreds of LUPs have been prepared, including impact assessments. In the 'KASEVA project', draft guidance was applied and tested (linking the assessments with planning procedures, public participation and consultation, reporting) for the following plans:

- Regional Plan for Uusimaa Region;
- Master Plan for Sipoo municipality;
- Detailed Plan for Northern Vuosaari (part of the city of Helsinki).

France

Hundreds of SEAs had been prepared by mid-2006.

Germany

The EEB report 'Biodiversity in SEA' (2005) (www.eeb.org/activities/biodiversity/Final-SEA-report-271205.pdf) mentions around 25 SEAs, however, these were not specified and there are no reliable statistics for Germany. The first Directive-based SEAs for state development plans, regional plans and preparatory land use plans were carried out in 2006, however, none had been finished by mid-2006. Hundreds of SEAs for binding land use plans were being conducted. These can frequently be downloaded from the municipalities' homepages. Known post-Directive SEAs mainly include those for small-scale master plans, that is, 'big project SEAs', including two for the city of Duesseldorf (2004):

- Master plan extension Boehlerstrasse (area of 30,500m^2 or 3ha);
- Master Plan North of Vogelsanger Weg (area of 107,200m^2 or 11ha).

An SEA for the spatial development programme of Lower Saxony was started in 2005. This can be accessed at www.ml.niedersachsen.de/master/C11234 917_N11234568_L20_D0_I655.html#

Greece

No assessments have been prepared in Greece following the requirements of the SEA Directive. Three cases, however, have been quoted in the literature that were prepared by the Ministry of the Environment, including:

- Deviation of Acheloos River;
- Development of Piraeus Port Facilities;
- 2004 Olympic Games Programmes.

However, none of them incorporate all SEA Directive provisions, such as public consultation or systematic assessment.

Hungary

A few pilot studies have been conducted.

Ireland

By mid-2006, there had been 14 statutory and two pilot/non-statutory SEAs completed, for which the corresponding land use plans had been adopted. There were also around 20 SEAs in the process of being adopted. SEA case studies include:

- DDDA Master Plan 2003 by Dublin City Council;
- Waste Management Plan for the Midlands Region 2005 by North Tipperary, Laois, Longford, Offaly and Westmeath county councils;
- Ennis and Environs DP Variation No. 4 2006 by Clare County Council;
- Kilrush DP Variation No. 3 2005 by Clare County Council;
- Ballymun Local Area Plan 2005 by Fingal County Council;
- Fingal DP Variation No. 1 2005 by Fingal County Council;
- Galway County Development Plan Variations No. 5 and 6 by Galway County Council;
- Limerick CDP Variation No. 1 2005 by Limerick County Council;
- North Drogheda Environs Masterplan 2006 by Louth County Council;
- Dundalk South West Local Area Plan 2006 by Louth County Council;

161

- Meath County Development Plan 2006 by Meath County Council.

Italy

By mid-2006, a few regional pilot studies had been conducted within the context of the ENPLAN project (www.interreg-enplan.org). These include SEAs were in the regions of Emilia Romagna, Lombardy and Tuscany.

Latvia

To obtain more information on SEA case studies in Latvia, a government web site can be consulted: www.vidm.gov.lv/ivnvb/sivn/Latzin.htm

There were a number of plans/programmes that had been subject to SEA in 2005 and 2006. For these plans/programmes, the State Environment Bureau had issued an evaluation opinion.

Lithuania

A number of SEAs are currently under preparation:

- 51 SEA of Comprehensive Plan of Klaipeda County;
- SEA of Special Plan of National Bicycle Route;
- SEA of Comprehensive Plan of Panevezys County;
- SEA of Comprehensive Plan of Alytus County;
- SEA of Comprehensive Plan of Siauliai County;
- SEA of Comprehensive Plan of Siauliai District;
- SEA of Comprehensive Plan of Klaipeda District.

Malta

In mid-2006, there were only two ongoing SEAs:

- The Structure Plan Review by Ministry of the Environment in-house personnel;
- SEA following a tender for an SEA of an EU project, issued by the Office of the Prime Minister. This was conducted by a local group aided by foreign consultants.

The Netherlands

Hundreds of EIA Act-based SEAs have been conducted in The Netherlands since 1987. In mid-2006, some 10–20 plan SEAs had been started for housing, industrial estates, recreation, (road) infrastructure and other spatial developments regarding regional plans, land use plans, provincial transport and traffic plans. For more information, the website of the Dutch EIA Commission can be consulted: www.eia.nl

Poland

A voivodship officer who was interviewed estimated that in the Wielkopolskie voivodship, about 300 SEAs for local land use plans are conducted every year (Poland has 16 voivodships). About 95 per cent of all environmental reports are prepared for land use purposes and the rest for sectoral plans or programmes (for example waste management programmes). Relevant SEA examples include:

- Strategic environmental assessment for the National Development Plan 2004–2006; pilot project coordinated by the regional Environment Center (REC). This is known as a good practice example for SEA. See www.rec.org/REC/Programs/ EnvironmentalAssessment/pdf/Poland -SEAiNPR.pdf

- Environmental impact prognosis of the project strategy of the tourism development in the Silesian voivodship in 2004–2013 (Prognoza oddziaⅡywania na Êrodowisko Projektu strategii rozwoju turystyki w województwie Êlàskim na lata 2004–2013). See www.silesia-region.pl/stratur/srt_pr.pdf
- Environmental impact prognosis of the Waste Management Plan for Kujawsko – Pomorskie voivodhship (Prognoza oddziaⅡywania na Êrodowisko planu gospodarki odpadami województwa kujawsko – pomorskiego), Toruƒ, 2003. See www.kujawsko-pomorskie.pl/files/ srodowisko/program-ochrony/ prognoza-planu-ochr-sr.pdf

Portugal

By mid-2006, three pilot SEAs had been conducted:

- High speed railway (2003);
- Tourism investment strategy (2004);
- Portuguese operational programming proposals under the IV Framework Programme, Cohesion Policy 2007–2013.

Slovakia

There is just one case study of a 'full SEA' following the SEA Directive:

- The SEA for the Bratislava land use draft plan.

Slovenia

A few pilot studies were said to have been conducted by mid-2006.

Spain

By mid-2006, several case studies had been carried out under local regulations/legislation:

- SEA of Regional Development Plan and Structural Funds Programmes, 2000–2006;
- SEA of urban development plans and the wind energy plan in Castilla y León (2000);
- SEA of the urban plan (2002) for Puerto de la Cruz, Islas Canarias;
- SEA of wind energy plans in Valencia and Cataluña;
- SEA of territorial plans in the Basque Country;
- SEA of the Review of the Municipal Plan of Málaga;
- SEA of Infrastructure Plan 2000–2007.

Sweden

Since the introduction of SEA Directive requirements, hundreds of SEAs are thought to have been started for both municipal comprehensive plans and detailed development plans.

UK

Several hundred of Directive-based SEAs had been started by mid-2006. Examples include:

- Bracknell Forest Borough Council (2005). Bracknell Forest Local Development Framework scoping report – baseline data, characterization, indicators and trends,

www.bracknell-forest.gov.uk/
baseline-data-and-trends.pdf

- Thurrock Borough Council (2005). Thurrock Borough Council LDF Scoping Report, www.thurrock.gov.uk/planning/ strategic/pdf/sc_report_appendixb.pdf
- The Royal Borough of Kensington and Chelsea (2005). LDF Interim Sustainability Appraisal Report, www.rbkc.gov.uk/Planning/local developmentframework/rbkc_vol_II_ baseline_figures.asp
- Teignbridge District Council (2005). Integrated SEA/SA of local development documents to be included in the Teignbridge LDF 2001–2016, initial options to core strategy, www.teign bridge.gov.uk/media/pdf/r/j/Core_ Strategy_Sustainability_Appraisal_ Information_-__Report_24-05-2005. pdf
- West Midlands Regional Assembly (2005). West Midlands Regional Spatial Strategy – SA of the Black Country Study, www.black countryconsortium.co.uk/consult phase3.asp?ses=

Annex 3

Suggestions for exercise questions

Chapter 1

1 What is SEA? What are its main components?
See Box 1.1 'Definition of SEA'.

2 What can be said to be the generic stages of an EIA-based SEA process, and what do the different stages mean/involve?
See Figure 1.1 'EC SEA Directive-based process for improving plan and programme making'.

3 What are the characteristics of SEA, based on which benefits are thought to result?
See Box 1.2 'Characteristics of SEA, based on which benefits are thought to result'.

4 What are the differences between SEA and EIA?
See Table 1.1 'The changing focus of SEA from lower tiers to higher tiers'.

5 What is the rationale behind the use of SEA?
See Chapter 1, section 'Rationale for applying SEA'.

6 What does a tiered approach to SEA mean, and what is tiering said to include?
See Figure 1.4 'Strategic planning framework provided by SEA'.

7 How can SEA help to make decision-making more efficient?
See Chapter 1, section 'The need for more efficient decision-making'.

8 How does SEA support good governance and sustainable development?
See Chapter 1, section 'The need for

supporting good governance and sustainable development in decision-making'.

9 How is SEA thought to function and why is it thought to be able to be effective in supporting due consideration of environmental aspects?
See Chapter 1, section 'Why is SEA thought to be effective in improving the consideration of the environmental component in PPP making?'.

10 What are the conditions for effective SEA application?
See Box 1.3 'SEA effectiveness criteria advertised in the professional literature'.

Chapter 2

1 What is the purpose of the SEA process?
See Chapter 2, section 'The SEA process: Its role and purpose'.

2 What does screening mean in SEA and what does it involve?
See Chapter 2, section 'Screening'.

3 What does scoping mean in SEA and what does it involve?
See Chapter 2, section 'Scoping'.

4 Please list the different forms of SEA follow-up and monitoring
See Chapter 2, section 'Follow-up and monitoring'.

5 Describe the differences between consultation, participation, communication and reporting.
See Chapter 2, section 'Consultation, participation, communication and

reporting'.

6   What should methods and techniques aim to achieve?
See Chapter 2, section 'What methods and techniques should aim to achieve in SEA'.

7   Name and summarize descriptive methods/techniques for use in SEA.
See Chapter 2, section 'Most commonly used methods and techniques'.

8   Name and summarize analytical methods/techniques for use in SEA.
See Chapter 2, section 'Most commonly used methods and techniques'.

9   Name and summarize involvement methods/techniques for use in SEA.
See Chapter 2, section 'Most commonly used methods and techniques'.

10 Why are techniques, such as LCA and risk assessment, suitable for use in policy SEA?
See Chapter 2, section 'Additional methods and techniques'.

Chapter 3

1   What are the main differences of policy, plan and programme SEA in terms of: first, concrete, site-specific issues; and second, the range of possible alternatives considered?
See Figure 3.3 'Focus, tasks, alternatives, impacts, role of different administrations and methods/techniques within the system-based SEA framework'.

2   Map out the transport planning system in your country in terms of policies, networks plans, corridor plans, programmes and the various administrative levels (national, regional, local). Allocate issues and

alternatives considered at the different stages. Use the frameworks introduced in Figures 3.2 and 3.3 as examples. How would you integrate SEA into this system?

3   Map out the spatial/land use planning system in your country. Use figures 3.10 and 3.11 as examples. How would you integrate SEA into this system?

4   How would you try to convince a private company to conduct SEA? Name some of the potential advantages of SEA for private companies.
See Chapter 3, section 'SEA framework developed by ScottishPower'.

Chapter 4

1   Name at least one SEA system for each of the following SEA categories:
•   Administration-led SEA:
–   EIA-based SEA;
–   Non-EIA-based SEA;
•   Cabinet SEA.
See Chapter 4, section 'Review methodology'.

2   What are the context-related enabling factors that appear to have particular importance for effective SEA?
See Chapter 4, section 'Review methodology'.

3   Name those procedural factors that appear to be closely related to a perception that SEA is likely to lead to a better consideration of the environment.
See Box 4.1 'Factors for evaluating SEA systems' and Table 4.2 'SEA systems' performance and existence of context and procedural factors'.

4   How does cabinet SEA appear to differ from administration-led SEA?
See Chapter 4, section 'Observations on cabinet SEA'.

Chapter 5

1 What are the six main themes covered by the SEA Directive?
  See Chapter 5, section 'The European SEA Directive'.
2 What plans and programmes are covered by the SEA Directive?
  See Chapter 5, section 'The European SEA Directive'.
3 Name the different ways in which the SEA Directive has been transposed by EU members states.
  See Chapter 5, section 'Transposition status'.
4 What other directives are closely related to the SEA Directive?
  See Figure 3.3. 'Focus, tasks, alternatives, impacts, role of different administrations and methods/techniques within the system-based SEA framework'.

Chapter 6

1 Summarize the main features of the five different methodological approaches to administration-led spatial/land use SEA outlined in Chapter 6.
  See Chapter 6, 'Spatial and land use case studies'.
2 Which one of the five SEAs presented in Chapter 6 does not fall under the requirements of the SEA Directive? Explain!
  See Chapter 6, section 'Development Vision Noord-Holland'.
3 What SEA approach of those presented in Chapter 6 appears to becoming widespread? Explain why you think this may be the case.
  See Chapter 6, 'Spatial and land use case studies'.
4 Which SEA of those presented in Chapter 6 was conducted following project EIA requirements?
  See Chapter 6, section 'SEA for new housing and business development areas in Rotterdam and Leiden, The Netherlands'.

Bibliography

Akademie der Wissenschaften (2006)
Handbuch Strategische Umweltprüfung,
Akademie der Wissenschaften, Vienna,
http://hw.oeaw.ac.at/sup_collection?frames
=yes, last accessed: 29/12/2006

Amt Ketzin (1996) *Landschaftsplan
Gemeinden Ketzin / Etzin / Falkenrehde /
Tremmen / Zachow*, Gemeinde Ketzin,
Brandenburg

Annandale D, Lantzke R and Skinn M (2003)
*Making Good Waste Management
Decisions*, www.inem.org (go to
'knowledge' and then 'general knowledge
base' and 'waste'), last accessed:
29/12/2006

Arbter K (2005) 'SEA of waste management
plans – an Austrian Case Study', in Schmidt
M, João E and Albrecht E (eds),
*Implementing Strategic Environmental
Assessment*, Springer-Verlag, Berlin,
pp621–630

Arts J, Tomlinson P and Voogd H (2005) *EIA
and SEA Tiering: The Missing Link?*
Position Paper prepared for the meeting on
SEA of the International Association for
Impact Assessment (IAIA), Prague,
September

Arts J and Morrison-Saunders A (eds) (2004)
Follow-up in Environmental Assessment,
Earthscan, London

Aschemann R (1999) *Endbericht zum
Pilotprojekt Strategische Umweltprüfung
(SUP) des Flächenwidmungsplanes 3.0
(FWP) der Stadtgemeinde Weiz*,
Arbeitsgruppe Wissenschaftsladen Graz /
Büro Arch. DI Hoffmann, Graz

Aschemann R (2004) 'Lessons learned from
Austrian SEA', *European Environment*, vol
14, no 3, pp165–174

Au E and Hui S (2004) 'Learning by doing:
EIA follow-up in Hong Kong', in Arts J

and Morrison-Saunders A (eds) *Follow-up
in Environmental Assessment*, Earthscan,
London, pp197–223

Banister D (1994) *Transportation Planning in
the UK, USA and Europe*, E&FN Spon,
London

Barker A and Fischer T B (2003) 'English
regionalism and sustainability: Towards the
development of an integrated approach to
SEA', *European Planning Studies*, vol 11,
no 6, pp697–716

Barker A and Wood C (2001) 'Environmental
assessment in the European Union:
Perspectives, past, present and strategic',
European Planning Studies, vol 9,
pp243–254

Barrett J (2002) 'The application of the
ecological footprint: A case of passenger
transport in Merseyside', in Möhlenbrink
W, Bargende M, Hangleiter U and Martin
U (eds), *Networks for Mobility*,
Proceedings International Symposium,
18–20 September, Stuttgart, Centre of
Transportation Research, University of
Stuttgart, pp507–517

Bartlett R V and Kurian P A (1999) 'The
theory of environmental impact
assessment', *Policy and Politics*, vol 27, no
4, pp415–433

Bell S and Morse S (2003) *Measuring
Sustainability*, Earthscan, London

Bina O (2001) *Strategic Environmental
Assessment of Transport Corridors:
Lessons Learned Comparing the Methods
of Five Member States*, European
Commission, Directorate General for the
Environment, Brussels,
http://europa/eu/environment/eia

Bina O (2003) *Re-conceptualising Strategic
Environmental Assessment: Theoretical
Overview and Case Study from Chile*,

unpublished PhD Thesis, Geography
Department, University of Cambridge,
Cambridge

BMV (Bundesministerium für Verkehr) (1992)
Bundesverkehrswegeplan, BMV, Bonn

BMVBW (Bundesministerium für Verkehr,
Bau- und Wohnungswesen) (2003)
Bundesverkehrswegeplan 2003, BMVBW,
Berlin

Bond A and Brooks D (1997) 'A strategic
framework to determine the best
practicable environmental option (BPEO)
for proposed transport schemes', *Journal of
Environmental Management*, vol 51,
pp305–321

Bras-Klapwijk R (1999) *Adjusting Life Cycle
Assessment Methodology for Use in Public
Policy Discourse*, unpublished PhD thesis,
Delft University, Delft

Bunge T (1998) 'SEA in land use planning:
The Erlangen case study', in Kleinschmidt
V and Wagner D (eds), *SEA in Europe:
Fourth European Workshop on EIA*,
Kluwer Academic Publishers, Dordrecht,
pp86–89

Buschke M, Derwick B, Faust S, Finger A,
Flatow D, Funke J, Hudy S, Köller J,
Krsynowski A, Lermen A, Reinsch N, Stein
M, Sommer S, Träger N, Unsöld D and
Walter U (2002) *Ist der Landschaftsplan
zukunftsfähig als Plan-UVP? – Modell
Gemeinde Nauen*, Hauptstudienprojekt
2001/2002, Institut für Landschafts-und
Umweltplanung, Technical University of
Berlin, Berlin

Buselich K (2002) *An Outline of Current
Thinking on Sustainability Assessment*,
Government of Western Australia, Perth,
www.sustainability.dpc.wa.gov.au/docs/BG
Papers/KathrynBuselich.pdf, last accessed:
29/12/2006

Carter J G, Wood C M, Baker M (2003) 'The
environmental appraisal of national park
management plans in England and Wales',
*Journal of Environmental Planning and
Management*, vol 46, no 2, pp271–290

CEAA (Canadian Environmental Assessment
Agency) (1999) *Cumulative Effects
Assessment Practitioners Guide*, CEAA,
Ottawa, www.ceaa-acee.gc.ca/013/0001/
0004/index_e.htm, last accessed:
29/12/2006

Cherp A (2001) 'SEA in Newly Independent
States', in Dusik J (ed.), *Proceedings of the
International Workshop on Public
Participation and Health Aspects in
Strategic Environmental Assessment*,
Regional Environmental Center for Central
and Eastern Europe, Szentendre, Hungary

Cherp A (2004) *The Promise of Strategic
Environmental Management*, Working
Paper of the MiST-Programme, www.sea-
mist.se, last accessed: 29/12/2006

Cowell R and Martin S (2003) 'The joy of
joining up: Modes of integrating the local
government modernisation agenda',
Environment and Planning C, vol 21,
pp159–179

CSIR (2000) *Strategic Environmental
Assessment in South Africa*, guideline
document, Department of Enviromental
Affairs and Tourism, Pretoria

Culhane P J, Friesema H P and Beecher J A
(1987) *Forecasts and Environmental
Decision Making*, Westview Press, Boulder,
CO

Czada R (1998) 'Neuere Entwicklungen der
Politikfeldanalyse', *POLIS*, vol 39,
pp47–65

Dalal-Clayton B and Sadler B (2005) *Strategic
Environmental Assessment: A Sourcebook
and Reference Guide to International
Experience*, Earthscan, London

Dalkmann H and Bongardt D (2004) 'Case
study: The German Federal Transport
Infrastructure Planning (FTIP)', in Caratti
P, Dalkmann H and Jiliberto R (eds),
*Analysing Strategic Environmental
Assessment*, Edward Elgar, Cheltenham,
pp123–153

Danish Ministry of Environment and Energy
(1993) *Guidance Procedures for
Environmental Assessments of Bills and
other Government Proposals*, Ministry of
Environment and Energy, Copenhagen

De Roo G (2000) 'Environmental conflicts in
compact cities: Complexity, decision-
making and policy approaches',
Environment and Planning B, vol 27,
pp151–162

De Roo G (2003) *Dutch Environmental
Planning: Too Good to be True*, Ashgate,

Aldershot

DEFRA (Department for Environment, Food and Rural Affairs) (2004) *Guidance to Operating Authorities on the Application of SEA to Flood Management Plans and Programmes*, www.defra.gov.uk/environ/fcd/policy/sea.htm, last accessed: 29/12/2006

DETR (Department of the Environment, Transport and the Regions) (1998) *Strategic Environmental Appraisal, Report of the International Seminar on SEA*, Lincoln, 27–29 May, DETR, London

Diamantini C and Geneletti D (2004) 'Reviewing the application of SEA to sectoral plans in Italy: The case of the mobility plan of an Alpine Region', *European Environment Journal*, vol 14, no 2, pp 123–133

DoE (Department of the Environment) (1991) *Policy Appraisal and the Environment*, HMSO, London

DoE (Department of the Environment) (1992) *Planning Policy Guidance Note 12: Development Plans and Regional Guidance*, The Stationary Office, London

DoE (1993) *Environmental Appraisal of Development Plans: A Good Practice Guide*, The Stationary Office, London

Dovers S (2002) 'Too deep a SEA? Strategic environmental assessment in the era of sustainability', in Marsden S and Dovers S (eds), *Strategic Environmental Assessment in Australasia*, The Federation Press, Annandale, NSW, pp24–46

DTI (Department of Trade and Industry) (2001) *SEA of the former White Zone I: An Overview of SEA Process, Key Issues and Findings*, www.offshore-sea.org.uk/sea/dev/html_file/library_sea1.php, last accessed: 29/12/2006

DTI (2005) *Strategic Environmental Assessment UK Public Consultation for Energy Licensing Webside*, www.offshore-sea.org.uk, last accessed: 29/12/2006

Dusik J, Fischer T B and Sadler B, with Steiner A and Bonvoisin N (2003) *Benefits of a Strategic Environmental Assessment*, REC, UNDP, http://europeandcis.undp.org (go to publications), last accessed: 27/12/2006

EEB (European Environment Bureau) (2005) *Biodiversity in Strategic Environmental Assessment*, EEB, Brussels, www.eeb.org, last accessed: 29/12/2006

Elling B and Nielsen J (1997) *Environmental Assessment of National Policies*, European Commission, DG XI Environment, Brussels

Environmental Protection Department (2004) *Strategic Environmental Assessment Manual*, Government of Hong Kong, Hong Kong

EPA (Environmental Protection Authority) (2005) *Environmental Guidance for Planning and Development – Part A: Environmental Protection and Land Use Planning in Western Australia*, EPA, Perth

European Commission (1985) 'Council Directive of 27 June 1985 on the Assessment of the Effects of Certain Public and Private Projects on the Environment', *Official Journal of the European Communities*, L 175, pp40–48

European Commission (1992) 'Council Directive 92/43/EEC of 21 May 1992 on the Conservation of Natural Habitats and of Wild Fauna and Flora', *Official Journal of the European Community*, L 2006, published 22/07/1992, as amended by 'Directive 97/62/EC of 27 October 2007', *Official Journal of the European Community*, L 305, p42

European Commission (1997) *Case Studies on Strategic Environmental Assessment – Final Report*, European Commission, DG XI Environment, Brussels

European Commission (1999) *Manual on Strategic Environmental Assessment of Transport Infrastructure Plans*, European Commission, DGVII Transport, Brussels

European Commission (2000) 'Directive 2000/60/EC of the European Parliament and of the Council of 23 October 2000', establishing a framework for Community action in the field of water policy, *Official Journal of the European Community*, L 327, published 22/12/2000, p.1

European Commission (2001a) *IMPEL Project: Implementing Article 10 of the SEA Directive 2001/42/EC*, Final Report, http://ec.europa.eu/environment/impel/sea_directive.htm, last accessed: 29/12/2006

European Commission (2001b) 'Directive 2001/42/EC of the European Parliament and of the Council of 27 June 2001', on the assessment of the effects of certain plans and programmes on the environment, *Official Journal of the European Community*, L 197, published 21/7/2001, pp30–37

European Commission (2006) *The SEA Manual: A Sourcebook on Strategic Environmental Assessment of Transport Infrastructure Plans and Programmes*, DG Tren, Brussels, www.transport-sea.net/results.phtml, last accessed: 29/12/2006

Faludi A (1973) *Planning Theory*, Pergamon, Oxford

Faludi A (2000) 'The performance of spatial planning', *Planning Practice and Research*, vol 15, no 4, pp299–318

FEARO (Federal Environmental Assessment Review Office) (1993) *The Environment Assessment Process for Policy and Programme Proposals*, FEARO, Ottawa

FGSV (Forschungsgesellschaft für das Straßen- und Verkehrswesen eV) (2004) *Merkblatt zur strategischen Umweltprüfung in der Verkehrsplanung (M SUP)*, FGSV, Cologne

Fischer T B (1999a) 'Benefits from SEA application: A comparative review of North West England, Noord-Holland and EVR Brandenburg-Berlin', *EIA Review*, vol 19, pp143–173

Fischer T B (1999b) 'The consideration of sustainability aspects within transport infrastructure related policies, plans and programmes', *Journal of Environmental Planning and Management*, vol 42, no 2, pp189–219

Fischer T B (1999c) 'Comparative analysis of environmental and socio-economic impacts in SEA for transport related policies, plans and programs', *EIA Review*, vol 19, pp275–303

Fischer, T B (2000) 'Lifting the fog on SEA: Towards a categorisation and identification of some major SEA tasks', in Bjarnadóttir, H (ed.), *Environmental Assessment in the Nordic Countries*, Nordregio, Stockholm, pp39–46, www.nordregio.se/Files/r0304.pdf, last accessed: 29/12/2006

Fischer T B (2001) 'How to effectively evaluate the performance of an assessment', in Furman E and Hilden M (eds), *Transport Planning: Does the Influence of Strategic Environmental Assessment / Integrated Assessment Reach Decision-making?*, report by the Finnish Environment Agency, Helsinki, pp38–41, www.ymparisto.fi/download.asp?contentid=19915&lan=en, last accessed: 29/12/2006

Fischer T B (2002a) *Strategic Environmental Assessment in Transport and Land Use Planning*, Earthscan, London

Fischer T B (2002b) *Mobilität, Verkehr und Umweltfolgen(-prüfung)*, Kurs Zukunftspiloten, Deutscher Natuschutzbund, Osnabrück, booklet of 72 pages, can be ordered at www.zukunftspiloten.de, last accessed: 29/12/2006

Fischer T B (2003a) 'Strategic environmental assessment in post-modern times', *EIA Review*, vol 23, no 2, pp155–170

Fischer T B (2003b) 'Die Folgenprüfung zum Entwicklungsplan Oldham: Ein positiv wahrgenommenes Verfahren auf dem Prüfstand', *UVP Report*, vol 17, no 1, pp29–33

Fischer T B (2003c) 'Environmental assessment of the EU Structural Funds Regional Development Plans and Operational Programmes: A case study of the German objective 1 areas', *European Environment*, vol 13, no 5, pp245–257

Fischer T B (2004a) 'Transport policy-SEA in Liverpool, Amsterdam and Berlin: 1997 and 2002', *EIA Review*, vol 24, pp319–336

Fischer, T B (2004b) 'SEA in the UK', in Schmidt M, João E and Albrecht E (eds), *Implementing Strategic Environmental Assessment*, Springer-Verlag, Berlin, pp83–98

Fischer T B (2005a) 'Having an impact? Context elements for effective SEA application in transport policy, plan and programme making', *Journal of Environmental Assessment Policy and Management*, vol 7, no 3, pp407–432

Fischer T B (2005b) *SEA Training Materials for the Web-based MA in Spatial Planning*,

OPDM/University of the West of England, 2005, www.built-environment.uwe.ac.uk/ spatialplanning/catalogue.asp, last accessed: 29/12/2006

Fischer T B (2005c) 'Germany', in Jones C, Baker M, Carter J, Jay S, Short M and Wood C (eds), *Strategic Environmental Assessment and Land Use Planning*, Earthscan, London, pp79–96

Fischer T B (2006a) 'SEA and transport planning: Towards a generic framework for evaluating practice and developing guidance', *Impact Assessment and Project Appraisal*, vol 24, no 3, pp183–197

Fischer T B (2006b) 'Opportunities and pitfalls of sustainability assessment in spatial planning: Reflections on the UK experience', in Korea Environment Institute (KEI) (ed), *SEA and Future-Oriented Policy*, Proceedings of the International Symposium on the 13th Anniversary of KEI, 26–27 January, Seoul, pp191–216

Fischer T B (2006c) 'SEA in spatial/land use planning in the 25 member states: A July 2006 update', *UVP report*, vol 20, no 3, pp127–131

Fischer T B and Gazzola P (2006a) 'SEA good practice elements and performance criteria: Equally valid in all countries? The case of Italy', *EIA Review*, vol 26, no 4, pp396–409

Fischer T B and Gazzola P (2006b) *Conclusions of the Joint RTPI (Royal Town Planning Institute) – North West Region, and IAIA (International Association for Impact Assessment) – Ireland-UK Branch Conference on Sustainability Appraisal (SA) and Strategic Environmental Assessment (SEA) at the University of Liverpool on 31 October 2006*, www.liv.ac.uk/civdes/research/ Conclusions_of_the_joint_RTPI_(3).pdf, last accessed: 29/12/2006

Fischer T B and Seaton K (2002) 'Strategic environmental assessment: Effective planning instrument or lost concept?', *Planning Practice and Research*, vol 17, no 1, pp31–44

Fischer T B, Kopp C, Pung N and Lade M (1994) 'Umweltverträglichkeitsstudie vierstreifiger Ausbau der B 96 mit den Ortsumgehungen Glasow and Dahlewitz, km 224+000 bis km 229+230, GUT Gesellschaft für Umweltplanung mgH, Potsdam', in Fischer, T B (ed) (2002) *Mobilität, Verkehr und Umweltfolgen(- prüfung)*, Kurs Zukunftspiloten, Deutscher Natuschutzbund, Osnabrück, www.zukun ftspiloten.de, last accessed: 29/12/2006

Freie und Hansestadt Hamburg – Baubehörde (1995) *Verkehrsentwicklungsplanung Hamburg – Letlinien und Handlungskonzept für eine an Arbeit und Umwelt orientierte Verkehrpolitik in Hamburg*, Entwurf, Bauehörde Hamburg

Furman E and Hilden M (eds) (2001) *Transport Planning: Does the Influence of Strategic Environmental Assessment / Integrated Assessment Reach Decision- making?*, report by the Finnish Environment Agency, Helsinki, pp38–40, www.ymparisto.fi/download.asp?contentid =19915&lan=en, last accessed: 29/12/2006

Fürst F, Himmelbach U and Potz P (1999) 'Leitbilder der räumlichen Stadtentwicklung im 20. Jahrhundert – Wege zur Nachhaltigkeit?', *Berichte aus dem Institut für Raumplanung 41*, Fakultät Raumplanung, University of Dortmund, www.raumplanung.uni-dortmund.de/ irpud/pub/ber_e.htm#ber41, last accessed: 29/12/2006

Gazzola P, Caramaschi M and Fischer T B (2004) 'Implementing the SEA Directive in Italy', *European Environment*, vol 14, no 2, pp188–199

Gemeente Hilversum (1998) *Toekomstvisie Hilversum 2015*, Hilversum

George C (2001a) 'Testing for sustainable development through assessment', *Environmental Impact Assessment Review*, vol 19, pp175–200

George C (2001b) 'Sustainability appraisal for sustainable development: Integrating every- thing from jobs to climate change', *Impact Assessment and Project Appraisal*, vol 19, pp95–106

German Presidency of the EC Council of Ministers (1999) *Conclusion on the International Workshop on 'Best Practices for Integration of Environmental Protection Requirements into Other*

Policies, Draft, 25–26 May, Bonn

Gibson R (2004) *Specification of Sustainability-based Environmental Assessment Decision Criteria and Implications for Determining 'Significance' in Environmental Assessment*, Research and Development Monograph Series, 2000, Canadian Environmental Assessment Agency Research and Development Program, www.ceaa-acee.gc.ca/015/0002/0009/index_e.htm, last accessed: 27/12/2006

Glasson J and Gosling J (2001) 'SEA and regional planning – overcoming the institutional constraints: Some lessons from the EU, *European Environment*, vol 11, no 2, pp89–102

Glasson J, Therivel R and Chadwick A (1999) *Introduction to Environmental Impact Assessment: Principles and Procedures, Process, Practice and Prospects*, 2nd edition, University College London Press, London

Gullon N (2004) 'Links between the Water Framework Directive and SEA', in Schmidt M, João E and Albrecht E (eds) (2005) *Implementing Strategic Environmental Assessment*, Springer-Verlag, Berlin, pp513–522

Hanssen M A (2003) 'The plans and programmes directive in Norway', in Hilding-Rydevik T (ed.), *Environmental Assessment of Plans and Programmes: Nordic Experiences in Relation to the Implementation of the EU Directive 2001/42/EC*, Nordregio, Stockholm, www.nordregio.se/Files/r0304.pdf, last accessed: 29/12/2006

Healey P (1997) *Collaborative Planning, Shaping Places in Fragmented Societies*, Macmillan, London

Heikinheimo A (2003) *The Value Added in Mediation Processes Created by the Mediator and By the Process Itself*, www.cedr.co.uk/library/articles/default.htm, last accessed: 29/12/2006

Hilden M (2005) 'SEA experience in Finland', in Sadler, B. (ed.) *Strategic Environmental Assessment at the Policy Level*, Ministry of the Environment, Czech Republic, pp55–63

Hilden M and Jalonen P (2005) 'Implementing SEA in Finland: Further development of existing practice', in Schmidt M, João E and Albrecht E (eds), *Implementing Strategic Environmental Assessment*, Springer-Verlag, Berlin, pp159–167

Hilden M, Furman E and Kaljonen M (2004) 'Views on planning and expectations of SEA: The case of transport planning', *EIA Review*, vol 24, no 5, pp519–536

Hilding-Rydevik T (ed.) *Environmental Assessment of Plans and Programmes: Nordic Experiences in Relation to the Implementation of the EU Directive 2001/42/EC*, Nordregio, Stockholm, www.nordregio.se/Files/r0304.pdf, last accessed: 29/12/2006

Hironaka A and Schofer E (2002) 'Loose coupling in the environmental arena: The case of EIA', in Ventresca M and Hoffman A (eds) *Organizations, Policy and the Natural Environment*, Stanford University Press, Stanford, pp214–234

HMSO (Her Majesty's Stationary Office) (1989) *The Electricity Act 1989*, HMSO, London

HM Treasury (2004) *Barker Review of Housing Supply, Final Report: Recommendations*, www.hm-treasury.gov.uk/consultations_and_legislation/barker/consult_barker_ index.cfm, last accessed: 29/12/2006

Holling C S (ed.) (1978) *Adaptive Environmental Assessment and Management*, Wiley, New York

House of Lords Select Committee on the European Communities (1981) *Environmental Assessment of Projects*, HMSO, London

IAIA (International Association for Impact Assessment) (2002) *SEA Performance Criteria*, Special Publication Series No. 1, www.iaia.org, last accessed: 29/12/2006

IEMA (Institute of Environmental Management and Assessment) (2005) *Strategic Environmental Assessment (SEA) Environmental Report (ER) Review Criteria*, www.iema.net/download/membership/corporate/SEA-SA%20Review%20Criteria.pdf, last accessed:

27/12/2006

ISO (International Organization for Standardization) (1996) *Environmental Management Systems: Specification with Guidance for Use*, ISO, Geneva.

IUCN (International Union for Conservation of Nature and Natural Resources), United Nations Environment Programme and World Wildlife Fund (1980) *World Conservation Strategy: Living Resource Conservation for Sustainable Development*, IUCN, Gland

Jacoby C (2000) *Die Strategische Umweltprüfung (SUP) in der Raumplanung. Instrumente, Methoden und Rechtsgrundlagen für die Bewertung von Standortalternativen in der Stadt- und Regionalplanung*, Erich Schmidt Verlag, Berlin

Jansson A H H (2000) 'Strategic environmental assessment for transport in four Nordic countries', in Bjarnadóttir H (ed), *Environmental Assessment in the Nordic Countries*, Nordregio, Stockholm, pp39–46, www.nordregio.se/r003.htm, last accessed: 29/12/2006

Jansson A M, Hammer M, Folke C and Constanza R (eds) (1994) *Investing in Natural Capital – The Ecological Economics Approach to Sustainability*, Island Press, Washington DC

Jones C, Baker M, Carter J, Jay S, Short M and Wood C (eds) (2005) *Strategic Environmental Assessment and Land Use Planning*, Earthscan, London

Jones S A and Mason T W (2002) 'Role of impact assessment for strategic environmental assessment at the firm level', *Impact Assessment and Project Appraisal*, vol 20, no 4, pp279–285

Jonsson D K and Johansson J (2006) 'Indirect effects to include in strategic environmental assessment of transport infrastructure investments', *Transport Reviews*, vol 26, no 2, pp151–166

Kaljonen M (2000) 'The role of SEA in planning and decision making: The case of the Helsinki Area Transport System Plan, 1998', in Bjarnadóttir H (ed.), *Environmental Assessment in the Nordic Countries*, Nordregio, Stockholm,

pp107–116, www.nordregio.se/Files/r0304.pdf, last accessed: 29/12/2006

Kessler J J (2000) 'Strategic Environmental Analysis (SEAN): A framework to support analysis and planning of sustainable development', *Impact Assessment and Project Appraisal*, vol 18, no 4, pp295–307

Kidd S and Fischer T B (2007) 'Integrated appraisal in North West England', *Environment and Planning C*, vol 25, no 2, pp233–249

Kirkpatrick C and George C (2004) 'Trade and development: Assessing the impact of trade liberalisation on sustainable development', *Journal of World Trade*, vol 38, no 3, pp441–469

Klees R, Capcelea A and Barannik A (2002) *Environmental Impact Assessment (EIA) Systems in Europe and Central Asia Countries*, World Bank, Washington DC

Kleinschmidt V and Wagner, D. (1996) 'SEA of wind farms in the Soest district', in Thérivel R and Partidário M (eds), *The Practice of Strategic Environmental Assessment*, Earthscan, London

Knieps E and Welp A C (1991) 'UVS im Straßenbau', *UVP Report*, vol 1, pp28–34

Kørnøv L and Thissen W A H (2000) 'Rationality in decision- and policy-making: Implications for strategic environmental assessment', *Impact Assessment and Project Appraisal*, vol 18, pp191–200

Land Brandenburg (1995) *Landesstraßenbedarfsplan des Landes Brandenburg*, Ministerium für Stadtentwicklung, Wohnen und Verkehr, Potsdam

Lee N (2006) 'Bridging the gap between theory and practice in integrated assessment', *EIA Review*, vol 26, no 1, pp57–78

Lee N, Bonde J and Simpson J (1999) *Reviewing the Quality of Environmental Statements and Environmental Appraisals*, Occasional Paper 55, School of Planning and Landscape, University of Manchester, Manchester

Lee N and Walsh F (1992) 'Strategic environmental assessment: an overview', *Project Appraisal*, vol 7, no 3, pp126–136

Levett-Therivel, Treweek Environmental
Consultants and Land Use Consultants
(2006) *Appropriate Assessment of Plans*,
www.landuse.co.uk/Downloads/Appropria
teAG.pdf, last accessed: 29/12/2006

Linderhof V, Lise W and Oosterhuis F (2003)
*Recommendations for Environmental
Policy in a Liberalised Electricity Market*,
Summary Report of the 4th 'GRENELEM'
Project Meeting, 29–30 September,
Amsterdam, www.dii.uchile.cl/progea/
proyectos/grenelem/fourth/Summary
Amsterdam.pdf, last accessed: 29/12/2006

March J G and Olsen J P (1989)
*Rediscovering Institutions: The
Organizational Basis of Politics*, Free Press,
New York

Marsden S and Ashe J (2006) 'Strategic
environmental assessment legislation in
Australian states and territories',
*Australasian Journal of Environmental
Management*, vol 13, pp6–16

Marsden S and de Mulder J (2005) 'Strategic
environmental assessment and
sustainability in Europe: How bright is the
future?', *Review of European Community
and International Environmental Law*, vol
14, no 1, pp50–62

Marsden S and Dovers S (eds) (2002) *Strategic
Environmental Assessment in Australasia*,
The Federation Press, Annandale, NSW

Marshall R and Fischer T B (2006) 'Regional
electricity transmission planning and tiered
SEA in the UK: The case of ScottishPower',
*Journal of Environmental Planning and
Management*, vol 49, no 2, pp279–299

Marshall R and Baxter (2002) 'Strategic
routeing and environmental impact
assessment for overhead electrical transmission lines', *Journal of Environmental
Planning and Management*, vol 45, no 5,
pp747–764

McNamara C (2006) *Strategic Planning (in
nonprofit or for-profit organizations)*,
www.mapnp.org/library/plan_dec/str_plan/
str_plan.htm, last accessed: 29/12/2006

Merseyside Passenger Transport Authority
(1993) *MerITS - Merseyside Integrated
Transport Study*, Merseyside Passenger
Transport Authority Liverpool

Milner S J, Bailey C, Deans J, Pettigrew D
(2003) *Integrated Impact Assessment UK
Mapping Project Report*, Health Impact
Assessment Research and Development
Programme, Northumbria University,
Newcastle upon Tyne

Minister für Stadtentwicklung, Wohnen und
Verkehr des Landes Nordrhein-Westfalen
(1990) *Gesamtverkehrsplan Nordrhein-
Westfalen*, Minister für Stadtentwicklung,
Wohnen und Verkehr des Landes
Nordrhein-Westfalen Dusseldorf

Ministerium für Wohnungswesen, Städtebau
und Verkehr (1995) *Verkehrsuntersuchung
Nordost - Kurzfassung*, MWSV,
Magdeburg

More T A, Averill J R and Stevens T H (1996)
'Values and economics in environmental
management: A perspective and critique',
Journal of Environmental Management,
vol 48, pp404–406

Morrison-Saunders A and Fischer T B (2006)
'What is wrong with EIA and SEA anyway?
A sceptic's perspective on sustainability
assessment', *Journal of Environmental
Assessment Policy and Management*, vol 8,
no 1, pp19–39

MUNR (Ministerium für Umwelt,
Naturschutz und Raumordnung) (1995)
*Landesentwicklungsplan Brandenburg –
Zentralörtliche Gliederung*, MUNR,
Potsdam

MVW (Ministerie van Verkeer en Waterstaat)
(1989) *Second Transport Structure Plan
(SVVII), part d: Government Decision*,
MVW, The Hague

MVW (1995) *Beleidseffectmeting verkeer en
vervoer, beleidseffectrapportage 1995*,
MVW, The Hague

Niekerk F and Voogd H (1996) *Impact
Assessment for Infrastructure Planning:
Some Dutch Dilemmas*, paper presented at
the ACSP-AESOP Congress, July, Toronto

Nielsson M N and Dalkmann H (2001)
'Decision making and strategic
environmental assessment', *Journal of
Environmental Assessment Policy and
Management*, vol 3, no 3, pp305–328

Nitz T and Brown L (2001) 'SEA must learn
how policy-making works', *Journal of
Environmental Assessment Policy and*

Management, vol 3, pp329–342

Noble B F (2002) 'The Canadian experience with SEA and sustainability', *Environmental Impact Assessment Review*, vol 22, pp3–16

Noble B F and Storey K (2001) 'Towards a structured approach to strategic environmental assessment', *Journal of Environmental Assessment Policy and Management*, vol 3, no 4, pp483–508

Nooteboom S (1999) *Environmental Assessments of Strategic Decisions and Project Decisions: Interactions and Benefits*, DHV Environment and Infrastructure, The Netherlands

Nooteboom S and Teisman G (2003) 'Sustainable development: Impact assessment in the age of networking', *Journal of Environmental Policy and Planning*, vol 5, no 3, pp285–309

NWRA (North West Regional Assembly) (2003) *Action for Sustainability*, NWRA, Wigan

ODPM (Office of the Deputy Prime Minister) (2005a) *Sustainability Appraisal of Regional Spatial Strategies and Local Development Documents*, ODPM, London

ODPM (2005b) *Local Development Framework Monitoring: A Good Practice Guide*, ODPM, London

OECD (Organisation for Economic Co-operation and Development) (1990) *Environmental Policies for Cities in the 1990s*, OECD, Paris

OECD (2006) *Strategic Environmental Assessment Network*, www.seatasktweam.net, last accessed: 29/12/2006

Oldham Metropolitan Borough Council (2001) *UDP First Deposit Draft Sustainability Appraisal*, Oldham Metropolitan Borough Council, Oldham

OPSI (Office of Public Sector Information) (2004) *The Environmental Assessment of Plans and Programmes Regulations 2004, Statutory Instrument 2004 No. 1633*, www.opsi.gov.uk/si/si2004/20041633.htm, last accessed: 29/12/2006

Ortolano L (1984) *Environmental Planning and Decision Making*, Wiley, New York

Partidário M R (1997) 'Case studies on strategic environmental assessment in land-use planning: A comparative review', in NATO-CCMS (ed.), *Strategic Environmental Assessment in Land-Use Planning*, Report No 218, Brussels, pp138–145

Partidário M R and Fischer T B (2004) 'SEA', in Arts J and Morrison-Saunders A (eds), *Follow-up in Environmental Assessment*, Earthscan, London, pp224–247

Perdicoúlis A, Hanusch M, Kasperidus, H D and Weiland U (forthcoming) 'The handling of causality in SEA guidance', *Environmental Impact Assessment Review*

Petts J (1999) 'EIA versus other decision tools', in Petts J (ed.), *Handbook of EIA*, vol 1, Blackwell Science, Oxford

Pope J, Annandale D and Morrison-Saunders, A (2004) 'Conceptualising sustainability assessment', *Environmental Impact Assessment Review*, vol 24, no 6, pp595–616

PowerSystems (2003) *The Preliminary Establishment of Need*, SP PowerSystems Ltd, ScottishPower

Pröbstl U, Jiricka A and Stöglehner G (2006) 'Die SUP-Umsetzung in der örtlichen Raumplanung in Österreich', *UVP Report*, nos 1 and 2, pp52–55

Provincie Noord-Holland (1997) *Ontwikkelingsvisie Noord-Holland 2030 – verkenningen*, Provincie Noord-Holland, Haarlem

Rees W and Wackernagel M (1994) 'Ecological footprints and appropriated carrying capacity: Measuring the natural capital requirements of the human economy' in Jansson A M, Hammer M, Folke C and Constanza R (eds), *Investing in Natural Capital: The Ecological Economics Approach to Sustainability*, Island Press, Washington DC, pp362–390

Repubblica (19 April 2004) 'Sullo stretto di Messina - il ponte delle illusioni', www.repubblica.it/online/lf_dietro_il_ listino/ 040419ponte/ponte/ponte.html, last accessed: 29/12/2006

ROCOL (Road Charging Options for London Working Group) (2000) *ROCOL Report*, www.gos.gov.uk/gol/transport/161558/228

862/228869/, last accessed: 29/12/2006

Roussow N and Wiseman K (2004) 'Learning from the implementation of environmental public policy instruments after the first ten years of democracy in South Africa', *Impact Assessment and Project Appraisal*, vol 22, no 2, pp131–140

Sabatier P A and Jenkins-Smith H C (1993) 'Evaluating the advocacy coalition framework', *Journal of Public Policy*, vol 14, no 2, pp175–203

Sadler B (1996) *International Study of the Effectiveness of Environmental Assessment – Final Report: Environmental Assessment in a changing world: Evaluation Practice to Improve Performance*, International Association for Impact Assessment (IAIA) and Canadian Environmental Assessment Agency (CEAA), Ottawa

Sadler, B. (ed.) (2005) *Strategic Environmental Assessment at the Policy Level*, Ministry of the Environment, Czech Republic, Prague

Sadler B and Verheem R (1996) *Strategic Environmental Assessment – Status, Challenges and Future Directions*, No. 53, Ministerie van Volkshuisvesting, Ruimtelijke Ordening en Milieubeheer (VROM), The Hague

Schijf B (2002) *A New Model of EIA-based Decision Making: Implications for EIA Effectiveness*, paper presented at the International Association for Impact Assessment Meeting, 19–21 June, The Hague, on CD-Rom from www.iaia.org

Schmidt M, João E and Albrecht E (eds) (2005) *Implementing Strategic Environmental Assessment*, Springer-Verlag, Berlin

Scholles F, Haaren C, Myrzik A, Ott S, Wilke T, Winkelbrandt A and Wulfert K (2003) 'Strategische Umweltprüfung und Landschaftsplanung', *UVP Report*, vol 17, no 2, pp76–82

Scholten J J and Post R A M (1999) 'Strengthening the integrated approach to impact assessments in development cooperation', *EIA Review*, vol 19, no 3, pp233–243

Schomerus T, Runge K, Nehls G, Busse J, Nommel J, Poszig D, Burandt S, Lund B

and Kraetzschmer D (2006) *Strategische Umweltprüfung für die Offshore-Windenergienutzung*, Verlag Dr Kovac, Hamburg

Schön D A and Rein M (1994) *Frame Reflection. Toward the Resolution of Intractable Policy Controversies*, Basic Books, New York

ScottishPower (2001) *Mid-Wales System Development Proposals*, SP PowerSystems, Prenton

Scrase J I (2006) *Assessment and Appraisal Concepts in Environmental Policy and Management*, unpublished PhD thesis, Centre for Environmental Policy, Faculty of Natural Sciences, Imperial College, London

Sheate W (1992) 'Strategic environmental assessment in the transport sector', *Project Appraisal*, vol 7, no 3, pp170–174

Sheate W R, Byron H J and Smith S P (2004) 'Implementing the SEA Directive: Sectoral challenges and opportunities for the UK and EU', *European Environment Journal*, vol 14, no 2, pp73–93

Shepherd A and Ortolano L (1996) 'Strategic environmental assessment for sustainable urban development', *Environmental Impact Assessment Review*, vol 16, no 4, pp321–335

Smith S P and Sheate W R (2001) 'Sustainability appraisal of regional planning guidance and regional economic strategies in England: An assessment', *Journal of Environmental Planning and Management*, vol 44, no 5, pp735–755

Song Young-Il (2006) 'Development and implementation of strategic environmental assessment (SEA) in Korea', in Korea Environment Institute (KEI) (ed.) *SEA and Future-Oriented Policy*, Proceedings of the International Symposium on the 13th Anniversary of KEI, 26–27 January, Seoul, pp226–237

Stead D, Geerlings H and Meijers E J (eds) (2004) *Policy Integration in Practice: The Integration of Land Use Planning, Transport and Environmental Policy-making in Denmark, England and Germany*, DUP Science, Delft

Stein W, Smeets F, Wolff F and Danninger H (1993) 'Beitrag zur

Umweltverträglichkeitsprüfung bei der Fortschreibung des Landesstraßenbedarfsplans NRW', *UVP Report*, vol 4, pp184–188

Tait, J (1995) 'Sustainability: Some questions for planners', *Report for the Natural and Built Environment*, no 5, June

Tang Tao, Zhu Tan and Xu He (forthcoming) 'Integrating environment into land-use planning through strategic environmental assessment in China: Towards legal frameworks and operational procedures' *Environmental Impact Assessment Review*

Taylor S (1984) *Making Bureaucracies Think: The Environmental Impact Statement Strategy of Administrative Reform*, Stanford University Press, Stanford, CA

Thérivel R and Wood G (2004) 'Tools for strategic environmental assessment', in Schmidt M, João E and Albrecht E (eds), *Implementing Strategic Environmental Assessment*, Springer, Berlin, pp349–364

Thérivel R and Partidário M (eds) (1996) *The Practice of Strategic Environmental Assessment*, Earthscan, London

Thissen W and Van der Hijden R (2005) 'The Netherlands', in Jones C, Baker M, Carter J, Jay S, Short M and Wood C (eds), *Strategic Environmental Assessment and Land Use Planning*, Earthscan, London, pp146–158

Tomlinson P and Fry C (2002) *Improving EIA Effectiveness Through SEA*, paper presented at the International Association for Impact Assessment Meeting, 19–21 June, The Hague, on CD-Rom from www.iaia.org

Tonn B, English M and Travis C (2000) 'A framework for understanding and improving environmental decision making', *Journal of Environmental Planning and Management*, vol 43, pp163–183

UNCED (United Nations Conference on Environment and Development) (1992) *Agenda 21*, United Nations Publications, New York

UNECE (United Nations Economic Council for Europe) (2003) *Protocol on Strategic Environmental Assessment to the Convention on Environmental Impact Assessment in a Transboundary Context*,

www.unece.org/env/eia/sea_protocol.htm, last accessed: 29/12/2006

UNECE (2004) *Convention on Access to Information, Public Participation in Decision-making and Access to Justice in Environmental Matters*, www.unece.org/env/pp/treatytext.htm, last accessed: 29/12/2006

UNECE (2006) *Resource Manual to Support Application of the Protocol on SEA* (Draft for Consultation), www.unece.org/env/eia/sea_manual/welcome.html, last accessed: 29/12/2006

United States Environmental Protection Agency (1998) *Guidelines for Ecological Risk Assessment*, Washington DC

United States Government (1969) *National Environmental Policy Act*, Public Law 91-190, 91st Congress, S. 1075, 1 January 1970, Washington DC

UVP (2006) 'Special issue on emerging post Directive SEA practice', *UVP Report*, nos 1 and 2

Valve H (1999) 'Frame conflicts and the formulation of alternatives: Environmental assessment of an infrastructure plan', *Environmental Impact Assessment Review*, vol 19, pp125–142

Van den Berg J and Nooteboom S (1994) *SEA: Existing methodology*, European Commission, DG XI, Brussels, http://europa.eu.int/comm/environment/eia/, last accessed: 27/12/2006

Van Eck M and Scholten J J (1997) *Effectiveness of Environmental Impact Assessment*, briefing paper by the Dutch EIA Commission, Utrecht

Van Straaten D, Smolders K and Verheyen R (2001) *Strategic Environmental Assessment of the Master Transport Plan in Flanders*, presentation at the IAIA Cartagena meeting, 27 May to 1 June, Catagena

Verheem R (1996) 'SEA of the Dutch ten-year programme on waste maanagement', in Thérivel R and Partidário M (eds), *The Practice of Strategic Environmental Assessment*, Earthscan, London

Verheem R (2005) 'The challenge of implementing the European SEA Directive in the Netherlands – a personal reflection', in Dalal-Clayton B and Sadler B (eds), *The*

Status and Potential of Strategic Environmental Assessment, draft 65, IIED, London

Verkehrsministerium (1995) *Generalverkehrsplan Baden-Württemberg*, Verkehrsministerium Baden-Württemberg, Stuttgart

VROM (Ministry of Public Housing, Physical Planning and Environmental Affairs) (1984) *Prediction in Environmental Impact Assessment*, vol 17, VROM, The Hague

VROM (1993) *Vierde nota over de ruimtelijke ordening Extra (VINEX)*, deel 4, VROM, The Hague

VROM (1996) *(Milieu-) effectrapport over de Leidse en de Rotterdamse Regio, deel I*, VROM, The Hague

Wackernagel M and Rees W (1996) *Our Ecological Footprint: Reducing Human Impact on the Earth*, New Society Publishers, Gabriola Island, BC

Wallagh G (1988) *Tussen wens en werking*, unpublished Master's thesis, University of Amsterdam, Amsterdam

Ward M, Wilson J and Sadler B (2005) *Application of SEA to Regional Land Transport Strategies, Land Transport New Zealand*, Research Report, Wellington, New Zealand

Wende W, Hanusch M, Gassner E, Guennewig D, Köppel J, Lambrecht H, Langenheld A, Peters W and Roethke-Habeck P (2004) 'Requirements of the SEA Directive and the German Federal Transport Infrastructure Plan', *European Environment*, vol 14, no 2, pp105–122

Wood C (2002) *Environmental Impact Assessment, a Comparative Review*, Prentice Hall, New Jersey

Wood G, Glasson J and Becker J (2006) 'EIA scoping in England and Wales: Practitioners approaches, perspectives and constraints', *Environmental Impact Assessment Review*, vol 26, pp221–241

Wood C and Jones C E (1997) 'The effect of environmental assessment on UK planning authority decisions', *Urban Studies*, vol 44, no 8, pp1237–1257

Wood C and Djeddour M (1992) 'Strategic environmental assessment: EA of policies, plans and programmes', *Impact Assessment Bulletin*, vol 10, pp3–22

World Bank (2005) *Integrating Environmental Considerations in Policy Formulation – Lessons from Policy-based SEA Experience*, Environment Department, World Bank, Washington DC

World Bank Group (2006) 'Strategic Environmental Assessment (SEA) Distance Learning Course', World Bank, Washington DC, http://info.worldbank.org/etools/docs/library/107861/sea/sea/materials.html, last accessed: 29/12/2006

Wright F (2006) *The Purposes and Benefits of Understaking Strategic Environmental Assessment: The Case of Scotland in the Mid–Late 1990s*, unpublished PhD thesis, University of Strathclyde, Glasgow

Zdrazil V and Martis M (2001) *SEA in the Czech Republic, Experience, Open Issues, Background*, presentation at the IAIA Cartagena meeting, 27 May to 1 June, Catagena

Index